Essays on Modern Quebec Theater

❖ ❖ ❖ ❖ ❖ ❖ ❖ ❖ ❖ ❖ ❖ ❖ ❖ ❖ ❖ ❖ ❖ ❖ ❖

E. Photograph by Michel Brais.

Essays on Modern Quebec Theater

❖ ❖ ❖ ❖ ❖ ❖ ❖ ❖ ❖ ❖ ❖ ❖ ❖ ❖ ❖ ❖ ❖ ❖ ❖ ❖

Edited by

Joseph I. Donohoe Jr.

and

Jonathan M. Weiss

Michigan State University Press
East Lansing
1995

All Michigan State University Press books are produced on paper which meets the requirements of the American National Standard of Information Sciences—Permanence of paper for printed materials ANSI Z23.48-1984.

Michigan State University Press
East Lansing, Michigan 48823-5202

02 01 00 99 98 97 96 95 1 2 3 4 5 6 7 8 9 10

Library of Congress Cataloging-in-Publication Data

Essays on modern Quebec theater / edited by Joseph I. Donohoe Jr. and Jonathan M. Weiss
    p.   m.
  Includes bibliographical references and index.
  ISBN 0-87013-388-8 (hard cover : alk. paper)
  1. Theater—Québec (Province)   I. Donohoe, Joseph I.   II. Weiss, Jonathan M.

PN2305.Q4E88   1995   95-14382
792'.09714—dc20   CIP

Essays on Modern Quebec Theater was published with the assistance of the Quebec Government and the Government of Canada.

Photographs courtesy of *Les Cahiers de théâtre Jeu.*

For Victor M. Howard and Laurent Mailhot with the respect and affection of the authors.

Contents

❖ ❖ ❖ ❖ ❖ ❖ ❖ ❖ ❖ ❖ ❖ ❖ ❖ ❖ ❖ ❖ ❖ ❖ ❖

III. Quebec Theater in a Contemporary Context

IV. Interpretive Essays

Preface

❖ ❖ ❖ ❖ ❖ ❖ ❖ ❖ ❖ ❖ ❖ ❖ ❖ ❖ ❖ ❖ ❖ ❖ ❖

The present volume arises from an effort to bring together the best people working in the area, independently of critical stance or national origin, to celebrate the arresting development and undeniable richness of Quebec theater as it has emerged over the last three or four decades. To that end, we invited essays from a group of publishing scholars from Quebec, Anglophone Canada, France, and the United States. While imposing no rigid criteria on the collection, other than the inherent interest of the piece and the use of the cultural revolution of the 1960s as a common point of reference, we were able nonetheless without great difficulty to organize the articles submitted under the rubrics of culture, language, contemporary critical perspectives, and essays on individual plays or authors. We believe that we have succeeded in including, if not everyone whose work we value, at least a number of the most thought-provoking contemporary critical voices. The final product is a wide-ranging, comprehensive mosaic of ideas and insights which we hope will prove stimulating not only to the student of Quebec theater but, to the extent that Quebec will be seen to have broken new ground in dramatic theory and stage practice, to students of theater in general.

The often-remarked sympathy between growing national consciousness and the vitality of the stage would most probably have cast the Quiet Revolution—had we not done so—in the role of organizational center for the essays of this collection. No surprise then that a number of the essays concern themselves with the interrelated issues of language (including translation) and cultural identity which lay at the heart of the dialogue of theater and society in the 1960s, as well as with the re-invention of the Quebec stage in response to the singular intensity of that dialogue. In spite of the cooling of the nationalist debate, after the failure of the 1980 referendum, the stage innovations and the acquired insights of the earlier period will continue, as other essays make clear, to influence the preoccupations and techniques of the theater. Among these latter, the identity-related concerns of women, experiments with improvisation, the reassessment of the dramatic text and the heightened importance of *mise en scene*.

Owing to the international nature of the collection and our pragmatic decision to use English as lingua franca, the entirety of the original French texts—excluding direct citations which have been conserved out of a concern for accuracy—have been translated into English. For this daunting task, executed with grace and precision, we owe a debt of gratitude to our translators: Professors Dean Detrich and Leonard Rahilly of Michigan State University and Professor Keith Palka of Central Michigan University. May their reward hereafter be the equal of the time and energy here expended.

As is always the case with the realization of projects of this nature, the editors find themselves indebted to numbers of other individuals and organizations whose support has been crucial to the completion of the task. Among these, we should like especially to thank the *Cahiers de théâtre Jeu* for access to its photographic archives, Victor Howard, the general editor of the Canadian Studies Series, Fred Bohm, director of the Michigan State University Press, and the Press's incomparable editor in chief, Julie Loehr.

Finally, we are pleased to acknowledge the generous support of the research, preparation and publication of the manuscript by the Quebec Government and the Government of Canada.

Introduction

Jonathan M. Weiss

Of the forms of artistic expression, theater is among the most elusive. Unlike print literature or cinema, stage productions are ephemeral and differ from themselves, to a greater or lesser degree, according to the circumstances (audience, stage, actors) that attend them. The written text is but one element of the whole; varying conceptions of the theater can make it either one of the most important or least important elements. To attempt to examine the theater, therefore, we must also take into account aspects of the phenomenon that are evident only fleetingly, while the play is being performed.

The essays in this volume attest to the complexity and elusiveness of the theater of Quebec. This complexity stems in part from the circumstance in which Quebec finds itself: a French-speaking society within an English-speaking country that, on numerous occasions, has attempted to snuff out the use of the French language. It is difficult enough to assemble all the elements necessary for theater to take place in a society whose culture is unambiguously national; in Quebec it was necessary to put together these elements in the context of a society whose culture was, for a long time, undefined and unrecognizable. It is no wonder then that, from its beginnings in the eighteenth century until the middle of the twentieth, the theater of Quebec was mostly preoccupied with local problems. While foreign plays (principally from France) were very popular, plays written in Quebec concerned historical events (such as the 1837 revolt) or, in a few instances, the linguistic divisions of Quebec society. However, these were primarily circumstantial plays, and neither their appeal nor their

1

quality transcended their time. It was not until the middle of the twentieth century that theater in Quebec came into its own, with playwrights composing texts of dramatic quality and directors staging these texts in productions that showed creative originality.

Like most aspects of modern Quebec culture, theater has been informed, until quite recently, by nationalism. Far more than American, French, or British theater of recent times, drama in Quebec has been part of a constantly changing effort to define and redefine a national identity. In the eighteenth and nineteenth centuries, the principal obstacles to cultural independence were the Catholic church and the English power structure. It was, of course, hardly possible to contradict the church in so public a forum as theater; as for the power structure itself, it was mainly indirectly, through the use of the French language, that Quebec dramatists asserted their national and cultural identity. As Quebec moved into the twentieth century, the influence of American culture became more pervasive replacing, at the popular level, European (French) influences. Quebec theater soon responded to this influence with shows inspired by stage reviews in New York and other cities, but with a notably Quebec flavor. These productions and the plays of Gratien Gélinas and Marcel Dubé, during the 1940s and 1950s, produced the first authentically twentieth-century *québécois* characters. The period immediately following World War II saw examples of plays reflecting the social reality both of the working and middle classes, but this theater, interesting though it was, receded into the background when, in 1968, the first plays of Michel Tremblay were presented in Montreal.

When Tremblay's plays arrived on the scene it was as if the entire history of drama in Quebec needed to be rewritten, so responsive a chord did this playwright strike in his audience. Suddenly Quebecers saw themselves reflected on the stage, both in the decor of the plays (the kitchen, center of the family, presided over by women), in their subject matter (the trials and tribulations of everyday life—including the seamier aspects of life), and in their language. This last point deserves some clarification. Although not the first dramatist to present popular forms of speech on stage, Tremblay was the first to integrate *joual*, a form of French used in working-class neighborhoods of Montreal, into his theater. Even though a few critics were dismayed, audiences and, later critics, would all recognize in Tremblay one of the most original and authentic voices on the stage.

2

What helped Tremblay's theater resonate throughout so many layers of Quebec society was that it came into being at a time of cultural as well as political awakening and nationalist ferment. The 1970s saw the rise to power of the independentist party, the *Parti québécois*, and the flowering of *québécois* culture in numerous areas (literature, art, cinema). Both to *québécois* audiences within the province and to Canadian and U.S. audiences outside, Tremblay became the symbol of the reawakening of Quebec as a distinct (not French, not Canadian, not U.S.) culture. A great many other dramatists presented their plays during the 1970s in Montreal; some of these were overtly political, others more psychological. One playwright, Jean-Claude Germain, attempted to re-write Quebec's cultural history on the stage and in so doing give voice to forgotten figures of the past. But it is Tremblay, more than any of his contemporaries, whose plays both reflect the birth of a renewed Quebec culture and transcend the specificity of Quebec to convey a universal message.

By the end of the 1970s the nationalist fervor in Quebec was dimmed by the defeat of the referendum that would have given the government the power to negotiate independence from Canada. The tone of theater in Quebec quickly changed. Gone were the plays whose text (or sub-text in many cases) argued Quebec's cultural, historical, or political separateness from Canada. The 1980s saw plays that responded rather to the specific concerns of various segments of Quebec society. Feminists, particularly, began to write and produce plays about women, confirming a trend that had begun in the 1970s with a collective creation called *La Nef des sorcières*. Collective creation in general became popular, giving rise to such dramatic exhibitions as Le Grand Cirque Ordinaire and La Ligue Nationale d'Improvisation, the latter modeled after a hockey match, and with no fixed text.

The 1980s and 1990s have seen, on the one hand, the continual development of experimental and collective theater, and, on the other, the resurgence of the author-dramatist. Whereas the authors of the 1970s all seemed to be heading together toward a national and at times nationalist awakening, more recent authors are introspective, and each seems headed toward his or her own reality. Whether it be plays about power relationships between men and women, or about the struggle of gay men to define their own world, or about militaristic tendencies in society, contemporary Quebec theater is more concerned with universal problems than with particular ones.

3

As Quebec theater developed, beginning in the 1970s, it also became exportable. Translated into English, plays of Michel Tremblay and others were performed in Toronto and elsewhere in English Canada, in a few places in the United States and, on numerous occasions (and in the original), in France. Whether or not the message conveyed by the translations was the same as that perceived by Quebec audiences is a matter of some dispute; there can be no doubt, however, that Quebec drama is now known in many places outside the province. There is also much evidence that Quebec playwrights and producers have become sensitive to drama throughout the world—especially Europe and the United States. At the same time Canadian Anglophone theater has exercised little influence on the theater of Quebec. This is a phenomenon that parallels the situation in other cultural areas, particularly in literature, wherein the prevalence of Quebec texts (in translation) in the rest of Canada is not matched by the availability of translated Canadian texts in Quebec. In many instances, what happens across the Atlantic Ocean or south of the border holds far more interest for Quebec than what happens culturally to the west of the province.

What is striking above all in the recent history of Quebec theater is the way in which, beginning in the 1970s, playwrights, directors, and actors have defined their own aesthetic. The great separatist movement of the period induced, in the theater—for the first time—a style and especially a language that was *québécois*. It is no wonder then that even the defeat of the referendum on sovereignty-association did not plunge Quebec theater into a reexamination of its identity. On the contrary, Quebec theater today shows an aesthetic originality and a consciousness of itself that puts it in the forefront of world theater.

With the growth of theater in Quebec has come a great deal of critical and theoretical literature. By the 1970s, already, theater had become the subject of critical analysis: Laurent Mailhot's and Jean Cléo Godin's *Théâtre québécois* was the first attempt systematically to put the drama of the post-1940s into perspective. At the same time, the Centre d'Essai d'Auteurs Dramatiques was affording the opportunity for Quebec's young playwrights to create productions that they otherwise would have been unable to fund. The combination of talented, young dramatists and critics alike was to confer on Quebec theater of the 1970s an intellectual respectability not previously accorded to drama in the province.

4

The theater review *Jeu* has also played an important role in the development of theater in Quebec. Founded in 1976, this quarterly publication not only presents analysis of current and past productions in Quebec, but also brings to its readers the most important theatrical trends from Europe and elsewhere. It would be difficult to underestimate the importance of *Jeu* in the development of a theatrical consciousness in Quebec.

The essays that follow are an attempt to continue the tradition of critical analysis of Quebec theater by bringing together ideas from Quebec, English Canada, the United States, and France. There is no attempt to cover all periods of theater or to provide a historical introduction to the subject; rather, the essays reflect a wide variety of interpretative techniques and theoretical underpinnings. Despite their diversity, however, these essays all attest to the rich imagination and innovative techniques of Quebec's playwrights and directors.

The Cross-Fertilization of Cultures in Quebec Theater[1]

Alonzo Le Blanc

❖ ❖ ❖ ❖ ❖ ❖ ❖ ❖ ❖ ❖ ❖ ❖ ❖ ❖ ❖ ❖ ❖ ❖ ❖ ❖

When the word *half-breed* strikes the ear of a Quebecer, the image it prompts is that of a hero, Louis Riel, the leader of an important rebellion in the Canadian West, arrested by order of John A. MacDonald, founder of the Canadian Confederation, and executed for murder after sentence was pronounced in 1885. Louis Riel's identity depended on the fact that he was a half-breed, born of a father of mixed blood and a mother of French ancestry. His execution was regarded as a national insult in the province of Quebec, where Riel had received his secondary education, for it put an abrupt end to the dream of a Native North American and Francophone community in western Canada. A whole century would pass before the memory of Louis Riel would be rehabilitated and the legitimacy of his cause recognized by the Federal Government in Ottawa. Yet his struggle had always seemed exemplary in the eyes of Quebecers because, despite his status as a half-breed, he embodied resistance to political homogenization. No doubt there was in this recognition an instinctive solidarity and a spontaneous identification with an Indian brother.

Contrary to what is commonly believed outside of Canada, Quebec has been the locus of an extraordinary racial mixing of the population. When you hear, as in a recent advertisement, "Nous sommes six millions de presque parents"—indeed seven million now—you might imagine, on the basis of genealogies neatly conserved through baptismal records, that old Quebec families with names like Tremblay, Lévesque, Bouchard, Côté, Gagnon, Charest, Lachance, Lacroix,

7

Lapointe, Cloutier, Dubé, Leblanc, Simard, Latulippe, Lavigueur, Laviolette, and others, are "homogeneous," that is of French heritage, to which other cultural traits such as the Catholic faith have been added to make up what is often called "des Québécois pure laine." This is a mistaken notion inasmuch as Quebec has known, ever since its beginnings, through marriage with Natives and people of other ethnic backgrounds, a racial intermixing in the population not found in many other countries. In the veins of 80 percent of Francophone Quebecers flows some Native blood; and very often, among the remaining 20 percent, the blood of some other group—English, Scottish, Irish, or Italian.

In Quebec as elsewhere, crossbreeding takes place in people before being inscribed in texts. Demographically there are two kinds of crossbreeding: the one visible and sometimes problematic, the other invisible but not necessarily innocuous. Should we project this distinction onto the textual plane and distinguish between visible and invisible hybridization? For the time being, let us reserve judgment and first examine the cultural circumstances peculiar to Quebec that have left traces in the birth and development of its theater.

Quebec has always been at the crossroads of three distinct cultural influences: French, British, and American. French culture constitutes the taproot, the site of its ethnic and linguistic grounding in the French language, laws and customs transmitted from generation to generation for nearly four centuries. British culture has made a deep impression on our political, economic, and industrial institutions, through both a style of public and private administration and commercial practices and day-to-day habits that still characterize us today.

The American culture has been an overwhelming influence. In his doctoral dissertation entitled *L'image des Etats-Unis dans la littérature québécoise* (1775-1930),[2] my colleague Guildo Rousseau has shown how, from 1775 to 1930, the United States exerted an enduring fascination on the people of Quebec, drawn by a form of freedom, an affluence, and a democratic lifestyle that struck them as authentic. The whole of America appealed to our taste for risk, for adventure, and the picturesque. The idea of annexation has been a constant temptation to certain Canadian political figures, including Louis-Joseph Papineau who was disappointed by the social inequalities he had witnessed in England. This attraction, intensified or dampened by the great Francophone migration toward the U.S. at the turn of the century, was soon seen as a threat to the distinctive values of the French Canadian community: the Catholic faith, French language, family, agriculture, parish unity, and the sense of a messianic vocation. After 1860, a resistance developed against the American temptation and provided the recurring themes of most of the works of Canadian writers who denounced the money worship, materialism, immorality, gangsterism, or simply the empty superficiality of the American way of life. Yet, despite our attempt to retreat into ourselves and all our defense mechanisms, American culture has long since managed to overtake our daily lives, by means of items we consume every day: cars, movies, music, songs, magazines, comic strips, books, and now television series that flood our markets just as everywhere else in the world, including France.

Quebecers are, therefore, North Americans by their lifestyle and by a set of behaviors that constitute what the social psychologist Ralph Linton might call a "basic personality," as suggested by the title of his book from the 1950s: *The Cultural Background of Personality*.[3] Living in their homeland and adopting this cultural attachment, belonging, the people of Quebec have been able to maintain an identity that distinguishes them from the Americans, the French, and the British alike.

This identity is comprised of homegrown elements and outside influences, of a popular oral tradition and an elitist academic tradition, which together, perhaps, explain its inner tensions, cultural vigor, and in particular the vitality of our theater. I shall try to describe how such a mixing of cultures came to be in Quebec's theatrical repertoire by looking at the following topics: 1) the French tradition and Montreal's theatrical institutions; 2) popular inspiration, where cultural hybridization occurs; 3) Quebec and "Americanness," according to Jacques Languirand; 4) parody; 5) the question of *joual*; and 6) hybridization and theatricality.

French Dramatic Tradition and Montreal's Theatrical Institution

Historians of Quebec theater are of one mind in that at the beginning of the twentieth century, Quebec hosted the foundation of a permanent French-language theatrical institution. This process of becoming autonomous occurred as a result of repeated visits by important French actors and actresses (Sarah Bernhardt came to Montreal at least seven times between 1880 and 1916), as part of tours arranged by an American distribution network. Other French actors moved to Quebec during the period from 1890 to 1914, becoming involved in collaborative efforts with Canadian actors, first amateur then professional. Out of this collaborative union arose such institutions as the Théâtre des Variétés and the Théâtre National, founded by Julien Daoust in 1900 and later managed and directed by the Frenchmen Paul Cazeneuve and Antoine Godeau. This period therefore witnessed the creation of a theatrical tradition, audiences of theater-lovers, and acting companies and playhouses catering to the varied tastes of the public.

Another result of the union is the attempt to create an original repertoire. Several Canadian plays are produced at the Théâtre National and other theaters, but on the whole they simply translate the language, the form, and even the content of European models. These attempts to imitate the great French playwrights, with or without the characteristic twelve-syllable line, five-act structure, and trimmings of neoclassicism, romanticism, melodrama, or other traditions, gave rise to plays in which, as far as I am concerned, one cannot really discuss cultural cross-fertilization. In fact, for 150 years Quebec was the locus of a constant introduction of learned, essentially imported culture, an implantation that contributed to the maintenance of French language and grammar, the classics, and a rudimentary education in science but did not always reach the heart of the popular soul or contribute to its expression or representation in original works. This gap was especially evident in the theater, the artistic genre slowest to take root and flourish in Quebec soil.

Popular Inspiration

It is in the popular sector of Quebec's theatrical life that we can begin to discuss cultural cross-fertilization. This is the word that immediately comes to mind in relation to the subject of burlesque theater. In both her M.A.[4] and her Ph.D. theses,[5] Chantal Hébert has shown how the burlesque repertoire was imported from the United States at the beginning of the twentieth century by a few pioneers. A prime example is Olivier Guimont, nicknamed "Ti-Zoune," who first acted in English, specifically in spoken American English, then felt the need to translate his variety sketches for French-speaking audiences. Comparing these two repertoires, of which precious examples have been conserved on both sides of the border, Hébert shows that the texts were subjected to typical transformations that explain the enduring success of this genre in the period from 1920 to 1950, the golden age of burlesque theater in Quebec. This process of appropriation entails not just the switch from American English to Canadian French (the transcriptions are dreadful), but also certain changes in the subject matter. For instance, one can observe a displacement of axiological and ideological values. In several of the American comic sketches, the family is ridiculed and marital squabbles, rife with ridiculous situations, often end in divorce, which is acceptable in Protestant American society. In front of Quebec audiences, where these endings ran the risk of being negatively received or inviting the rebuke of the clergy, hybridization consisted of safeguarding marriage and family values. Instead, the accent was placed on other national foibles (thank heaven, we are not without them!) thanks to the verve and improvisational skills of burlesque actors and actresses, the best known of whom, the incomparable Rose Ouelette (also known as "La Poune") is still popular today despite her advancing years. The same popular tradition played a role in the flowering of melodrama, many examples of which were adapted for the screen by film industry pioneers. Should one see an instance of cross-fertilization in the melodrama *Aurore, l'enfant martyre*.[6] This play was inspired by a Canadian *fait divers*, co-written by two actors, the Montréaler Henri Rollin, whose real name was Willie Plante and the Frenchman Léon Petitjean, the better read of the two, who worked and died in Quebec. This was the most frequently performed in Quebec—an absolute record with some 5,000 performances between its opening in 1921 and its film première in 1952—and contains a few textual signs of their collaboration, e.g., the use of the non-contemporary Quebec word *barlander* in the first scene to mean hesitate or languish. Various productions of this play often include songs and comic scenes and interludes that justify the name of the genre whose etymology—*melos, drama*—suggest a form of hybridization.

Running parallel to the rise of burlesque and melodrama, the phenomenon of the revues began circa 1900 in Montreal, New York, and

Paris. By definition, the revue is a catch-all of elements as diverse as monologues, sketches, songs, and variety numbers; it often included a "leg show" or chorus line. This theatrical genre is a constant of the first half of the century, with authors like Henri Deyglun and Henri Letondal. In the dialogues written for these revues one can identify the textual signs of a cross-fertilization between the two cultures, French and Canadian (French-Canadian), in what is distinctive to the latter, i.e., based on observation of the facts of life in Montreal and Quebec and on the description/representation of these realities in appropriate terms.

It was in this typically popular vein, started before his birth, that Gratien Gélinas won his fame. Born in 1909, lavishly fêted by theater people, Gélinas is still alive and active today and is widely considered to be the founding father of Quebec's present-day theatrical repertoire. This acknowledgement does not in any way diminish the role of or the credit due to Father Emile Legault (1906-83) and his Compagnons de St-Laurent (1937-52), who contributed to the development of a more classical theatrical tradition. *Les Fridolinades,*[7] originally created on the radio, are revues that were first staged at the Monument National in 1938, and the play *Tit-coq,*[8] which had 200 performances on its first run, was staged in 1948 from a sketch entitled *Le Retour du conscrit.* The success of *Tit-coq* has been rightly viewed as a birthing act, for in the prolongation of Fridolin, observer and critic of local realities, took root a typically *québécois* character, a native-born bastard soldier who speaks a language at once correct and folksy, at the center of an original dramatic development which is the product of a long process of maturation.

Quebec and Americanness

Among Quebec playwrights of the first generation, Jacques Languirand no doubt appears to have been the most open to external influences. His first plays, *Les Insolites* and *Les Grands Départs*, are in their own way closely akin to the European theater of the absurd. The title and even the theme of *Les Grands Départs*[9] translate this desire to set off for some vague elsewhere on the part of characters quite incapable of actually moving, with the exception, at the end of the play, of the strange grandfather. In 1965, the play *Klondyke*[10]

12

reveals Languirand's previously repressed awareness of membership in a North American community. Just as the Klondike gold rush of 1896 attracted adventurers from many countries—Irish, Italian, French, British, Native North American, Canadian, Quebecer and others—so this play, in a class of its own (the author himself labeled it an "action dramatique"), brings to the stage picaresque characters whose French is marbled with English and Native American expressions. The play's twelve tableaux follow one another in rapid succession, interrupted here and there by dances, songs, colorful indoor and outdoor scenes which occur at different seasons of the year and are accompanied by the projection of historical photographs, which lend a certain epic character to the whole production.

In the midst of this proliferation, wherein the elements of spectacle prevail over psychological depth, the playwright means to express the American adventure, more extroverted than introverted, characterized by a predominance of the Dionysian tendency, essentially active and triumphant, the affirmation of a freedom of thought and action which appears unlimited and finds on this vast continent plenty of room to roam. Such a spectacle, successfully staged in Montreal and London in 1965, gave a hint of the eventual breakthrough of other Quebec artists who were deeply affected by Americanness, artists such as Robert Charlebois and a number of young musicians and cabaret singers from Quebec.

In an essay entitled *Le Québec et l'américanité*, published as a postscript to the play, Languirand tells the story of how during his first trip to Paris, in 1949, as a young man of eighteen, he began to discover America. Coming into contact with a French nation "already obsessed with America," his repressed Americanness rose to the surface and became clearer as he realized that he, a Quebecer, was a French-speaking inhabitant of an English-speaking continent. This realization seems to have been at the origin of his conception of *Klondyke*, sparking in him a creative tension between otherness and the inner self. Languirand quotes anthropologist Lionel Tiger as saying man is supposedly a "chasseur frustré," so that the rush to the Klondike, like the call to war is a "nouvel exutoire dionysiaque," a kind of magic ritual, including an exorcism and an initiation, and also a series of trials sometimes leading to sacrifice.[11] One of the characters in *Klondyke* puts it this way: "Il n'y avait pas de guerre, alors je suis venu au Klondyke."[12]

For a long time, this mixture of the Dionysian and the Apollonian went hand in hand in Quebecers: a feeling of insularity, enriched with a touch of xenophobia yet perfectly at home with a missionary spirit. It has also been observed by English Canadians, such as Northrop Frye and Margaret Atwood, who have called it a "garrison mentality": you protect the fort; you also yearn to leave it. These character traits have evolved over the past thirty years, giving way to a greater openmindedness with regard to others, including immigrants. This, too, has been evidenced in recent theatrical productions, for example in *Balconville*[13] a completely hybridized play that is written in two languages and so appeals to both cultural communities in Canada, written by the non-native French speaker David Fennario of Montreal. Here I could have evoked other plays as well, created out of a similar tension by a number of young Quebec playwrights who have come into contact with other aspects of the North American continent or with American culture itself.

Parody

In 1968, several Quebec plays took the form of parodies of works from the classical repertoire. In *Hamlet, prince du Québec*, which opened at Montreal's Théâtre de l'Escale on 17 January 1968, Robert Gurik stages a symbolic confrontation between the political forces at work in Quebec. Here is how he himself explains his intentions in the introduction to the play:

> Hamlet, c'est le Québec avec toutes ses hésitations, avec sa soif d'action et de liberté, corseté par cent ans d'inaction. Autour de lui se meuvent les masques des personnages qui conduisent sa destinée. Le Roi, l'anglophonie, qui tient les rênes du pouvoir politique et économique, la Reine, cette Eglise qui, dans notre histoire, a accepté tous les compromis, le Premier ministre, instrument exécutif du Roi. Il y a aussi les deux grandes tendances qui écartèlent le Québec, d'un côté les fédéralistes: l'aile québécoise du Parti Libéral du Canada (Trudeau, Marchand, Pelletier) qui, il y a bien longtemps, ont pu passer pour nationalistes, et de l'autre, les indépendantistes (Lévesque, Bourgault).[14]

14

In this parodic adaptation of *Hamlet*, the ghost of Hamlet's father is a screen projection of General de Gaulle just as he appeared in July 1967 on the balcony of Montreal's city hall, although the role can also be played by an actor. The specter will tell his son Hamlet/Quebec:

> J'ai été un mauvais père, tu as grandi orphelin, et aujourd'hui encore je me présente à toi le visage rougi par les flammes et la honte, aujourd'hui encore je viens la main tendue car j'ai bien peu à t'offrir et je te l'offrirai bien tard. Mais tu es ma chair et mon sang et si jamais tu aimais ton pauvre père, ce vieillard rongé par l'orgueil. . .venge un meurtre horrible.[15]

When referring to the King who stands for the Anglophone world, he will add: "Do not let Quebec rot beneath the boot of this profiteer who might manage to make you think he understands you and loves you."[16] As in Shakespeare's play, most of the protagonists die: Ophelia, Polonius, the King, the Queen, Laertes, and Hamlet himself who, as he dies, turns toward his friend Horatio (René Lévesque) as a source of hope and tells him:

> Je meurs. . .qui viendra nous conduire vers la lumière? . . .Qui. . . qui. . .nous sortira de la fange des compromis, de l'esclavage? Qui brisera les chaînes qu'hypocritement nous avons nous-mêmes formées? Il faut que ma mort serve aux autres. Il faut. . .que vive. . .un. . .Qué. . .bec. . . libre.[17]

What are we to think of such a parody? Does applying an old text to a contemporary political situation count as a form of hybridization? Does the radical change in the referential function still leave room for the initial text to be discovered beneath this palimpsest? I think the answer must be yes: parody is a kind of cross-fertilization and one of the pleasures it procures for us arises precisely from the possibility of identifying the two superimposed referents, that of text A and that of text B, as well as the gap between them.

Another example of parody occured was furnished in the same year, 1968, in Réjean Ducharme's play *Le Cid maghané*. "Maghané" is a Quebec word meaning "mistreated." Ducharme keeps pretty nearly the same plot, characters, and overall structure, but inserts several parodic differences. The most important of these are: 1) Constant allusions to the contemporary world. For example, Rodrigue refers to his Rolls Royce and wants to take Chimène to a motel. 2) A transformation of language, a deliberate break with tradition, a transition from the classical alexandrine to a completely degraded form of everyday speech: "qu'ils viennent les maudits, si c'est pas des peureux."[18] 3) On a deeper level, a transformation of the contents of the play whereby Rodrigue is no longer conquering hero but an antihero who, weakened by alcohol and wearing boxing gloves and skis, is finally put out of commission by Don Sanche. 4) From the tragicomedy it was for Corneille, the play becomes a vulgar comedy verging on farce, illustrating, much more than hybridization, Ducharme's desire to be done with the masterworks of imported culture once and for all.

This parodic vein runs through all of contemporary Quebec theater, including the works of Jean-Claude Germain, which he himself describes as an effort to liquidate the nation's "old stock," placing *homo quebecensis* face-to-face with what he is not, sometimes appropriating the image of the other, like a Halloween costume: dressing up like a skeleton in order to scare death. Inspired by the historical figure of Sarah Bernhardt (1844-1923) as well as by his own contemporary the Canadian soprano Emma Albani (1847-1930), Germain stages on 6 November 1974, *Les Hauts et les bas de la vie d'une diva: Sarah Ménard par eux-mêmes*.[19] Right at the start of the play, the description of the set emphasizes the kaleidoscopic dimension of the career of Sarah Ménard who is pictured on posters as Lili Marlene, as a Walkyrie, as a dancer, as a *fin de siècle* diva. The diva sings arias such as the *Oiseau de malheur*, the *Aria d'Eurydice au téléphone*, the *Duo d'Antoine et d'Eurydice*, the *Air du suicide d'Orphée*. In the second part of the play, the songs evoke realities much closer to the cultural past of Quebecers, e.g., the rise of Catholic guidebooks or the "deification" of Monseigneur Aubuchon. At the same time, a ledger line is drawn for Sarah Ménard: that of a life devoted to being someone other than oneself through the acting out of chunks of text received from a foreign culture. In the end she asks herself, "Oucé qu'j'en suis venue là?" and she recovers her train of thought, stands up, unfastens her cape, takes off her wig, looks out at the audience, comes down from the stage, changes her costume, puts on a long coat made of locally produced cloth, and finally recovers the voice and Gaspé accent of her father from Sainte-Marthe-sur-Mer. She becomes herself

Les Hauts et les bas de la vie d'une diva, 1975. Photograph by Daniel Kieffer.

again, recapturing her childhood memories, consecrated by the Gigue à Mononcque Simon, which she "now dances for herself." Sarah Ménard regains her true identity, what comes to her from her rooted-ness in a family and her native land. This one-character play starts to look very much like a victory over the possible forms of alienation that threaten the identity of a "great" actress.

Jean-Claude Germain revealed his thinking about otherness in a later, explicitly political play: *A Canadian Play/Une plaie canadienne,* performed for the first time on 26 April 1979, at the Théâtre d'Aujourd'hui, and which stages the ritual execution of Lord Durham, a proponent of assimilation identified with *Bonhomme Sept Heures,* a symbol of French Canadian alienation. This ritual is played out according to a ceremony inspired by a Freemasonry whose French-speaking adherents, now government ministers, often betrayed their fellow Quebecers. The author's message is spelled out in the preface and postface of the play.[20]

The work of Jean-Pierre Ronfard must be situated in another vein of parody. Born in France, married to Marie Cardinal, Ronfard has pursued a career as a director in Montreal since 1960. He is the

author of numerous translations and adaptations and for forty years
has been staging the most prestigious works of world theater. Acting
for Quebec audiences, he has necessarily become an expert on the
subject of hybridization, insofar as this term, in the context of the theater, can denote any form of appropriation meant to make a work
accessible to people of another era, another milieu, or another mentality. After reading the complete works of Shakespeare between January
and April 1980, the members of the *bande des quatre*—a collective of
the *Nouveau théâtre expérimental de Montréal* under the direction of
Ronfard—reached a point where they conceived of a collection, a
genealogy of characters and families who came into conflict over a
kingdom. In the wake of some writing workshops they all attended,
they assigned Ronfard the task of writing a play or rather a cycle of
plays inspired by Shakespeare but situated in a French-Canadian context of mockery and parody. Thus came into existence the six-play
cycle known as *Vie et mort du Roi Boiteux*,[21] whose main character
and basic plot, inspired in large part by *Richard III*, thrust onto the
stage a monster of ugliness and ambition. The text of the play
includes numerous cultural allusions to the whole of Western theatrical tradition ranging from Aristotle, Racine, and Bertolt Brecht to
Quebec authors such as Victor-Lévy Beaulieu.

By invoking well-known myths, literary works, and historical or cultural referents, Ronfard and his team gave birth to an entirely new
work, with a meaning all its own. The word that strikes me as the most
fitting to describe this creative process is "dérivation," with all the
meanings and shades the dictionary attributes to it. Dérivation is "un
procédé de formation de mots nouveaux par modification d'un mor-
phème (suffixe) par rapport à une base (radical)." Ronfard finds his
roots in the cultural heritage of Europe. He gives this heritage a new
meaning by incorporating it into a framework in which the morphemes
or suffixes are modified and transmogrified according to the contemporary context and the design pursued by the collective creator.[22]

There is no room here to examine in detail the historical context of
Quebec in which this play cycle was conceived and created in the
aftermath of the 1980 referendum. The 24 June 1982 production constituted a theatrical event of extraordinary significance. Six plays were
performed one right after the other, from ten o'clock in the morning
until one o'clock at night, at Montreal's Expo-Théâtre, in a variety of
stage settings, both indoors and outdoors, interspersed with meal

Vie et mort die Roi Boiteux, 1982. Photograph by Hubert Fielden.

breaks and informal gatherings of actors and spectators. The Quebecers in attendance felt as if they were reliving, in their own way, the high points of the Dionysia of ancient Greece. Yet in this fun fair that had every appearance of a carnival, they recognized themselves. In this great wayward current that toured the world as well as the collective theatrical space, in this cross-fertilization of theatrical cultures of multiple origins, the idea of a king and his kingdom became the stuff of an important metaphor. In the life of this lame, laughable, and weak-willed monarch who is Richard Premier, in the lives of the other characters both male and female, it was the human existence of each and every person that was emerging, the emptiness of each little individual kingdom, with its ridicule and its trivialities, at the center of the cultural hybridization of our century.

The Issue of *joual*

With the public reading of Michel Tremblay's *Les Belles-Sœurs*[23] on 4 March 1968, and its production by the Théâtre du Rideau-Vert in the following August, the working-class dialect of Quebec made its official début in the theaters of Montreal. The critics found themselves in a quandary: how were they to reject this blue-collar speech, *joual*, when quite obviously the play itself, thanks to its value as drama, was stirring the emotions and enthusiasm of the theater-going public? It was immediately clear that essentially working-class characters ought to express themselves as such people do, at home, in the street, in their kitchens, and in their living rooms. The rest is history: *joual* eventually emerged as the language of choice of most Quebec play-wrights, a preference that has lasted for two decades, although it seems to have declined somewhat in the last few years.

Should the use of *joual*—the word is a corruption of *cheval*, horse—be seen as an instance of hybridization? There are two aspects of *joual*: one of them is intrinsic, involving a deformation or modification of standard French from within, which appears first in the pronunciation of words and then in the transcription of speech; the other aspect is extrinsic, involving the introduction into French of heterogeneous elements most often coming from English, e.g., the verb *whatcher*, which means to watch over. Sometimes these borrowings come from elsewhere: *crisser quelqu'un dehors*, for instance, is the verbal extension of a swearword and means to expel or throw someone out. As far as I am concerned, *joual* represents without any doubt the collision of two cultures, learned and popular. Learned culture is linked to the use of the French language such as it is taught in school, with its grammar and its texts handed down as part of an elitist education based on norms, codes, and privileges. The popular culture of Quebec shows not only the influence of the *Americanité* discussed above, but also of a way of life, a geography, an invasion of daily life by consumer goods first given a name in British or American English.

The phenomenon of *joual* is indeed one of hybridization, and the takeover of this dialect by the contemporary theater movement was all the more spontaneous in that at the very same time, during the period between 1965 and 1968, Quebec was undergoing a profound shift in values and culture. Quebec society is located at the crossroads of several cultures, several influences, both American and European. It is the word *crossroads*, more precisely the word *trivium*, meaning three ways or paths, that provides the etymological source of the word *trivial*. The *trivium*, or crossing of several paths, became the meeting place of ordinary folks. *Trivialis*, trivial, defined the character of whatever was common, ordinary, of realities that were the most banal, the lowest, the most vulgar. The freedom of expression assumed by Aristophanes, allowing his lower-class characters to speak a language appropriate to their station in life (and God knows just how far he goes in this direction!), was demanded by Quebec writers in the name of their own freedom. Away with censorship, away with inhibitions! Today, this demand seems muted but it will never disappear altogether: in the minds of Quebec playwrights it is connected to freedom of speech and to the existence of a working class which, if I may put it euphemistically, does not mince its words.

Hybridization and Theatricality

Quebec dramatists of the period 1950–70 experienced early on the influence of theatrical innovations taking place in America and Europe. One such example that comes to mind is the influence of Bertolt Brecht, whose *Threepenny Opera* was being staged by this time. The plays of Dubé and Loranger evolve from a classical art of the crisis, built around the observance of the three unities of time, place, and action, toward an art of the tableau, with dramatic action moving from place to place and in some cases spreading out over a period of several years (e.g., *Un Simple Soldat*, in 1958). Loranger experiments with spectacular theatrical innovations. *Le Chemin du roy* (1968), following upon the historical visit of General de Gaulle, symbolically transposes the political conflict Canada vs. Quebec into a hockey game pitting the Federalists against the Separatists. *Double Jeu* (1969) and *Médium saignant* (1970) by the same author invite the active participation of the audience. The symbolism of play, which established a parallelism between hockey and drama, reappeared at the time the Ligue Nationale d'Improvisation was founded by Robert Gravel, 1976–77. This organization, which has given birth to many like it in various countries of the world, also embodies a form of hybridization, as the skating rink with its referees and its exact rules becomes the staging site of a joust between teams displaying a virtuosity that is theatrical in every sense of the word.

In the on-stage use of *joual*, certain observers, for example Bernard Dort, have seen a form of theatricality that expresses the will to mark one's difference from traditional theatrical models.[24] Freedom with respect to language goes hand in hand with a desire to appropriate dramatic codes and to undertake some rather extensive experimentation with form. The most striking plays of Michel Tremblay, e.g., *Les Belles-Sœurs* and *A toi pour toujours ta Marie-Lou*,[25] are set apart not only by the raciness and crudeness of their language, but also by their rather daring stagecraft, and their very structure, which has often been compared to that of a cantata. In the first of these plays, the figured bass of the stamp-licking party is periodically interrupted by blackouts that clear the stage for the dramatic monologues of each of the "belles-sœurs"; in the second one, a single stage set is the locus of a superimposition and crisscrossing of conversational exchanges between the parents, then between the daughters, conversations that in fact take place in different places and ten years apart.

In the theater, the cross-fertilization of texts is complemented by the cross-fertilization of styles of stage direction. Translating Shakespeare in her own way, then staging it in Japanese style, as she did *Henry IV* in 1984, Ariane Mnouchkine carries out a kind of hybridization by drawing upon signs that can be perceived as heterogeneous, as foreign: diction, gestures, costumes, masks, music, and stage design. The same could be said about her recent interpretation of the *Atreidae,* of which I have seen and admired the *Agamemnon.* In his production of *The Tempest* staged in Paris during the 1990-91 season, Peter Brook used actors of every race and color to draw upon African culture, Southeast Asian culture, the sobriety of English-speaking actors, and the vivacity of French-speaking ones. What an incredible mixing of convergent effects that was, placed at the service of a gigantic metaphor that constitutes a brand new reading of *The Tempest*!

In the past decade, new forms of theatricality have arisen in Quebec, notably in the production of Robert Lepage's Théâtre Repère, in the *Trilogie des dragon,* as well as in those of the Carbone 14 group spearheaded by Gilles Maheu: *Le Rail,* then *Le Dortoir,* among others, have gone on world tour. These productions have been favorably received in some fifteen countries because of their originality. Their success did not depend on written texts but on modern scenography and a wholly original, strongly metaphorical use of gestures, which caused reference to the written text to be relegated to second place by choreography, recorded background, and a visual message that are all highly stylized. Therein, of course, lies a form of

Le Rail, 1984. Photograph by Yves Dubé.

hybridization, if only through the emphasis on objects, gestures, music, and dance. The logos born of traditional Occidental culture gives way here to praxis, and the *poiein* of writing, to one of action. This recent development would have pleased Antonin Artaud, but it formalizes the divorce between theater and literature. The theatrical institution and the literary institution take divergent paths, each expressing the world with its own distinctive voice. Here of course I betray my own literary bias, but one can foresee that the art form liable to suffer more from this parting of the ways, in the long run, is the theater. Unless videotape is used to record its adventures, the theater is depriving itself of the material support of the text, which in our cultural tradition has always been the archive of memory.

The encounter between the self and the other is the first form of cross-fertilization. It takes place within the individual human being who, as he or she advances through life, must take on and assimilate diverse and sometimes disparate elements, welling up within the self or arising from the self's contacts with the world. Might there not be good reason here to suggest an analogy with love, where two distinct human beings come together? In this meeting between A and B, who have at first a distance between them, three possibilities can be envisaged. The first of these is the total fusion of A and B, an outcome difficult to envisage, either in human love or in divine love, since persons remain separate and distinct! The second possibility is an absorption whereby one partner, i.e. A, draws the other to itself: A swallows B. This involves the integration, the melting down and disappearance of B. Who would ever wish for such an unsatisfactory result? The third and final possibility is love, or a mingling based on closeness, encounter, and compromise, and where the partners, A and B, meet each other half way, in the middle, yet remain distinguishable to varying degrees, as in the staging of a written text. In this way the two partners can come together as one, without losing their separate identities.

Notes

1. Translated by Keith Palka, Central Michigan University.
2. Guildo Rousseau, *L'Image des Etats-Unis dans la littérature québécoise (1775–1930)* (Sherbrooke: Editions Naaman, 1981).
3. Ralph Linton, The Cultural Background of Personality (New York-London: Appleton-Century, 1945).
4. Chantal Hébert, *Le burlesque au Québec. Un divertissement populaire* (Montréal: Hurtubise HMH, 1981), 175–205.
5. Chantal Hébert, "Analyse comparée des modèles représentatifs du burlesque québécois et américain" (Ph.D. dissertation, Université Laval, Sainte-Foy, 1984).
6. Leon Petitjean and Henri Rollin, *Aurore l'enfant martyre*, Histoire et présentation de la pièce par Alonzo Le Blanc (Montréal: VLB Editeur, 1982).
7. Gratien Gélinas, *Les Fridolinades*, 4 vols. (1945-1946; 1943-1944; 1941-1942; 1938-1940) (Montréal: Les Quinze, éditeur, 1980, 1981, 1981, 1988).
8. Gratien Gélinas, *Tit-Coq* (Montréal: Beauchemin, 1950).
9. Jacques Languirand, *Les Grands Départs* (Montréal: Cercle du livre de France, 1958).
10. Jacques Languirand, *Klondyke* (suivi d'une étude: "Le Québec et l'Américanité") (Montréal: Cercle du livre de France, 1971).
11. Ibid., 225, 228.
12. Ibid., 230.
13. David Fennario, *Balconville: A Play* [1979] (Vancouver: Talonbooks, 1980).

14. Robert Gurik, *Hamlet, prince du Québec* (Montréal: Editions de l'homme, 1968), 5.

15. Ibid., 28.

16. Ibid., 30.

17. Ibid., 95.

18. Réjean Ducharme, *Le Cid maghané* (manuscrit conservé au Théâtre du Trident, Québec and in the archives of CRELIQ [Centre de recherche en littérature québécoise], Université Laval, Québec).

19. Jean-Claude Germain, *Les Hauts et les bas dans de la vie d'une diva: Sarah Ménard par eux-mêmes* (Montréal: VLB Editeur, 1976).

20. Jean-Claude Germain, *A Canadian play/Une plaie canadienne* (Montréal: VLB Editeur, 1979).

21. Jean-Pierre Ronfard, *Vie et mort du Roi Boiteux*, 2 vols. (Montréal: Leméac, 1981).

22. Alonzo Le Blanc, "Ronfard: dérive organisée et conflit des cultures," *Etudes littéraires* 18(3) (Winter 1985): 134.

23. Michel Tremblay, *Les Belles-Sœurs* (Montréal: Leméac, 1972).

24. Bernard Dort, "Sur le travail théâtral, entretien de Bernard Dort avec Thérèse Arbic et Robert Chartrand," *Chroniques* 1(4) (April 1975): 17.

25. Michel Tremblay, *A toi pour toujours ta Marie-Lou* (Montréal: Leméac, 1971).

The Theater: Sounding Board for the Appeals and Dreams of the *Québécois* Collectivity

Chantal Hébert

❖ ❖ ❖ ❖ ❖ ❖ ❖ ❖ ❖ ❖ ❖ ❖ ❖ ❖ ❖ ❖ ❖ ❖ ❖

One function of theater is to respond to the real world, and it is my intention here to look at the avatars of the modern Quebec stage in order to discover how this theater has interacted in recent times with a changing Quebec society. The "p'tit Québécois," known as "French-Canadian" until around 1960, has been witness to a spectacular evolution in all the categories of living during the last three decades. This period of evolution appears to parallel events in the theater where, in recent years and especially in the 1980s, important changes have taken place with respect to content as well as form and processes of dramatic writing and scenography.

In order better to appreciate the linkages between the history of Quebec and its theater, it will be useful to put recent changes into historical perspective by beginning our examination in the period of the 1960s before looking at the 1970s and the 1980s. While dividing history up into *tranches de vie* may seem arbitrary, I believe that certain salient political events, like the coming to power of the provincial Liberals in 1960, the October Crisis of 1970 and the Referendum of 1980, can serve as crucial reference points for the understanding of complex changes.

The 1960s: The Emergence of a *Québécois* Voice[2]

"C'est le temps que ça change" was the popular slogan of the so-called "du tonnere" team of Jean Lesage, who came to power in 1960 and inaugurated a remarkable new era in the history of Quebec, known thereafter as "The Quiet Revolution." The 1960s were an important crossover between the French-Canadian attachment to the past, and the discovery of a colonized collective consciousness, which led in turn to the emergence of a new mentality that demanded emancipation, modernization, and liberalization. As a result, great changes marked Quebec's political, economic, social, and cultural life in the decade of the 1960s.

With the Quiet Revolution, the theater, following the example of a number of other artistic practices in Quebec, denounced its French-Canadian status the better to affirm its *québécois* identity. During this period, the theater experienced a remarkable growth, manifested in the founding of basic, permanent theatrical institutions like the Centre d'Essai des Auteurs Dramatiques (1965) or the various theater programs and schools which, in addition to having a direct effect on training, stimulated the creation of new drama. To these initiatives may be added the construction of theaters which furnished the basic material support necessary for theatrical activity. In Montreal alone, more than fifteen new theaters were constructed or converted between 1967—the year of "Expo 67"—and 1980. Concurrently, the appearance of new and dynamic troupes bore witness to exceptional creativity: Les Saltimbanques (1962), the Nouvelle Compagnie Théâtrale (1964), the Théâtre du Vieux-Québec (1967), Le Grand Cirque Ordinaire (1969), and the Trident (1969), among others. At the same time, new and diverse audiences emerged.[3] This explosion of activity was also reflected in the quality and quantity of dramatic productions by such authors as Marcel Dubé, Jacques Languirand, Françoise Loranger, and Robert Gurik.[4]

It was, however, with the creation of Michel Tremblay's *Belles-Sœurs*[5] in 1968 that a downtrodden nation became defiantly aware of itself. Sharing the same *maudite vie plate*, prisoners of their own banality and of a spatial universe lacking in perspective and variety, the sisters-in-law are stuck together with the glue of a common alienation. The play contributed to the *prise de conscience* of Quebec society by denouncing its minority reflexes and a past molded by dependence on religious and rural values anchored in the traditional family. The Tremblay work is an acerbic critique of the *Québécois*, a people shown to be economically and culturally poor and having as its only treasure *joual,* that "bastard" language which in the play becomes the object of a genuine consecration.

The dramaturgy of Tremblay, without doubt the most important author of the period, refocused Quebec's self-image, igniting in the process a new consciousness of social and cultural realities. The old self-image, grounded in alienation, became the principal target of the partisans of the Quiet Revolution. The *Québécois* were alienated from every point of view: on the one hand their economic assets were controlled by Anglo-Saxon companies, on the other they were culturally colonized by France.

Evidence of alienation can also be found in the history of Quebec theater dating from the Conquest until well into the modern era. Indeed, until the beginning of the twentieth century all commercial theaters belonged to English-Canadian or American interests. In cities with a majority of French speakers, like Montreal and Quebec City— the only theatrical centers in Quebec—the plays done by professionals were invariably performed in English. During this period, in short, New York extended its hegemony over things theatrical throughout the North American continent. Until 1880, plays mounted in French in Quebec comprised less than 5 percent of local theatrical activity. The result, as Jean-Marc Larrue[6] has shown, was that the professional French-speaking theater in Quebec was of necessity born of Anglo-American parents. With respect especially to production values (special and technical effects, large casts), American influence was enormous. Aesthetically, however, the value of the repertory was measured against continental French standards. The history of Quebec theater was as a result destined to become a long search for dramatic integrity and autonomy; this, despite our fascination with "Americanness" during the 1960s, when the hippie counter-culture made especially strong inroads into Quebec.

What has been called, since the late 1960s, "new theater" or "new *québécois* dramaturgy," pointedly rejected foreign influences, especially French, and served as a cure for alienation as well as an impetus for collective affirmation. We have already seen that French-Canadian theatrical practices since the 1890s (when Francophone professional activity first appeared in Quebec) had been subjected to French standards. As of 1965, we began to see traces of the indigenous imagination at work in popular theater forms.

One of the particularities of the "new theater" was that it housed a vast gallery of portraits of "little people"; when the "greats" of this world did appear in it, as Jean-Cléo Godin[7] has shown, they were completely divested of their solemn finery. The phenomenon is hardly surprising when viewed in a wider historical context. The "North American French," scarred by the Conquest of 1760, had come to see themselves as "an insignificant people of water carriers and wood cutters." They tended to construct, as a result, a dramatic universe in which the recurrent protagonist was the anti-hero, a parodic and parodied version of the invincible hero. From Tit-Coq in the play by Gratien Gélinas[8] to the marginal characters of Michel Tremblay and the parodic heroes of Jean-Claude Germain, the anti-hero dominated the dramaturgy of identity until about 1980, the end of a period of intensely nationalistic, introspective theater.

While the break with traditional attitudes relied heavily on the figure of a "hero" who spoke the language of the Quebec public, it also depended on dramatic writing that invented themes and symbolism and created a mythology identifiable with the voice of Quebec.

The 1970s: Shaping Forms and Values

Quebec subscribed easily to modernity and, as the nation recovered its collective voice, a strong tendency toward theatrical autarky emerged. The wholesale introduction of *joual* to the stage corresponded to the need for self-expression. Several prominent playwrights appropriated this voice and were joined by the young companies of "collective creation" that appeared during the period.

From the late 1960s to the 1980 Referendum, Jean-Claude Germain was undoubtedly the person who, more than anyone, personified the wish for the *québécisation* of our culture. Germain carried out a scathing examination of traditional theater and its mythified forms.[9] While challenging the family, religion, and social institutions, he was undoubtedly one of those who, with Tremblay, caught most accurately the popular speech and imagination of the 1970s. Aligned with Germain was Jean Barbeau, another prolific author of this effervescent period, known especially as a representative of populist dramaturgy. Through humor, Barbeau portrayed his version of the anti-hero and in turn denounced alienating traditional values in plays like *Ben-Ur, Goglu,* and *Joualez-moi d'amour.*[10]

The prominence of *joual* and the use of popular speech on stage during this period cannot be ignored. Language incorporates a vision of the world and playwrights chose to put on stage the common people speaking their everyday language as an unequivocal sign of their cultural and economic underdevelopment. While this choice suggests a Marxist perspective on the alienation of an entire society, another reason for the use of *joual* can be found in theatricality itself, and can be explained in the desire to mark a distance from traditional theatrical models, and most especially the French model.

The Feminist Struggle

At the beginning of the 1970s, the questioning of traditional values, in particular those relating to family and religion, also colored the feminist agenda. *La Nef des sorcières,*[11] a collective dramatic work signed by seven women, marked the beginning of "women's theater." Seven women/sorceresses are presented successively in a juxtaposition of varied monologues. The monologue had long been important in the theater of Quebec, with roots in the indigenous oral tradition, but here it acquired an importance on par with the emergence of popular speech to which we have already referred.[12]

If *La Nef des sorcières* and Denise Boucher's *Les Fées ont soif*[13] have acquired the reputation of manifestos, it should be noted that among the texts representative of this remarkable battleground of the 1970s, *Un reel ben beau, ben triste,*[14] by Jeanne-Mance Delisle, represents another high point of "*Québécois* dramaturgy" *au féminin*.

By deciding to speak out publicly on stage, the women of Quebec denounced their alienation, their dispossession, their submission to a world of men. In the theater, collective creation, as practiced in the Théâtre des Cuisines or the Théâtre Expérimental des Femmes became an important vehicle of self-awareness among women whose activity stood out as if in counterpoint to the political questions of the day.[15] Without being directly linked to nationalist aspirations, this important emancipation movement participated in a parallel search for identity. Women's dramaturgy—an important facet of Quebec theater in the 1960s —was a dramaturgy of struggle. Furthermore, the majority of Quebec feminists of the period were linked to the nationalist movement. The very name of the Front de libération des femmes du

Québec, moreover, recalls the Front de Libération du Québec (FLQ), which would itself also impact the contemporary stage.

At the beginning of October 1970, one cell of the FLQ kidnapped a British diplomat, while another cell abducted a recently elected minister of the Bourassa government. The FLQ had embarked on extremist measures in the effort to free Quebec from the capitalist and colonialist yoke. When the Bourassa government appealed to the Canadian Army, the Ottawa Parliament proclaimed the War Measures Act, which suspended civil liberties and permitted the arbitrary detainment of more than four hundred fifty "suspects": trade unionists, poets, singers, and left-leaning intellectuals. The October Crisis of 1970 made a strong impression on the cultural output of the period, inspiring among others, on the stage, *Les Tas de siège* by Robert Gurik,[16] Jean-Claude Germain's *Les Tourtereaux,*[17] and *La Complainte des hivers rouges* by Roland Lepage,[18] a play that deals with the October Crisis while alluding to the revolt of the Patriots of 1837–39.

Dramatic discourse in these pivotal years of the evolution of modern Quebec was permeated with and obsessed by the question of nationalism. Caught between the events of October 1970 and the election of René Levesque's *Parti québécois* on 15 November 1976, the theater continued to be the privileged weapon against the national tragedy of alienation. It reproduced on stage political and sometimes humorous confrontations of the people of Quebec wherein the city council meeting room, the skating rink (La Ligue Nationale d'Improvisation), and the public square replaced the kitchens and living rooms of earlier works. In my opinion, Françoise Loranger's *Médium saignant*[19] remains the best example of this kind of militant theater. As documentary theater and theater of participation, the play attempted to exorcise the trepidation of a Quebec nation still caught in the agonizing search for identity.

The three currents of committed political theater, improvisation, and collective creation manifested themselves forcefully throughout these years. In particular, the phenomenon of collective creation, a true medium of spontaneous popular culture, could be found just about everywhere in Quebec. Under the impetus of a desire for autonomy and in the spirit of a redefined national dramaturgy set in motion in the 1960s, collective creation (whose golden age extended roughly from 1968 to 1978) was the path taken during the 1970s by several young companies repelled by what they saw as the worn-out conventions of the theater. While the voice of the collective happening strove to be both egalitarian and popular, relatively few of the texts produced have been published.

La Ligue Nationale d'Improvisation

The spell cast by improvisation was illustrated by the creation in 1977 of La Ligue Nationale d'Improvisation (LNI), a theatrical game inspired by hockey, which has remained an extremely popular form of entertainment.[20] The point of LNI, which now enjoys an international reputation, is to present improvisation as a theatrical product. In other words, the improvisation workshop itself becomes the play: the spectator witnesses a process of discovery, which is also the product. As Pierre Lavoie points out, the fascination exercised by improvisation arises from a distinctly theatrical phenomenon, that of the compelling rapports between actor and spectator, but he emphasizes, citing Lorraine Camerlain, "la création, qu'elle soit le fait d'un auteur

Ligue Nationale d'Improvisation, 1982. Photograph by André Panneton.

33

ou d'un collectif, demeure encore et toujours l'élément clé de la dramaturgie québécoise, le cheval de Troie de notre imaginaire."[21]

"La création . . . L'élément clé de la dramaturgie québécoise, le cheval de Troie de notre imaginaire"

The 1970s were thus strongly characterized by experimentation both on stage and with the use of language. A host of collectives created during this period opened themselves up to various kinds of exploration, increasing experiments with physical acting, expanded space, and multidisciplinarity, while looking as well into new perceptual fields. The involvement of new companies, such as the Grand Cirque Ordinaire (1969–77), the Théâtre Euh! (1970–78), the Omnibus group of Jean Asselin (1970), Gilles Maheu's Carbone 14 (1975), Eskabel (1971), the Théâtre Parminou (1974), and La Veillée (1973), to name just a few, undoubtedly contributed to the dynamism of dramaturgical and theatrical creation and to a redefinition of both national dramaturgy and theatricality. The project of the Nouveau Théâtre Expérimental, founded in 1975 under the name Théâtre Expérimental de Montréal, is explicit along these lines:

> Fondé pour remettre en question—par la pratique—tous les formalismes dans lesquels se sont enfermés la création et la pratique théâtrales, le TEM s'est donné pour but de mettre en scène des thèmes rarement exprimés au théâtre, tels l'onirique et le fantastique, d'accorder une place prépondérante à l'imaginaire et ce par un travail en commun axé sur un théâtre "physique" et le jeu du comédien, provoqué et nourri par l'improvisation.[22]

These experimental Quebec troupes truly transformed theater praxis, liberating it through research from—among other things—the omnipotence of the text. Their pioneering work was at the root of the emergence of a new type of text that director Jean-Luc Denis, recalling Richard Schechner, referred to as *texte représentationnel*:

> Par "texte représentationnel" (performance text), Schechner entend un produit indissociable de sa mise en scène et de ses conditions de création: un théâtre d'image, multidisciplinaire et multivectoriel,

façonné en cours de répétition, qui ne se codifie pas (donc, ne se perpétue pas) aussi facilement que le texte dramatique conventionnel.[23]

The "performance text" so defined is representative of the paths taken by the young innovators of the 1970s, who cleared the way for the experimental theater of the 1980s.[24] It is clear henceforth that the dramatic text will no longer necessarily be considered the vital source of a play, and that the will exists to take the spectator to the very heart of theater as a living art.

One needs also to mention in this context of theatrical renewal the growth of theater for younger audiences (children and teenagers), which enjoyed a remarkable expansion and a renewal of creativity during the 1970s.[24] Profiting from the climate of research and experimentation, several companies contributed to the reinvention of theater for the young, with respect both to content and theatrical presentation; these include the Théâtre de la Marmaille (1973), the Théâtre de Carton (1973), the Théâtre du Carrousel (1975), and the Théâtre des Confettis (1977). At the same time, playwrights like Marie-Francine Hébert,[25] Suzanne Lebeau,[26] Gilles Gauthier,[27] and Louis-Dominique Lavigne,[28] contributed to the emergence of a dramaturgy for younger audiences.

Between 1960 and 1980, according to the critic Gilbert David, "la société québécoise a changé et, avec elle, le théâtre qui la désigne." And, like Quebec, he adds, "La création dramatique nationale a fait un bond remarquable."[29] At the end of the 1970s, the image of Quebec that emerges in this theater is that of a nation no longer idealized in any sense, but rather a real entity in the process of actualizing itself. From this point, the theater will move to open up new worlds for itself, and the ongoing struggle for identity will henceforth be accompanied by an opening outward toward the world and toward the international vocation of Quebec.

The 1980s: New Forms of Writing to Change Our Perception of the World

As we have seen, theatrical praxis for some years now has been non-traditional. The work of the theater is no longer necessarily dependent on texts written beforehand by an author, nor does it need ideas intended for realization in a space—"empty" if possible—by collective creation. As a result, relationships between text (dramaturgy) and stage have been transformed and have become more complex. What is more, the distinction between text and stage has all but disappeared as each attempts to represent the world according to rules that Aristotle would have difficulty recognizing.

Following closely on previous experimentation, other changes occurred, among them a swing from a political to a formal focus. Creators who sought new theatrical paths and new forms found an original way to create meaning by signing *different* kinds of texts. While the 1960s and 1970s had helped to delineate the contours of a new identity, the 1980s shaped a discourse oriented toward the multiple tendencies of human experience (no longer simply toward a collective definition) and above all toward the insertion of Quebecers into the international scene.

We have seen that from 1970 to 1980, an astonishing number of young troupes had as their goal the promotion of an innovative theater in Quebec. Although fifty-three troupes were created in the period between the October Crisis and the Referendum, the most fertile years for exploration and innovation were those immediately following the failure of the Referendum. (It should be recalled that the Referendum of May 1980 did not bear on the independence of Quebec, but simply on the right to negotiate sovereignty association with the Canadian confederation. The majority of *Québécois* rejected what was in fact a simple request to negotiate, showing instead their confidence in the "fédéralisme renouvelé" of Pierre Elliott Trudeau.)

Did the disappointment and distress engendered in certain playwrights by the Referendum exacerbate their need for expression? Such a question may seem inappropriate for the sociologist lacking a method to relate social questions to artistic creation. It seems nonetheless probable that a shock to Quebec society, on the scale of the defeat of the 1980 Referendum, would have had repercussions in the discourse of the theater, in which that society saw itself mirrored. Whatever the case, between 1980 and 1985, a new generation of dramatic authors appeared, and no less than forty-seven new theatrical groups were created.[30] It is clear that for a number of those innovative, young companies producing theater based on images, there was a strong desire to break with the work of institutionalized troupes.

Their own work was after all oriented more toward creation goals than toward the polished, public staging of a production; the term used to describe this approach is "experimental theater,"[31] a term that well describes the path taken by the dramatic authors of the 1980s.

It should also be noted that, with the beginning of the 1980s, there was a shift with respect to themes: the figure of the artist, in particular, tended to supplant family portraits. New writing styles must also be taken into account: a form of dramatic composition opposed to the older dramaturgy emerged, as well as an original theater that contributed to a revaluation of formal considerations. In short, the public was confronted with new dramatic forms and texts. As a result, the reader and/or spectator could no longer refer to an old conception of the theatrical machine any more than he or she could fall back on traditional dramaturgy.

"Performance Text" . . . Provides a Glimpse of What is Stirring within the Depths of the Mind

This new form of theater is in fact related to the "performance text" of Schechner referred to above: the experimental theater, freed from the all-importance of the text, creates in general with *tangible resources* made up of *all* the elements at the roots of creation (e.g. objects, actors, text, lighting, sound, and space). The theatrical project is shaped according to choices made, the arrangement and interrelationships of the *various* elements, rather than according to some predetermined goal set forth in a text. In short, it takes form and meaning thanks to particular processes of organization brought into play by creative activity, that is to say, contact among heterogeneous elements inherent to theatrical art forms. In this context, the organization of meaning is a function of sometimes erratic relationships that are built during the interactive and dynamic explorations controlled by the imagination and intuitions of the group of creators and that depend on the particular circumstances of creation in the immediate. The organization of meaning is no longer tied to the preeminence of the narrative form in the organization of traditional knowledge. "C'est un processus dynamique," explains director Jacques Lessard:

On explore. . .sans se donner de limites et sans but précis, ce qui nous amène à des expériences complètement libres. Par exemple, lors des explorations pour *En attendant,* l'une des partitions consistait à ouvrir plusieurs fois la valise en disant à chaque fois le premier mot qui nous venait à l'esprit. Tout à coup, pendant cette fête du délire, une image est apparue et s'est imposée.[32]

From the creative explorations typical of the performance text of experimental troupes, there emerges an imaged language whose syntax is formed before the very eyes of the spectator, delivering the code simultaneously with the message. The originality of this moving combination of words, gestures, and images lies in the fact that the content of the message—which is most often indefinite at the beginning—can sometimes take on several meanings, each originating in the models of interaction of the participating elements. These elements, with their multiple potentialities, solicited by the creators in order to bring out their meaning, enter into the structure of the play by virtue of this meaning, rather than by way of a preestablished content. In other words, instead of formulating discourse with things based on ideas (a theater of the *logos,* of rational discourse), our artists have rethought theatrical language by letting things "speak," by exploring them *sans a priori,* as Pierre A. Larocque explains in describing the work undertaken by Eskabel in 1977:

Le travail que nous poursuivons à l'Eskabel cette année [1977] est de cet ordre; sans texte préalable, sans scénario si mince soit-il, sans schéma de base, aller à la recherche d'images nouvelles, d'un monde ou de mondes se dégageant progressivement des rares éléments choisis et créer une réalité aussi forte, aussi dense, aussi imaginaire, aussi totale (pleine de revirements, de contradictions, de faux-semblants, de sensations, de perceptions multiples . . .) sans faire appel, ou le moins possible et si ce n'est pour renforcer la vision du "percepteur" à quoi que ce soit d'extérieur: texte, décors, costumes, objets . . .

Ces signes tangibles—ainsi notre idée de base est-elle de «nous laisser conduire» par ces éléments—provoquent des liens que nous tentons d'actualiser, de rendre le plus perceptible possible sans pour autant en limiter le sens, lui donner une seule signification, à l'aide de la parole—qui devient un moyen entre autres, de même que l'acteur, et non le centre de tout, la cause et la finalité—de la musique, de

> l'éclairage, jamais figés, immobilisés. Tout est changeant, polymorphe
> et proche du fonctionnement métaphorique de la poésie où un drap
> devient un linceul, un écran, une pure teinte, un voile . . . .[33]

In this connection, let us recall the similar use of privileged visual elements like the sheets, shoe boxes, and their contents, in the *Trilogie des dragons* of the Théâtre Repère. Another example is the measuring tape, the modest object with which Robert Lepage, in *Vinci*,[34] takes us on a voyage from the Pyramids to the Great Wall of China, leading us from Picasso to radio and television, from jazz to *Jaws* and the moonwalk of Michael Jackson, proving that objects can act as key vectors of theatrical activity and offering us what has been called a theater of images, while leading us into unsuspected universes and revealing what lies stirring within the depths of the mind.

Current performance text uses the logic of dreams, creating its context or contexts as it is carried along by correspondences, shifts, and various other connections among disparate entities. The originality of this interactive writing in theatrical space consists of the fact that the content of the message can take on numerous variations and meanings. The Quebec theater of the 1980s spoke in a different way, said new things; the text no longer dominated the stage—to the detriment of other means of theatrical expression. We have exchanged a praxis in which only the text provided meaning, for a praxis wherein everything contributes to meaning. Henceforth, the organization of meaning will depend at the very same time on a network of heterogeneous crossover points, in the chimeric relationships that occur among them, in short on the multiple possibilities offered by the interaction, and on the dynamic and creative relationship that will ensue between spectator response and theatrical reality. It can be seen that the understanding of the performance text depends on the coming together of sender and receiver, who find themselves cooperating, for the purpose of modeling, indeed remodeling, a universe of meaning.

It is tempting to look for a connection between the performance texts of experimental troupes and the fascination exercised by improvisation, which, as has been noted, offers the same sort of privileged relationship between the actor and the spectator. Beyond the pleasure of his or her participation, however, we must insist on the preponderant role of the spectator with respect to the organization of meaning in present-day theater. The spectator can no longer be considered in the traditional way to be a passive presence, and communication can no longer happen according to the classical model. It is striking that of all the arts requiring visual perception, only the theater continues to be defined as the art of active viewing. By raising the curtain on productive meandering, as it were, by affirming itself to the point of becoming an essential referent of individual and collective cognitive structures, did the theater of the 1980s uncover a new art of viewing?

What is clear is that this new theater, by establishing new ways of seeing and interpreting reality, created a feeling of suddenly escaping the habitual limits of perception in order to penetrate into another order. Present-day Quebec dramaturgy accomplishes the same thing by breaking with a certain rigidity of traditional representation and by instituting new modes of representation and writing that reorder our perception of the world.

New Theatrical Writing . . . Allows the Cry of the Artist To Be Heard

The text, neglected in the 1970s in favor of body language and a theater of images, was reactivated in the 1980s. Liberated by the abandonment of (partisan) political subjects and the weakening of ideologies, the "nouvelle dramaturgie québécoise"[35] (that is, the dramaturgy of the young playwrights of the 1980s) now explored other paths, among them the path of introspection; the imagination of the collective project has thus given way to the introspective questionings of the artist. If there were in fact one theme that took center stage during the 1980s, it was that of artistic creation. To familiarize one's self with the dramaturgy dealing with the role of the artist in society, one might read *26 bis, Impasse du Colonel Foisy* by René-Daniel Dubois,[36] *Provincetown Playhouse, juillet 1919, j'avais 19 ans* by Normand Chaurette,[37] or *Le Syndrome de Cézanne* by Normand Canac-Marquis.[38] These texts, which some have called unstageable, are fascinating if on occasion disconcerting. Disconcerting because they break with familiar dramatic models and develop a new theatrical writing involving numerous *mises en abîme,* the mixing of genres and styles, the special use of monologue and narrative, the upsetting

40

and telescoping of time, the fragmentation of space, discontinuity of the story-line, modification of the notion of suspense, and the questioning of the notions of character.

The thematic range of creation is, to be sure, inscribed in the text itself. The search for identity passes into the very act of writing, of recounting one's self: the creative act thereby becoming political in the larger sense. Finally, what characterizes this contemplation of the self is that it is no longer concerned with the question "Who am I?" which was, in fact, very much a part of the great socio-political problematic peculiar to the 1970s; this time the question centers on "What am I doing?" The young creators and writers of today raise questions with respect to themselves and their function as artists in society.

Throughout the crisis of a dramaturgy at odds with previous conventions, we are witness to a crisis of reality, or rather of the death of reality in reality, as it is defined by traditional artistic codes. In other words, we are confronted with a reaction against a representation of a world considered outmoded. While realism had as its task the furnishing of objective reality, "préserver les consciences du doute, . . . de stabiliser le référent, de l'ordonner à un point de vue qui le dote d'un sens raisonnable,"[39] as Lyotard explains it, the post-modern consciousness admits henceforth to being totally subjective. To grasp an unstable world, caught between order and disorder, one needs recourse to multiple points of view, to the dramaturgy of the fragment, that is, a splintered writing that refuses to present a definitive point of view on the world.

Should not the recurrent use of *mise en abîme* and of the theater within the theater throughout the 1980s be read as the effect of a new awareness, of self-questioning by the theater with respect to its ways of communicating reality . . . and the imaginary? These efforts at breaking with the past have brought a self-consciousness to dramatic writing, which goes so far as to bring us the voice of the author in the midst of creation, dismantling, as in René-Daniel Dubois' *26 bis,* *Impasse du Colonel Foisy,* any progressive story and leading us to the very source of creation, the consciousness of the creator. In this text, Dubois puts on stage two actors who play their characters: an exiled Russian princess, whom the author calls Madame, and her faithful valet. Madame is awaiting her young lover who plans to assassinate her. To pass the time, she tells the sequences of her life in a long monologue containing flashbacks: her voyages, her loves, and so on.

We then witness the explosion of this dramatic line as the author, overtaken by anguish and doubts, intrudes upon his own text, calls Madame "ma grosse," undermines the plot, addresses the audience, and "sabotages" the play which will end with a tirade by Madame on theatrical illusion. Her last words are: "Je ne suis qu'un personnage." After having resisted, the illusion crumbles.

By bringing to the stage both character and author, by forcing a direct relationship with the spectator, by juxtaposing reality and fiction back to back, Dubois creates a situation in which "reality" is no longer an issue. All at once, the central concept of classical aesthetics is brought into question. The plausible, resting on the principle of mimetic illusion, sees its field of application pushed to the limit, while the plays of the 1980s, like the Dubois play cited above, explore the boundary between fiction and reality. With respect to the realist aesthetic, we find ourselves confronted by strange distortions. The major change in present-day creation resides precisely in the relationship between the real and its representation: what is at stake is no longer the representation of a supposedly objective world, recognizable to all, but rather the reconstruction of the real from another perspective, whose purpose is to offer a new way of looking at the world.

Thus, Normand Chaurette's *Je vous écris du Caire*[40] provides another example of this new artistic logic, which marks the end of our narrative culture (or that of the great unifying narrative), placing the ball definitively in the court of the reader or spectator. In the play, an agent of the Italian cultural ministry encloses Verdi in a room, ordering him to write an opera within forty-eight hours. Verdi finds himself in the company of a failed baritone, Terziani, a successful opera singer with whom he had an affair, Stölz, and a prompter who, toward the middle of the play, pretends to be Verdi. There follows an argument between the two "Verdis" as to their respective identities. At the end of the play, the truth is not established, and ambiguity and opacity remain. The prompter might be someone who personifies Verdi to get out of his "rut," just as he might be the real Verdi. From the point of view of the singer, there are two false Verdis, while the agent and the baritone believe themselves to be in the presence of the real Verdi and of a prompter. It is up to the spectator to decide if he or she has seen either the "true" or the "false" Verdi, one "true" and one "false," two "trues," or two "false". . . . From this open writing, without *dénouement*, so to speak, there can result a destabilizing effect on the perception of the reader or spectator who is finally confronted with a "new" truth: the truth of his or her existence within the discourse of the work. Indeed, the play substitutes for mimetic illusion the play of a continual provocation that incites the audience to assume its function as first receiver-interpreter of the theatrical act, recalling that the objective and "universal" reality of so-called "reality" plays has been replaced by the subjective and individual realities of the "new" dramaturgy.

Present-day Quebec dramaturgy tends in this way to destabilize the spectator and put him in a position of discomfort. It tries to bring the spectator to modify his or her own representations of the world. The spectator is no longer in front of a coherent object (or text) presented for reading, but is projected into the midst of fragments of a confused world in which, in the face of the impossibility of arriving at any ordered vision, diverse fragments seem to be arranged helter-skelter. While the classical model reposes on the obvious clarity of the story-line, contemporary writings must be approached and accepted like a game; indeed, like a puzzle missing some pieces. In truth, the approach to contemporary writing is only possible to the extent that the reader or the spectator accepts playing the game, which consists precisely in working on what is missing and in constructing a text by introducing into it his or her own imagination and meaning.

Having directed its gaze for a time toward itself, an essential step in the conquest of its identity during the 1960s and 1970s, *québécois* society is now ready to redefine its relationship with the world. Thus the discussion of *poiesis*, which focuses on the preoccupations of the creators of contemporary Quebec theater and transcends the narrow limits of "art for art," as well as those of purely local concerns. If formal and thematic innovations pinpointed in contemporary dramatic and performance texts have profoundly disturbed our theatrical landscape by questioning what speaking, telling, writing, playing, and staging mean, they testify as well to the evolution of Quebec society in a rapidly changing world. So it is that the introspective detour has become, at the moment of internationalization, a window from which to scan the world outside. In any case, at the dawn of the third millennium, it is a space that seems to have been appropriated by the creators of Quebec theater in order to stage a possible if difficult rendez-vous of the individual and History.[41]

Notes

1. Translated by Leonard Rahilly, Michigan State University.
2. The part of this text bearing on the 1960s and 1970s resumes in its essential parts a portion of a text entitled "Une Mutation en cours," which I wrote with Irène Perelli-Contos, and which appeared in *Théâtre/Public* 117 (May-June 1994): 64-73.
3. For further details, read the article by Gilbert David, "Un nouveau territoire théâtral, 1965–1980" in: René Legris, et al., eds., *Le Théâtre au Québec 1925–1980* (Montreal: VLB Editeur, 1988), 141–71.
4. Regarding the work of each of these authors and of others mentioned throughout the text, I suggest consulting the *Dictionnaire des œuvres littéraires du Québec*, 6 vols., edited by Maurice Lemire (Montréal: Fides). Especially: vol. 4: 1960–1969 (published 1984), vol. 5: 1970–1975 (published 1987), and vol. 6: 1976–1980 (published 1994). The introduction to each of these volumes gives a good idea of the literary and theatrical landscape of the periods treated.
5. Michel Tremblay, *Les Belles-Sœurs* (Montréal: Leméac, 1972).
6. On this topic, see the article by Jean-Marc Larrue, "Entrée en scène des professionels 1825–1930." This article appeared in: Renée Legris, Jean-Marc Larrue, André-G. Bourassa, and Gilbert David, *Le Théâtre au Québec 1925-1980* (Montréal: VLB Editeur, 1988), 25–60.
7. See Jean-Cléo Godin, "Héros ambigus, rois sans royaumes," in *Small Is Beautiful*, under the direction of Claude Schumacher and Derek Fogg (Glasgow University: Theatre Studies Publications, 1990), 243–51.
8. Gratien Gélinas, *Tit-Coq* (Montréal: Editions de l'Homme, 1968).
9. Among the writings of Jean-Claude Germain are, *Les Hauts et les bas de la vie d'une diva: Sarah Ménard par eux-mêmes* (Montréal: VLB Editeur, 1976); and *Si les Sansoucis s'en soucient, ces Sansoucis-ci s'en soucieront-ils? Bien parler, c'est se respecter!* [preceded by] *Diguidi, ha! ha! ha!* (Montréal: Leméac, 1972).
10. Jean Barbeau, *Ben-Ur* (Montréal: Leméac, 1971); *Goglu* [preceded by] *Le Chemin de Lacroix* (Montréal: Leméac, 1971); *Joualez-moi d'amour* [preceded by] *Manon Lastcall* (Montréal: Leméac, 1972).
11. *La Nef des sorcières*, texts by Luce Guilbeault, Marthe Blackburn, France Théoret, Odette Gagnon, Marie-Claire Blais, Pol Pelletier, and Nicole Brossard (Montréal: Quinze, 1976).
12. Consider, among others, the monologues of Yvon Deschamps, Marc Favreau (Sol), Clémence Des Rochers, and Jacqueline Barette. For additional information, consult *Monologues québécois 1890–1980*, by Laurent Mailhot and Doris-Michel Montpetit (Montréal: Leméac, 1980). It should be noted that solo performances were commonplace during those years.

13. Denise Boucher, *Les Fées ont soif: Théâtre* (Montréal: Editions Intermède, 1978).

14. Jeanne-Mance Delisle, *Un reel ben beau, ben triste* (Montréal: Editions de la Pleine Lune, 1980).

15. With regard to the place of women in Quebec theater—and in our society—consult *Jeu* 16 and *Jeu* 66. These two numbers of the *Cahiers du théâtre Jeu* (Montréal: Editions les Cahiers du théâtre Jeu, 1980 and 1993) are devoted to the role and place of women in the theater.

16. Robert Gurik, *Les Tas de siège* (Montréal: Leméac, 1971).

17. Jean-Claude Germain, *Les tourtereaux* (Montréal: l'Aurore, 1974).

18. Roland Lepage, *La Complainte des hivers rouges* (Montréal: Leméac, 1974).

19. Françoise Loranger, *Médium Saignant* (Montréal: Leméac, 1970).

20. For a description of the LNI, see Joyce Cunningham and Paul Lefebvre, "La ligue nationale d'improvisation," *Jeu* 11 (Montréal: Les Cahiers de théâtre Jeu, 1979), 5–9. Also: Robert Gravel, Jean-Marc Lavergne, *Impro II, Réflexions et analyses* (Montréal: Leméac, 1987); Robert Gravel and Jean-Marc Lavergne, *Impro II, Exercices et analyses* (Montréal: Leméac, 1989).

21. Pierre Lavoie, "L'Improvisation: l'art de l'instant," *Etudes littéraires* 18 (3) (Québec: Presses de l'Université Laval, 1985). This number was prepared under the direction of Gilles Girard, and is entitled *Théâtre québécois: tendances actuelles.*

22. Robert Gravel, TRAC 3, a document filed in the National Archives of Québec, Montréal.

23. Jean-Luc Denis, "Savoir préparer l'avenir ou des effets du manque de clairvoyance sur la régression du théâtre d'expérimentation au Québec," *Jeu* 52 (Montréal: Les Cahiers de théâtre Jeu, September 1989), 178–79.

24. See *Le Théâtre pour enfants au Québec: 1950–1980,* by Hélène Beauchamp (Montréal: Hurtubise, 1985).

25. Marie-Francine Hébert, *Cé tellement "cute" des enfants* (Montréal: Quinze, 1975).

26. Suzanne Lebeau, *Une lune entre deux maisons* (Montréal: Québec/Amérique, 1980), and *La Marelle* (Montréal: Leméac, 1984).

27. Gilles Gauthier, *On n'est pas des enfants d'école* (Montréal: Québec/Amérique, 1984).

28. Louis-Dominique Lavigne, *Où est-ce qu'elle est ma gang?* (Montréal: Québec/Amérique, 1984).

29. David, "Un nouveau territoire théâtral," 164.

30. "Le théâtre expérimental et la fin de l'unique," Solange Lévesque, *Jeu* 52 (Montréal: Les cahiers de théâtre Jeu, September 1989), 41.

31. For example: the "Théâtre Repère," the "Théâtre Niveau Parking," the "Théâtre Sortie de Secours", the "Arbo-Cyber Théâtre," and the "Théâtre Recto-Verso," among others.

32. Hélène Beauchamp et Jean-Marc Larrue, "Les Cycles Repère. Entrevue avec Jacques Lessard," *L'Annuaire théâtral* 8 (Montréal: Société d'Histoire du Théâtre du Québec, 1990), 139.

33. Pierre A. Larocque, "Projet pour un bouleversement des sens ou visions exotiques de Maria Chaplin," *Le Baroque*, Cahier 2 (April 1977), 3–4. Document on file in the National Archives of Quebec.

34. Created in 1986, at the Théâtre de Quat-Sous in Montréal, *Vinci* is a production conceived, produced, and acted by Robert Lepage.

35. Among the young authors who belong to this "nouvelle dramaturgie" are René-Daniel Dubois, Normand Chaurette, and Normand Canac-Marquis.

36. René-Daniel Dubois, *26 bis, Impasse du Colonel Foisy* (Montréal: Leméac, 1982).

37. Normand Chaurette, *Provincetown Playhouse, juillet 1919, j'avais 19 ans* (Montréal: Leméac, 1981).

38. Normand Canac-Marquis, *Le Syndrome de Cézanne* (Montréal: Les Herbes Rouges, 1988).

39. Jean-François Lyotard, *Le Postmoderne expliqué aux enfants* (Paris: Galilée, 1987), 19.

40. *Je vous écris du Caire,* by Normand Chaurette, was created in the autumn of 1993 at the Théâtre d'Aujourd'hui in Montréal. Publication by Editions Leméac is expected in late 1995.

41. The author of this article received grants to carry out research on *Les tendences actuelles de l'écriture scénique* (Hébert and Perelli-Contos, CRSH, 1992–95) and on *Le théâtre de recherche et la référence aux formes populaires du spectacle* (Hébert, FCAR, 1990–93).

Hysterical Pregnancies and Post-Partum Blues: Staging the Maternal Body in Recent Quebec Plays

Jane Moss

Over the last twenty years, feminist theorists on both sides of the Atlantic have engaged in a critique of gender roles and sexual difference from anthropological, economic, historical, literary, sociological, and psychoanalytic points of view. Much of the debate has focused on mothering since it has been identified as the central factor leading to asymmetry in the gender system. The term "mothering" is here used to describe the biological capacity to procreate and the primary responsibility for parenting which has been traditionally assigned to women. The debate over mothering has been far-reaching and disturbing: we have been reminded that the foundation of Western Culture was the murder of the mother, Clytemnestra in the *Oresteia*; that the Christian ideal of femininity is the *mater dolorosa*, the Virgin Mary; that Freudian theory explains motherhood as the passive masochistic gratification which compensates for the lack of a penis; that the capacity to reproduce as controlled by patriarchy leads to women's powerlessness and oppression. The critique of mothering has also been divisive: feminist daughters have often found liberation in matrophobia; partisans of *l'écriture féminine* or *l'écriture au maternel* have redefined maternity as a source of *jouissance* only to be criticized as essentialists; the issue of motherhood has often separated heterosexuals from lesbians, mothers from the childless.[1]

Changing attitudes toward sexuality in general and motherhood in particular have had profound effects on Quebec society in the past several decades. As the Catholic Church's influence diminished, the sexual revolution and the availability of contraception and abortion made it possible for women to take advantage of new educational and job opportunities by delaying or refusing motherhood. *La revanche du berceau* was forgotten and the birth rate plummeted. Functioning as a mirror of social concerns, Quebec theater has echoed the on-going debate over gender roles and reflected the new understanding of parenthood as choice.[2] In this essay, I propose to study a number of plays by women who have used the maternal body as a symbol of femininity. We will see that in the last two decades, women's theater has staged the maternal body in many different ways: as a fetished body-text that performs its own humiliation, as a sign of compulsory motherhood, as a symbol of women's desire to be both independent and emotionally connected.[3] Transcending the matrophobia of early feminist plays which protested coercive maternity, women's theater has turned to examining women's continued desire to have children and how mothering can attain status in a more gender equal society. Julia Kristeva's comments in "Women's Time" anticipate the dramatization of the maternity question in Quebec women's theater:

> The desire to be a mother, considered alienating and even reactionary by the preceding generation of feminists, has obviously not become a standard for the present generation. But we have seen in the past few years an increasing number of women who not only consider their maternity compatible with their professional life or their feminist involvement. . .but also find it indispensable to their discovery, not of the plenitude, but of the complexity of the female experience, with all that this complexity comprises in joy and pain.[4]

The early work of feminist theater collectives illustrates the virulent attack on compulsory maternity, repressive mothering, and exploited motherhood. In 1974, a group of leftist activists formed the Théâtre des cuisines and presented their first play, *Nous aurons les enfants que nous voulons,* on the issue of abortion on demand. The "Manifeste du théâtre des cuisines" (1975) underscored the centrality of women's reproductive capacity in the critique of women's oppression:

> Notre exploitation, nous la vivons quand nous sommes tout simplement "femmes." Le contrôle de nos corps nous est refusé . . . nous ne pouvons décider nous-mêmes du choix de nos maternités; nous ne pou-

vons jouir ni de nos maternités ni de nos corps. La société nous a si bien dévalorisées que nous avons honte d'être des femmes.[5]

The group's next two works, *Môman travaille pas, a trop d'ouvrage* (1976) and *As-tu vu? Les Maisons s'emportent* (1980) deal with mothering, dramatizing the household burdens that fall almost exclusively on women, even those who work outside the home. In staging the exploitation of women in the domestic sphere, the Théâtre des cuisines calls for drastic revisions in the way government, business, and society view the family. The plays demand political action (childcare, school lunches, health clinics), economic opportunity (equality in the workplace), and changes in gender roles (shared parenting).

A ma mère, à ma mère, à ma mère, à ma voisine (1978), by the founders of the Théâtre Expérimental des Femmes, grew out of Pol Pelletier's desire to put motherhood on trial. The verdict was a foregone conclusion: mothers were guilty of collusion with patriarchy, conditioning their daughters to be subservient, passing on a heritage of shame and powerlessness.[6] The patriarchal mother had to be condemned and put to death. In dramatizing mother-daughter relations, *A ma mère* illustrates how a certain idea of mothering is reproduced. Instructing her daughter on proper behavior for girls, the Reine-Mère of the first tableau makes it clear that she is training her for her maternal role: "N'oublie pas que tu es une future mère. . . . Une femme n'est vraiment femme que lorsqu'elle est mère. . . . Ma fille est une vraie petite mère."[7] In the second tableau, the daughter assumes her role as a young married woman with alarming results. The actress performs a pantomime of the wedding ceremony, marital sex, pregnancy, and childbirth. As she tends to the rag ball that represents her baby, the new mother begins to train her daughter as she was trained by her mother, but as she does so, she strangles to death hysterically. The stage directions describe her demise: ". . .elle monologue, s'étrangle et meurt, hystérique. Sa tâche est accomplie. Elle se jette dans le même trou qui a englouti la reine-mère."[8] The maternal body is also the focus of the fourth tableau in which an actress struggles with a large laundry ball that represents her womb, the reproductive capacity that determines women's experience.[9] A song composed by one of the actress/authors (but not performed with the play) expresses the daughter's dream of reunion with the maternal body, perhaps of a return to the womb:

49

> Je rêve de toi ma mère
> L'union de la chair à accomplir
> Le plaisir défendu
> Et ton corps s'est raidi.
> Je rêve de toi ma mère
> Le désir de ton ventre jeune
> L'énergie dans ton corps d'enfant
> Au service du sourire aveugle.[10]

A ma mère did not exorcise the maternal body from the theatrical imagination of Pol Pelletier. In 1981, she wrote *La Lumière blanche* which was performed at the Théâtre Expérimental des Femmes. One of the three female stereotypes deconstructed in the play is represented by the pregnant woman, Leude. In addition to her huge belly, her fetishized maternal body carries the weight of the patriarchal construction of motherhood. Initially, Leude seems quite pleased with her situation, apparently accepting reification as she boasts of the courage and certainty that come with reproductive powers:

> Je suis une usine de transformation qui secrète son propre système d'autoprotection. Comme une sphère légère et enveloppante et invincible. Rien ne peut m'atteindre. Depuis que je suis enceinte, je ne connais plus la peur ni le doute, ni l'angoisse.[11]

The aggressive, ugly Torregrossa conveys a different image of the maternal body, listing all the prohibitions placed on pregnant women who must be sequestered for the protection of "le précieux bébé de la précieuse tribu."[12] According to Torregrossa, the pregnant woman is a burden, "un gros fagot, un gros tas d'eau" who has chosen to subordinate self in order to fulfill her biological destiny as ". . .la procréatrice de l'humanité, . . .la grosse génitrice qui macère dans son jus au service de la collectivité."[13] The implication is that by choosing maternity, a woman surrenders selfhood and control over her body to a society that sees only her womb.

Recounting the story of her life, Leude describes how her mother trained her for motherhood by making her responsible for younger siblings.[14] Although she tries to convince herself that parenting has evolved with the times into a freely chosen, joyous experience of shared responsibility,[15] her post-partum appearance belies her words.

After giving birth, she is transformed into a haggard, hollow-eyed, unkempt, exhausted woman with baby dolls hanging from her clothes and sleepless nights inscribed on her maternal body.[16] In response to the question "C'est quoi une mère?", she says "Une servante sacrifiée et bien enrubannée. . . ."[17] She foresees motherhood as an eternel present between the stove, refrigerator, and crib; "un immense quotidien."[18] Torregrossa predicts a life of domestic slavery ("Elle sera enterrée vivante sous cinq tonnes de couches Pampers") for an ungrateful family.[19] Despite her post-partum blues and Torregrossa's sarcasm, Leude is overwhelmed by maternal love and wistfully imagines mother-daughter intimacy:

> . . .toi sur mon coeur, toi, mon bébé, tète, tète, mon bébé, toi couchée, moi couchée, dans mon-ton lit à l'abri du besoin et de la peur, tes membres noués aux miens, ta salive dans mon lait, ça coule sur mon corps, gluantes et collées, oh le plaisir, le bien-être. . . . Pourquoi le plaisir et le bien-être sont-ils des valeurs rétrogrades et anti-civilisation?[20]

With full knowledge of the burdens of motherhood as constructed by patriarchal society, the play's third stereotypical character, B.C. Magruge, the beautiful coquette, proclaims "Je veux un bébé."[21] This leads to a discussion of why women desire to have children: to please their male partners, to strengthen the couple's bond, to fulfill their female vocation, or to fill the void.[22] Torregrossa's critique of what she calls "l'invention de la maternité" cites feminist theorist Shulamith Firestone in blaming maternity for the exploitation and oppression of women,[23] who have allowed reproductive capacity to become the definition of femininity.[24] The ambivalent attitudes expressed during the lengthy discussion of maternity in *La Lumière blanche* underscore the point referred to above in Kristeva's "Women's Time": that having exposed all the oppressive aspects of motherhood as socially constructed, feminists need to theorize the continued desire for maternity.

The feminist project of rethinking maternity and mothering also influenced Jocelyne Beaulieu's psychodrama, *J'ai beaucoup changé depuis. . .*, performed at the Théâtre d'Aujourd'hui in 1980. The play takes place in a mental hospital where "F" (as in "Femme" and "Folle") is being treated for a hysterical pregnancy, one symptom of her third nervous breakdown following an abortion her boyfriend forced her to have. As she acts out her traumas and delusions, it becomes clear that she has experienced two kinds of maternal models—the eternal victim Mère Blanche, who offers castrated love, and the strong-willed Mère Noire, who gives castrating affection. The lack of good role models has not diminished her desire to give birth, a desire made more poignant by the fact that her psychiatrist, Marguerite, is very pregnant and on the verge of a maternity leave. F dreams of having a baby to fill the emptiness inside her,[25] of giving her daughter the love she never received as a child.[26] She also fantasizes about being the fetus inside Marguerite,[27] a fantasy that underscores conflicting attitudes toward maternity since "Un ventre est une grosse machine pour garder les bébés au chaud,"[28] but it is also vulnerable to those jealous of women's procreative powers.[29] F's paranoid delusions are clearly connected to the oppression of women in a society that reduces women to their reproductive roles, but then denies maternal power and love. The voices she hears echo the slogans of pro-natalist politics, "On a besoin d'enfants, l'pays est grand. Faut qu'ça s'peuple,"[30] yet these voices also threaten her as she tells Marguerite, ". . .i'sont en train de nous enfermer avec nos gros ventres, dans une p'tite cage à l'écart, tu seules. J'les vois. I' viennent à tour de rôle pour nous prendre en pitié pis nous dire quoi faire."[31] Unlike the male medical establishment that prefers to treat female hysteria with drug therapy, Marguerite (described as an anti-psychiatrist) uses identification and transference in her treatment of F. As a woman, she understands the sexual repressions F has faced and shares F's ambivalence toward maternity. Torn between her professional responsibilities and her home life, distressed by her realization that she has repressed her female nature for the sake of her career, the pregnant Marguerite is reduced to silent tears.[32] What she has helped F to understand is that she must first give birth to herself before she will be ready for maternity. Freud notwithstanding, motherhood is no substitute for selfhood.

Several plays written by actress/writers in the early 1980s reinforce the notion that women often choose maternity for the wrong reasons and that they must not repeat the psychologically damaging mothering they experienced as daughters. Louisette Dussault, who played the role of the Virgin Mary Statue in *Les Fées ont soif* (1978), comments on the negative effects of female stereotypes in the introduction to her monologue *Moman* (1981): "L'archétype de la Sainte-Vierge, avec tout ce qu'on lui a mis sur le dos, débouche nécessairement sur le stéréotype de la mère qu'il faut absolument réussir à tuer en soi si on veut retrouver la femme."[33] In a passage toward the end of the first act, Dussault focusses on the maternal body in a flashback to her pregnancy. Caressing her belly, she feels her twins move inside her and she muses on the conflicting emotions aroused by impending motherhood:

> Depuis que vous êtes là, je m'occupe de mon corps comme je m'en suis jamais occupé. . . *(Elle rit)* Comme si mon corps avait enfin trouvé son utilité. . . *(L'air soudainement craintive)* C'est bête ce que je viens de dire là. . . . *(Un temps)* Ca serait que je n'accepte mon corps qu'en autant qu'il soit utile. . . Je serais en train de vous mettre au monde pour me sentir utile? Pour me déculpabiliser. . . De quoi, bon Dieu? De mes deux avortements? *(Elle berce son ventre)* Ah non! mes petits bébés, vous n'êtes pas juste des prétextes. . . Depuis que vous êtes là, j'ai l'impression que je vis à l'intérieur de moi avec vous autres, que j'existe pour la premiere fois de ma vie! Ah! J'ai hâte que vous sortiez, de vous prendre dans mes bras, de vous serrer, de vous aimer. . . J'ai besoin de vous autres. . . *(Un temps)* Ça n'a pas de bon sens. . . Est-ce que je serais en train de vous mettre au monde à la place de me mettre au monde, moi?[34]

Dussault's Mother understands that women must refuse to play at motherliness in order to make others love them;[35] they must reject the role of the over-protective "Mère-police" and the fantasy of the ideal mother.[36] In other words, if they are to lead satisfying independent lives, women must not define themselves by their maternal function.

While academic feminists argued over the meaning of the female body as the matrix of difference, Quebec theater women continued to stage their bodies as performable texts, to make spectacles of themselves we might say. The kind of maternal *jouissance* envisioned by Julia Kristeva is described by Francine Tougas in her solo piece, *Grandir*, first performed at the Festival Femmes en Solo in 1981 and later staged at the Théâtre Expérimental des Femmes in 1982. The monologue begins with a lyrical reenactment of the birth of her daughter. She evokes her pregnant body, her labor pains, the powerful feeling that comes with giving birth, her sense of connectedness with generations of women and with the universe, the surge of energy that comes at the moment of delivery:

La Saga des poules mouillées, 1981. Photograph by André Le Coz.

Une seconde. . .une seconde où je deviens le receptacle d'une énergie formidable, de toute l'énergie du monde! Une seconde où je n'ai plus de corps, où je suis comme du métal en fusion! Puis je pousse. Je pousse de toutes mes forces! Je m'ouvre, je me fais grande, immense, un feu doux coule partout en dedans de moi, je sens mon enfant monter lentement vers la lumière et j'ai des étoiles chaudes jusqu'au bout des cheveux! Une joie fantastique frissonne dans l'air. C'est la vie qui s'excite devant cette nouvelle vie qui arrive. Un enfant qui naît, c'est un rappel qu'on est vivants[37]

Without glossing over the hardships, Tougas speaks of the fears and anxieties that come with raising a child alone. She dramatizes the conflicts between work and motherhood, between her sexual needs and her maternal love, and, acknowedging the feminist revolt against compulsory motherhood, she talks about maternity as a choice.[38] The play ends with a poetic "lettre d'amour à ma fille," a celebration of maternity that recalls the *écriture maternelle* of Chantal Chawaf in its sensual descriptions of nursing the infant daughter:

Marie-Mousse. . .

Tu sens l'amour.

Ta bouche quand tu donnes des becs . . .

Te souviens-tu du temps où mon sein était ta seule nourriture,

Ton seul bonheur?

Tantôt sur mon lit, toutes nues toutes les deux,

Roulant de caresses en ti-galops, de chatouillements en baisers,

On retrouvait ce vieux souvenir-là. . .

Marie-Mousse, ma petite fille

Mon immense, mon éternel amour

Tu viens chercher en moi des trésors endormis

Tu me révèles à moi même.[39]

Unfortunately, Marie Laberge's women characters never seem to come to a feminist revision of maternity. I have argued elsewhere that Laberge's plays usually dramatize the daughter's negative view of mothering, but in this paper I would like to look briefly at her representation of the maternal body. In *Deux Tangos pour toute une vie* (written in 1982 and staged at the Théâtre du Petit Champlain in 1984), Suzanne Langlais Casgrain is a depressed thirty-three-year-old woman at a crisis point in her life and marriage. She must decide whether or not she will return to her nursing career, stay with her husband Pierre, and have a baby. Her mother argues that children cement marital bonds[40] and Pierre would like to have a child.[41] The choices are further complicated by a brief but passionate love affair with Pierre's office colleague, Gilles. Suzanne finally gives in, accepting her mother's traditional vision of a wife's conjugal role with a tearful promise to be "correque" and "raisonnable."[42] The play's "Epilogue" shows us Suzanne, several months pregnant and sadly resigned to the choices she has made.[43] Clearly, Laberge stages the maternal body as a symbol of defeat and surrender to traditional gender roles that repress female sexuality.

Renewed attention was focused on the maternal body as symbol of the female condition in two plays from the late 1980s: Carole Fréchette's *Baby Blues* (1988) and Maryse Pelletier's *La Rupture des eaux* (1989). Both pieces employ flashbacks which allow the female protagonists to come to terms with their family histories and domestic arrangements so that they can overcome ambivalence about the choice to give birth. Both plays dramatize the anxiety of career women who fear that motherhood and careers are incompatible, that maternal love will not be adequate compensation for lost freedom, that they will fail to fulfill the heavy emotional and material demands made upon them as mothers. *Baby Blues* was given a public reading by the Centre d'Essai des Auteurs Dramatiques and a Radio-Canada production in 1988 before being staged at the Théâtre d'Aujourd'hui in 1991. The English title refers both to the post-partum depression of Alice, a singer, and the musical quality of the text. Alice has not slept at all since giving birth forty nights ago and during her sleepless nights she struggles to adjust to her new career, motherhood, by conjuring up the women of her family—sister, mother, aunt, grandmother, and daughter. She identifies her dilemma at the beginning of the play, introducing herself as "la mille millionième nouvelle maman secouée par cette chose qui lui arrive."[44] Her descriptions of her pregnant body, her fear of labor and delivery[45] de-sentimentalize the birthing process while the loud, disturbing baby cries that punctuate the text underscore the unsettling effect that baby Amélie has had on Alice's life. In the end, Grandmother Antoinette's simple vision of the natural power of maternal love helps Alice accept motherhood:

> Les enfants qui pleurent, il faut les prendre dans nos bras. . . . Il faut les caresser, les cajoler, leur parler doucement dans l'oreille. On peut leur dire n'importe quoi, toutes les folies. On sent leur chaleur sur notre peau. Y a rien d'autre comme ça, comme cet abandon-là. Heureusement qu'ils pleurent. . . .[46]

La Rupture des eaux, staged at the Théâtre d'Aujourd'hui in 1989, centers around thirty-something-year-old Françoise in the hospital for the birth of her first child. With a chorus to accentuate her contractions, the first act climaxes as her water breaks and the play ends with the delivery of a baby boy. Unlike earlier feminist plays that gave us lyrical descriptions of pregnancy and birth, Maryse Pelletier deliberately de-romanticizes maternity as part of her strategy. As the play examines how male doctors treat pregnant women and how society constructs maternal roles, Françoise tries to reconcile her decision to become a mother with her bad memories of her own childhood and her fear of maternity. Her experience as a social worker makes her sensitive to the problems of dysfunctional families and she is determined to find a maternal praxis that is not emotionally or psychologically damaging.

The critics were not especially kind to either Fréchette or Pelletier, suggesting that the themes and issues raised by their plays were clichés left over from the militant feminist theater of the seventies.[47] That charge is particularly mean spirited in the case of Carole Fréchette who was a founding member of the Théâtre des cuisines and has clearly switched from agitprop to a poetic exploration of maternity as symbol of the search for origins.[48] Feminist critic Lynda Burgoyne argues that as long as the woman writer confines intimate thoughts to her private journal, she does not threaten the established male order. "Si par contre elle ose se dire publiquement, on l'accuse immédiatement de donner dans le *narcissisme* et le *nombrilisme,* termes aujourd'hui devenus les sombres synonymes *de féminisme.* "[49] While bemoaning the anti-feminist backlash of the early 1990s, we need to point out how these new plays differ from earlier works which dramatized traditional motherhood and what those differences mean in terms of the changing status of women in Quebec. Gone are the daughters' dramatic attacks on patriarchal mothers, the critiques of coercive motherhood and the humiliated maternal body. What we see now is a staging of *le discours maternel* through the intimate drama of women who have chosen to have children. Maternal figures on the Quebec stage are now speaking subjects who talk about their fears and anxieties, working out their relations with families and partners as they ready themselves for healthy relationships with their unborn or newborn children. Clearly, Quebec women's theater reflects changes in reproductive practices and women's status as well as feminist theorizing about *female jouissance,* maternal thinking, and the reproduction of motherhood. The mother is no longer a self-sacrificing masochist or a cold disciplinarian, she is a liberated career woman dealing honestly with her ambivalence about motherhood and trying to reconcile conflicts between her desires and others' demands in her search for happiness.

Notes

1. The literature on mothering is extensive. My thinking on the subject has been informed by Nancy Chodorow's *The Reproduction of Mothering*; Chodorow and Susan Contratto's "The Fantasy of the Perfect Mother"; Shirley Nelson Garner, Claire Kahane, and Madelon

Sprengnether's essay collection *The (M)Other Tongue*; Marianne Hirsch's *The Mother/Daughter Plot*; Julia Kristeva's "Stabat Mater," "About Chinese Women," "Women's Time"; Sara Ruddick's "Maternal Thinking"; Domna C. Stanton's "Difference on Trial: A Critique of the Maternal Metaphor in Cixous, Irigaray, and Kristeva."

2. My own work has frequently dealt with how Quebec playwrights dramatize changing gender and family roles. See in particular my "Living with Liberation: Quebec Drama in the Feminist Age"; "Fillial (Im)pieties: Mothers and Daughters in Quebec Women's Theatre"; "'All in the Family': Quebec Family Dramas in the 1980s."

3. See my "Fillial (Im)pieties: Mothers and Daughters in Quebec Women's Theater" *American Review of Canadian Studies* 19(2) (1989): 177–86 and "Marie Laberge and Women's Theater in Quebec," *Writing Beyond the Hexagon: Women Writing in French*, edited by Karen Gould, Mary Jean Green, Micheline Rice-Maximin, Keith Walker, and Jack Yeager [forthcoming].

4. Julia Kristeva, "Women's Time," *The Kristeva Reader*, ed. Toril Moi (New York: Columbia University Press, 1986), 205.

5. Théâtre des cuisines, *Môman travaille pas, a trop d'ouvrage!* (Montréal: Les Editions du remue-ménage, 1976), 5.

6. Dominique Gagnon, Louise Laprade, Nicole Lecavalier, and Pol Pelletier, *A Ma Mère, à ma mère, à ma mère, à ma voisine* (Montréal: Les Editions du remue-ménage, 1979), 4.

7. Ibid., 18–19.

8. Ibid., 26.

9. Ibid., 29–30.

10. Ibid., 53.

11. Pol Pelletier, *La Lumière blanche* (Montréal: Les Herbes rouges, 1989), 22.

12. Ibid., 32–33.

13. Ibid., 33.

14. Ibid., 49.

15. Ibid., 64.

16. Ibid., 59–60.

17. Ibid., 63.

18. Ibid., 65.

19. Ibid., 68–70.

20. Ibid., 73.

21. Ibid., 77.

22. Ibid., 78–79.

23. Ibid., 93.

24. Ibid., 130.

25. Jocelyne Beaulieu, *J'ai beaucoup changé depuis. . .* (Montréal: Leméac, 1981), 36.

26. Ibid., 92.
27. Ibid., 65.
28. Ibid., 66.
29. Ibid., 70.
30. Ibid., 74.
31. Ibid., 78.
32. Ibid., 99.
33. Louisette Dussault, *Moman* (Montréal: Boréal Express, 1981), 33.
34. Ibid., 34.
35. Ibid., 114, 130.
36. Ibid., 138.
37. Francine Tougas, *Histoires de fantômes, L'Age d'or, Grandir* (Montréal: Leméac, 1985), 98.
38. Ibid., 119–23.
39. Ibid., 134–35.
40. Marie Laberge, *Deux Tangos pour toute une vie* (Montréal: VLB éditeur, 1985), 74.
41. Ibid., 100.
42. Ibid., 157.
43. Ibid., 159-61.
44. Carole Fréchette, *Baby Blues* (Montréal: Les Herbes rouges, 1989), 13.
45. Ibid., 29.
46. Ibid., 80.
47. See reviews of Pelletier's play by André Ducharme in *Lettres québécoises* 54, Diane Pavlovic in *Jeu* 5 and of Fréchette's play by Yves Dubé in *Lettres québécoises* 58, Robert Lévesque in *Le Devoir* (30 March 1991), Gilles Lamontagne in *La Presse* (23 March 1991). Lynda Burgoyne's article in *Jeu* 61 is much kinder to Fréchette and her comments on critical reaction to feminist playwrights in *Jeu* 65 attack the sexism of the male critical establishment.
48. Lynda Burgoyne, "Carole Fréchette, Les Blues d'un chant intérieur," *Cahiers de théâtre Jeu* 61 (1991): 25.
49. Lynda Burgoyne, "Critique théâtrale et pouvoir androcentrique: Réception critique de *Leçons d'Anatomie* et de *Joie, Cahiers de théâtre Jeu* 65 (1992): 51.

Language and Collective Identity: When Translators of Theater Address the Québécois Nation

Annie Brisset

❖ ❖ ❖ ❖ ❖ ❖ ❖ ❖ ❖ ❖ ❖ ❖ ❖ ❖ ❖ ❖ ❖ ❖ ❖

Translation constitutes a discursive practice that is interesting to observe in as much as language and identity converge therein as both subject and object of discourse. It is easily understood that in intercultural transference the displacement of linguistic material may reveal a metadiscourse. It is less obvious that the subject who translates a foreign work engages the social group he represents or with which he identifies himself, just as the subject that was expressed in the original text was itself immersed in a social discourse.[1] Translation is thus a privileged place from which to observe the manner in which collective identity defines itself by and against what it is not. However, all the translations that characterize a society in a given period must be examined, and not just a particular translation of one work without regard for the discursive context in which it appeared.[2] This approach assumes that translation is interdependent with social discourse, that it participates in its organicity, that it shares its hegemonic traits.

Translation makes manifest the confrontation of the Self with the Other. The process begins with the cooptation strategies that precede the actual translation. Which texts, and thus which discourses, do we choose to translate from among everything a foreign language or society has to offer? In this sense the translator establishes hierarchies of otherness. The cooptation of certain elements of otherness presupposes some form of recognition. Strategies of identification thus correspond, inversely, to strategies of avoidance or rejection: which texts are ignored, but also and especially, which discourses are *silenced* in the texts that are translated?

61

In the confrontation between self and otherness, translation is also a privileged witness because it poses, in an unavoidable way, the question of language. Our intent here will be to analyze *québécois* society's questioning of its identity through the transformations of linguistic material, not by following the canonical opposition between source language and target language, but through the palimpsest of the translation language, by examining what it reveals or conceals in itself. We say palimpsest, not merely to convey that the target text exists in superimposition over the original text and replaces it, but to orient the analysis toward the effects of the upheaval theatrical language in Quebec underwent near the end of the 1960s. A new linguistic material erased the preceding one and launched a translation movement that consisted of rewriting certain plays of a Francophone—French and French-Canadian—background, of translating and especially retranslating the foreign repertoire into the new code of the Quebec stage. The affirmation of a distinct identity involved successive rewritings that produced a linguistic blossoming whose traces and effects will offer themselves for analysis.

The background for the present study is *québécois* society during one of the more troubled periods of its quest for national identity, the 1970s and 1980s. More specifically, the focus will be on the theater, because it is statistically the genre most translated during this period. This is no accident as theater is often regarded as the most national of genres; it is also, in the words of Antoine Vitez, "a place where a people come to hear their language." It is a social art, consumed *in vivo* and collectively, and it differs from the novel or from poetry in that these are perceived individually and at a person's own pace. Since theater addresses a group in a specific place, at a specific time, it resonates more immediately with social discourse, with the imaginary and the symbolic representations of society. The stage is, therefore, in a literal as well as figurative sense, the place *par excellence* for projections of identity.

The theater quite obviously performed this function for the *québécois* collectivity between the late 1960s and the mid-1980s, a period during which theater, like literature in general, took on the quality of political manifesto and action. During this entire period, playwrights invested the language with a new function. They no longer treated it as if it were a neutral medium. On the contrary, the material of discourse became the very object of discourse. Specifically, dramaturgy highlighted language as a reflection of the subaltern condition of Quebecers. This tendency is clearly evident in a quite representative single speech from *Les Belles-Sœurs* by Michel Tremblay, who spearheaded the trend:

> PIERRETTE GUÉRIN: . . .Pas moé! Chus trop vieille! Une fille qui a faite la vie pendant dix ans, ça poigne pus! Chus finie! Pis essayez donc d'expliquer ça à mes soeurs. Comprendront rien! J'le sais pas c'que j'vas devenir, j'le sais pas pantoute![3]

Momentum built up by naturalistic writing drawing on the vernacular led the theater to hurtle toward a new aesthetic. A new name, "théâtre québécois," underlined the change of paradigm that was taking place. The new theater was launched in the same year as the *Parti québécois,* the sovereigntist political group that, in choosing this name for itself, also linked *territoriality* with the affirmation of collective identity. Awareness of identity thus became inextricably linked to the representation of country and language through a common desire, that of recovering them both.

Les Belles-Sœurs, 1969. **Photograph by Guy Dubois.**

During the period under study, the language of theatrical translations is striking for its instability. Ordinarily, the language into which
one translates is a given that precedes the translation; the very existence of this language is the *sine qua non* of the act of translation.
When one looks at the translations produced during the two decades
considered, one gets the impression that the translators were constructing the target language, that they were seeking at least to codify,
to stabilize, it in writing, while at the same time reconstructing the
source text. Yet the heterogeneity of the linguistic material of theatrical translations arises from a single impulse, to make the specificity of
one's "own" particular language heard, to legitimize the existence of
the speaking collective. We will consider, firstly, the diverse codification procedures undertaken by translators. It is noteworthy that apart
from only a few rare exceptions, the theatrical translators of the time
were also the playwrights who made the emergence of *québécois* theater possible, people like Michel Tremblay, Jean-Claude Germain, and
Michel Garneau. Translations were usually presented as rewritings of
works selected from a foreign repertoire based on their similarity to
the new symbolic representation of *québécois* society. Translation was
deformative, hypertextual; it catalyzed dramatic creation by being
itself an act of dramatic creation.

For Michel Garneau, who translated *Macbeth* into "*québécois*,"
the language of translation *seems* obvious. Yet, in identifying the
work as being Shakespeare's text "translated into *québécois*" (ordinarily, the original language of the text is indicated, since its target
language is a given) he is effectively saying that although the *québécois* collectivity possesses its own language, that language has been
lost. The goal of translation must then be to reconstitute this element
of the collective heritage. The language of translation is thus a language of memory, reconstructed from the remaining vestiges of a
dialect identified as that of the Gaspé Peninsula, where Jacques
Cartier took possession of what would become New France. The language chosen to translate *Macbeth* is thus the original language of the
country-to-be, an ancestral, Edenic language. Note that the translator
deliberately chose to anchor his quest for an identifying language in
Macbeth, a text from the universal literary heritage based on the story
of a dispossession—which is ultimately overcome by the victory of the
dispossessed. Michel Garneau transforms the Shakespearean story, a
story of victimization congruent with the social discourse of the time,

into a myth of the origins of the *québécois* collectivity, a founding myth that the language of translation is instrumental in creating. For the *québécois* public, this language assumes an identification function from a perspective at once historic and contemporary, like superimposed representations of before and after the Conquest. At the outset of the play, the language projects the space-time of the Shakespearean text onto the actual History of *québécois* society. In its territorial and ancestral relationships, the "*québécois* language" is constructed as a natural language, free from any infiltration by the language of the British conqueror; it is, as we have said, an Edenic language, but it conveys not so much nostalgia for the early days of colonization as the "utopia" of liberation, with the solidarity mentioned earlier between the subject matter and the medium of discourse.

> Not'cause peut pas ête plus jusse! La victoére nous attend
> Au boutte d'la route!. . .
> Bon yeu qu'j'ai hâte qu'les temps changent!
> C'tes temps-citte sont en train d'nous virer en étranges![4]

This language, which symbolizes the language originally spoken by the founders of the country, is an *artifact,* a language reconstituted from a lexical base that has fallen into disuse. "I drew (as from an artesian well)," says Garneau, "from the ancestral springs of the *québécois* language. I rummaged around in the glossaries. . . ." His translation of *Macbeth* into *québécois* is an exhumation of linguistic memory that makes it possible to read the present identity into the past through the medium of the Shakespearean text, which the translation nudges toward an allegory of the Conquest and the possibility of revenge on History.

This process is characteristic of a good number of the theatrical translations from this period. Thus when Jean-Claude Germain describes himself as "paraphrasing" in *québécois* Félix-Gabriel Marchand's *Les Faux brillants*—a vaudevillian rendering of the theme of the *québécois* gentleman falling victim to a foreign swindler—Germain explicitly presents this process as a "real translation of now into back then," the inclusion in the text of a "bifocal vision," which consists of "mettre le présent dans le passé, là où il était d'ailleurs déjà virtuellement présent comme avenir"[5] That said, the *québécois* language of Michel Garneau's *Macbeth* has nothing in common with the naturalist mode of expression in the translation-adaptations of Jean-Claude Germain, even if a similar impulse inspired both. Take, for example, Germain's adaptation of Brecht's *A Respectable Wedding*:

LA MARIÉE: Çé Jérôme q'y a toutte faitte lui-même.

L'AMIE DFILLE: Toute! Même la panterée?

LA MARIÉE: Ah! oui. . .çé lui qu'y a eu l'idée pour toute han? . . .Y a tiré les plans, y a achté le bois, y l'a scié, y l'a sablé pis y l'a collé. . .parsque toute est embouffeté pis collé han. . .a parre les pantures, y a pas un clou. . .çé faitte rustique!

L'AMIE DGARS: Entoucas, çé-t-unique en son genre! Où çé qu't'as trouvé ltemps dfaire tout ça?[6]

Here, the codification of the *québécois* language results from a dual procedure. The first consists of the gap between the written and spoken language, between a language said to be imposed from outside, artificial and alienating, and a free language, natural and authentic, spoken in the home and in the street. In his translations as in his creations, Germain seeks, he says, to "restituer notre langue nationale dans la pleine mesure de sa vérité d'expression,"[7] which comes down to replacing the code of *Franceness* with the idiom that specifically defines *Quebecness*. It is at this point that the second process comes into play, which is making visible on the page the places where the two idioms diverge, or more exactly, that of emphasizing the difference, of marking it ostentatiously, of going so far as to invent it (*çé/c'est, achté/acheté, parsque/parce que, embouffeté/embouveté, à parre/à part, entoucas/en tout cas*), or to coin quebecisms by adapting the spelling of English words that pepper the speech of the characters (*panterée/pantry*). This work with the signifier manufactures a difference that is far from neutral. On the contrary, it is the vector of the victimization ideology that underlies their self-representation; when playwrights or translators modify the signifier to show that it is different from its French equivalent, they *proletarianize* it.

The proletarianization of the signifier performs various functions. Sometimes it makes the play seem true to life, marking, for example, the class difference between characters; in *Oncle Vania*, the servant Marina is the only character who uses the sociolect of *Les Belles-Sœurs*.

MARINA: T'as ben vieilli. T'es pus aussi beau. Faut dire, aussi que t'haïs pas ça prendre une p'tite vodka de temps en temps. . . . Tu voudrais peut-être manger quequ'chose? . . . Avant eux autres, on a toujours dîné à une heure, comme tout le monde. Depuis qu'i' sont là, c'est jamais avant sept heures! La nuit, le professeur lit pis écrit. . . .C'est comme là, là, le samovar est sur la table depuis deux heures; eux autres, i' sont partis s'promener![8]

And sometimes it is the characters who are moved to a lower social register than that which they occupied in the original play. Robert Lalonde's three sisters are no longer the daughters of a brigadier general, but of a country doctor; they live in a house whose modesty is underlined by the translator-adapter, in contrast to Prosorov's staterooms; despite of their condition (an academic environment replaces a military environment) their language remains that of poorly educated people:

GISÈLE: . . .Ah! Seigneur! En me réveillant à matin, quand j'ai vu qu'y faisait si beau, y m'est venu une de ces envies de m'en retourner au Québec, à Montréal. . . . A force d'enseigner tous les jours à l'école, j'ai assez mal à tête! A part de çà, j'commence à avoir de plus en plus l'air d'une vieille fille. C'est vrai! Ça fait déjà quatre ans que j'enseigne, pis j'me sens dépérir de jour en jour!. . . Pis y a rien qu'une affaire qui me trotte dans tête. . . . En tout cas, aujourd'hui chu en vacances, j'ai pas mal à tête pis j'me sens plus jeune qu'hier![9]

Instead of, as happens here, making the play less highbrow by lowering the social status and linguistic register of the characters, it is more common to find the *québécois* repertoire adapting foreign plays that already feature the proletariat, for example Brecht's "water seller" (from *The Good Person of Sechuan*) who is a mirror of the *québécois* "water carrier"; the latter cannot speak in any manner other than one would on Main Street or in the neighborhood of Plateau Mont-Royal, just as do the oppressed, exploited or "godforsaken" of Eugene O'Neill, Arthur Miller, Tennessee Williams, Paul Zindel or Sam Shepard.

LE VENDEUR D'EAU: Chu vendeur d'eau dans capitale du Setchouan . . . ya àpeu près rien que sués Dieux qu'on peut compter pour se

faire aider. . . . je suppose que le ciel s'est tanné de nous entendre
nous plaindre vers lui dins airs.[10]

Whatever the variants, the language of translation makes the language of the "*québécois* people" coincide with that of the proletariat; it is a metonymic language giving the illusion that the part is coincidental with the whole. Consequently, the representation of disadvantaged classes occupied most of the space on institutional stages for two decades. The sociolectal variants used to represent individual, familial, or social alienation have a perlocutionary, or persuasive, function inextricably linked to the identification project out of which emerged the new *québécois* theater, a theater "où le public non seulement peut se connaître, mais où il peut apprendre à se connaître—à se mieux connaître."[11] The image of society reflected in the mirror held up by the stage coincided almost perfectly with the history of victimization that formed the matrix of discourse on the condition of the *Québécois*.

Translation, instead of opening onto alterity, serves to confirm society's self-representation, while at the same time giving it a dimension of universal tragedy. This preoccupation influences the choice of texts to be translated, or rather to be recycled and reused to better serve the goal of self-representation. The foreign work (plot, name, and function of characters, etc.) is recontextualized in *québécois* society and inscribed with the quest for identity. It is called upon to lend a hand with the nationalist project: Shakespeare, Molière, Chekhov, Gogol, Brecht, O'Neill, Miller, Dario Fo, Garcia Lorca, and many others have the explicit and paradoxical function of awakening "la conscience d'être québécois"[12] in the audience.

A damaged language lends credibility and substance to the story of victimization around which the discourse on the *québécois* condition developed, and foreign plays seem to be staged for the purpose of fleshing it out. However, the commentaries with which the translators accompany their translations reveal an interesting diglossia: prefaces, afterwords, and stage directions are written in a French that is territorially neutral. In other words, when they speak for themselves, the translators do not include themselves in the *québécois* audience to whom their translations are addressed, even when the commentary is intended to explain that the decision to translate "into *québécois*" was inspired by the desire to use the language of the target society so as to ensure a better understanding of the text.[13] The argument often invoked to justify translations "into *québécois*" is the opacity of the French language "of France." "Si, par exemple, j'avais eu à jouer la traduction française [de *Mère Courage*]," explains Monique Mercure, "j'aurais eu besoin de lire la traduction anglaise pour saisir toutes les subtilités et toutes les nuances. C'est souvent ainsi pour presque toutes les traductions françaises d'auteurs étrangers."[14] This discourse on language reveals something new: the loss of intelligibility of the language in which up to now the translations, and, of course, the original creations, were presented in *québécois* theaters. This language has become unintelligible because it has become deterritorializing, at least as represented by the discourse on identity.

On the one hand, it should be understood that the change of language corresponds to a cultural reappropriation movement, to a real repatriation of translating activity. In 1968, 90 percent of foreign works presented on the institutional stages of Quebec were translations done in France. Twenty years later, the proportion was reversed: 93 percent of foreign works were presented in a *québécois* translation or adaptation. A feeling of cultural dispossession generated the new translations. Note, however, that these *québécois* retranslations did not necessarily differ from the corresponding French translations. Thus, when the director Gilles Marsolais underlines how "abnormal" it is for a dramatic text written in a foreign language not to be "translated or adapted by a *Quebecer* before being presented," he puts the nationality, or more precisely, the *ethnolinguistic identity* of the translator above any other consideration. Although he underscores the difference between the French of Quebec and the French of France, he takes no account of it when he himself is translating.[15] This clearly shows that the retranslation movement is fundamentally motivated by the desire to *reterritorialize* translation activity. This desire to recover "speech" is understandable, since Quebecers here came to consider it to have been *confiscated*. In fact, it was never actually claimed. Nevertheless, they speak of a cultural "colonization" by France, a spoliatory and coercive action. This conforms well with the victimization scenario in their self-representation.

On the other hand, it should be noted that beyond a simple wish for cultural "decolonization," the reappropriation of translation was rendered *necessary* by the upheaval in theatrical aesthetics occurring at the end of the 1960s. French translations, probably conforming to a dramatic aesthetic that then prevailed in France, appeared dated on

Quebec stages. Consider, for example, French translations of the American repertoire.[16] The feeling of alienation these translations provoked was at once linguistic and cultural; Quebecers could no longer identify with an *Americanness* revised and corrected by Parisian canons. If the French translations maintained the gap between the language of literature and that of everyday conversation, the new theatrical aesthetic dawning in Quebec rested, conversely, on the elimination of the distance that separated the spoken from the written word. It is important to note, however, that it is precisely this distance that is exploited to prove that an *intrinsic* difference exists between French in France and in Quebec. The intrasystemic difference drifts toward becoming an intersystemic difference:

> Thus, even for the most educated people in the country, there is still an exaggerated gap between spoken and written language and a kind of conflict that could cause great anguish and terrible feelings of dichotomy when a whole chagrin [*the Conquest and ensuing colonization*] tries to express itself. And it is true that in that light, the French language of France seems secondary and almost foreign to us because it does not have a strong emotional content and immediate allusions to our affects and experiences.[17]

The location of the conflict has shifted; it is not just the usefulness of two subcodes within the same language (*koiné* and literary language) that is disputed, but actually the existence of a code common to two different spaces, one of which no longer wishes to be in the cultural orbit of the other. Driving the French "of France" from the borders of Quebec is paramount to eliminating the "terrible feelings of dichotomy" engendered by internal bilingualism, that is, by the co-existence of two subcodes of the *same* language. This plea in favor of a *québécois* language distinct from "the French of France" rests on the argument that linguistic duality causes the subject's identity to be split, a split commonly illustrated in discourse by a series of metaphors referring to madness. One thinks of the "wild derangement" (*aliénation délirante*) of Gaston Miron, a paradigmatic essay in this regard:

> *Je m'en vas à la grocerie. . .*pitche-moi la balle. . .toé scram d'icitte. . .dans ta pensée polluée de dualisme de langage. . .tu ne sais

plus. . .qui tu es et si tu as une Personne Humaine et laquelle si c'est
oui. . .tu oscilles tu déraisonnes tu délires. . .ô mon schizophrène[18]

Gaston Miron stigmatizes the interference of the foreign language
with the native language because it corrodes the identity of the subject
like an acid, bringing with it the "négation de toute caractérisation"; the
subject becoming both one and the other is ultimately neither one nor
the other; "alors tu te mets à te chercher. . .tu disparais dans la densité
et le nombre indifférenciés dans l'informe l'incertain le vague. . .tu
touches avec ton moignon raccourci que tu ne peux dire qui tu es."[19]
Linguistic indifference is the symptom of progressive assimilation; it
relates to the condition of the "deficient man" (*l'homme carencé*),
deprived of a native language, of the only instrument that permits
total presence in the world.[20] Beyond what Miron already denounces,
Michèle Lalonde's discourse on language reveals something else: the
existence of an institutional conflict reflected in the instability of the
language of theatrical translations. This conflict also involves a power
struggle, no longer political but symbolic. It is a conflict between the
vernacular, designated the "*québécois* language," and the *referentiary*
language called "the French of France" or "International French,"
designations that essentially mark the extra-territoriality of this language, and consequently, its absence of legitimacy on *québécois* soil.
In the typology proposed by Henri Gobard, the vernacular corresponds to the "mother tongue" or "native language" while the referentiary language is the language of cultural traditions, notably that of
literature.[21] The referentiary or literary language is suddenly presented as a foreign language, that of another people and of another
land. This is equivalent to saying that it belongs to another ontology.
This is why it is, as we have seen, unintelligible and unsuited to
expressing Quebec "affects." By virtue of this principle, the value of
"the French of France" on the symbolic commodities market is trans-
ferred to the "*québécois* language," with every endeavour being made
to prove that the latter can replace French in its referentiary function,
that it is capable of designating everything, often better than French.
An extreme example would be the *Manuel pratique du français canadien*,[22] which, using dubious examples, tries to demonstrate
"Canadian French's" equality to, if not superiority over, "the French
of France," at least for designating North American realities or what
are supposed to be such. This is an extreme case, of course, but its

publication is indicative of the spirit that fuelled the current profusion of lexicographic texts. These works have several goals, not all of which the ideology of difference can clearly differentiate: to codify the specificity of *québécois* usages of French, and in so doing to lend support and scientific credibility to the reconquest of a language "of our own," certainly, but also to assert this language's ascendancy over both English and "the French of France." Difference is then endowed with a symbolic capital, it lends a new power to a new elite at the core of the institutions.

Thus, the adoption of the vernacular permits Quebec playwrights and translators to rise to the dominant institutional position, which was up to that point occupied primarily by "French Canadian" authors, or even by French authors and translators. At the end of the 1960s, 23 percent of plays and 90 percent of translations in the repertoire were of French origin; at the end of the 1980s, no more than 9 percent of plays and 6 percent of translations were imported from France. The desire for a language of one's very own fills a *distinctive* function necessary for the institutional recognition of the new playwrights. The numbers quoted mark the ground gained on the French repertoire which, either directly or indirectly through its models and translations, had occupied the greater part of the theatrical scene to the point of being experienced as a form of "colonialism." Language is the separating instrument that gave *québécois* theater its own identity and subsequently ensured its autonomy vis a vis the French playwrights.

The aesthetic break worked in tandem with the political claim by raising the territorial stakes. By adopting the thinking that underlay the literary production of the day, by making theater something other than a simple "expressivity," the new *québécois* playwrights took part in the reconquest of the discursive norm within the institution of the theater. As one reclaims a land submerged by the ocean, so one reclaims a cultural territory. If writing or translating for the stage becomes "un acte aussi probant que l'action politique"[23] in that it sets out to portray the socio-economic alienation of Quebecers, this also elevates *québécois* theater to the universal conscience. From this point of view, translating monuments of world drama "into *québécois*" is an act whose effect is more profound than that of simply writing plays in *québécois*; it achieves to the fullest extent the goal of wrenching "*québécois*" from its status of dialect and elevating it to the status of national language, of "native language." Thus, the new Quebec drama ranks with other national dramas thanks to the singularity achieved through a language that has been shown to be suitable not only for writing but also for translation. It acquires the property of being "*Québécois* in the world and to the world," fulfilling the vow made by Gaston Miron for all *québécois* literature.[24]

It is now clear that translation practices and arguments about language that directly or indirectly relate to these practices all hinge upon the principle of *individualization*. What is the purpose of theatrical translations if not to create a difference wherein the distinct identity of the *québécois* collectivity will be recognized? These translations aspire neither to be "transparent" nor "adequate" to the original text. On the contrary, the intervention of the translator is made obvious, and this intervention is considered to be a mark of creativity. The translator cannot consent to the type of inferiorization that, in his eyes, leaves someone trying to pass for someone else: "il se prendra pour un autre et n'existant que par l'Autre, il se condamnera du même souffle à n'exister que pour l'autre: en somme il s'apprête à devenir le double de son ombre."[25] Theatrical translations are hypertextual by design, intentionally "deformative"; they actualize, they adapt, they parody the original text. Here lies the paradox of the difference that ends up being what it was at the outset: otherness helps manufacture sameness because sameness was *already* within it. The other is not translated; rather, one translates oneself into the other by a mirror-like identification, by importing only those symbolic representations of the foreign text that belong to the constructions of the collective identity in the discourse of the target society. That is to say, in its emergent phase, "*québécois*" theater in part constructed its identity by doubling and appropriation of alterity, in opposition to and yet with it. By making the Other an analogue of the Self, it builds itself on the negation of the Other.

Language is in solidarity with these singularizing translation practices, it is pivotal to them. The basis of linguistic differentiation is not the language of the foreign text, radically other, but the referentiary code of French. The differentiation begins by attributing alterity to it: "the French of France," "International French," "hexagon French." These deterritorializing attributes have the effect of legitimizing the use of a distinct *québécois* language. In this case also, difference is produced through similarity, by means of two broad interrelated translation procedures that reinforce each other. The first follows from a genetic concept of language, relying on its diachronic dimension; the second makes the identity of the *québécois* collectivity coincide, here and now, with a symbolic system that could be called self-referential, a language to speak "among ourselves." Both procedures postulate the coextensivity of language, territory, and ethnicity. Both seek to establish the homogeneity of the group that must crystallize the "national conscience." Both have a *restorative* goal. The individualizing practices that express the quest for identity are fundamentally intended to erase the caesura embodied in the self-defining expression "nous autres" (we/people; we/others). The ethnocentrism that pervades theatrical translation does away with this constituent "ambiguity" of the *québécois* identity. Invested with the power to reimbue the group with the cohesion of identity that rests in its national conscience, language must be the *differentia specifica* of Quebecers, a territorial, ethnically identifying separator. This shows itself in Garneau's works by a return to the language of the original community, *Ursprache* or source language. The terms that describe this linguistic archaeology are eloquent: "I drew (as from an artesian well) from the ancestral springs of the *québécois* language."[26] This return to the mother tongue and its thematization by Michèle Lalonde in a text like *Défense et illustration de la langue québécoise* cannot fail to evoke the Fichtean concept of the rapport between language and national identity; the specificity of a nation, says Johann Gottlieb Fichte, is not "a question of the previous ancestry of those who continue to speak an original language; on the contrary, the importance lies solely in the fact that this language continues to be spoken, for men are formed by language far more than language is formed by men." Consequently, and importantly for this discussion, a language that adopts "something foreign" abandons "something native," cuts itself off from its "living root," and, in the end, becomes a "dead" language to its users. In other words, Fichte concludes, "when one looks at the matter closely, they are entirely without a mother tongue."[27] This is also the intent of the differentiating practices at work in the text and language of theatrical translations, since these practices consist of disengaging oneself from the *adulterating* alterity. The linguistic claims that form the doctrinal foundation of the discursive practices preoccupied with repossession have the same goal as well: "Actuellement nous avons besoin de plus que d'une langue maternelle pour nous épanouir, nous avons besoin d'une langue qui soit aussi natale. C'est par récupération que nous posséderons notre instrument de culture et que celle-ci pourra informer la réalité."[28] The distinction made between "mother tongue" and "native language" goes back to the doubly foreign status of the language that the *québécois* people inherit at birth. It is, on the one hand, the language of a conquered country, a language altered by that of the conqueror; on the other hand, it is the language of the French, anchored in another culture and ill-suited to name this place's realities. Thus, asks Michèle Lalonde, does there exist "une Langue Québecquoyse. . .distincte de la Française. . .dans laquelle je puisse m'exprimer?"[29] The Quebecer, "coupé de ses liens *écologiques* de droit, déculturé c'est-à-dire aliéné de sa culture," cannot be "au monde d'ici en l'absence d'une langue qui lui soit propre."[30]

Michel Garneau's translation "into *québécois*" is a paradigm of return to the "lifegiving" source of the native language, of the language of the country at its birth, this language that goes back to the point of origin of symbolic designation with its words "inventés pour nommer par exemple les bordages, les bordillons, les fardoches, les cédrières et autres choses si fréquentes en nos sauvages parages. . .qui tant émerveillaient nos aïeux sans pour autant les laisser bouche bée et impuissants à les nommer."[31] The updating of the original language with a view to restoring its true identity to the group shifts imperceptibly toward the idea of a *purification* of the language from which all "polluting" alterity must be removed, to use Miron's phrase—this is just one of many possible adjectives from the imagery of the time, where contact with alterity (construed, one might say, as *l'anglophonie*) equals sullying. In the same vein, moreover, the ethnocentric distortions in translations assist the new *québécois* theater in its task, which is to free the stage from the "encrassements" of traditional theater, or in other words to "nettoyer" the Quebec stage of foreign works.[32]

Believing, as Gaston Miron does, that "language and its speech. . .are the total presence of a man in the world" essentially establishes an ontological rapport between language and identity; it basically ties the constitution of the subject to the exclusivity of a symbolic system.[33] Wilhelm von Humboldt most fully developed the idea of an interaction between language and the subjectivity of perception of the real. For Humboldt, thought is closely related to the "specific" nature of the language serving as its vector; likewise, conceptualization of the content of internal perception and of affectivity "depends on the individual way of looking at things of an individual human being whose language is inseparable from him."[34] Is this not the same principle being applied in insisting that "the French of France" cannot legitimately serve to assert the Quebecer's presence in a *québécois* world, since the perception of the realities of Quebec is not adequate to their conceptual realization in this language forged elsewhere and from other affects? However, before concluding, in accordance with Fichte's teachings and as several Quebec language ideologists proclaimed during the 1970s, that the French "of France" is a dead language in Quebec, it should be noted that Humboldt's thinking is in opposition to that of the nationalist movement fueled by the Jena addresses.[35] If "language never ceases to be one with the nation," it is also, by definition, a crucible of heterogeneities,

> A crucible in which are decanted, mixed and transformed those representations which express age, sex, class, where all the rich diversity of character and of spirit shows itself, that of the group first, then, *to the advantage of this brew of terms and languages, that of each nation, that finally of all humanity,* with the growing extension of the boundaries of the human community—*language appears to be the place where the conversion of subjectivity to objectivity takes place, of constantly limited individual existence to totalizing unification.*[36]

The unique perspective each language offers on the world is far from permanently fixed. It is penetrated by constantly renewed alterities that embroider it with the perspective of other languages; each "reflects, under a firmly fixed aspect, an ideality and universality which refers us, beyond all individuation, to the simultaneous compatibility of all possible virtues."[37] We are, therefore, faced with an evolutionary concept of language, and, through it, just as evolutionary a concept of the presence of the subject in the world, its rapport with the world. Singularity is woven from alterities that, as such, continually modify the rapport between the subject and the symbols which connect it to the world. From this point of view, the language-centered concept of identity is demolished. One might in effect wonder, as Michel Foucault does, in what measure the subject supposedly constituted in a symbolic system that would entirely define it is not, rather, constituted "in real, historically analyzable practices":

> Il y a une technologie de la constitution de soi qui traverse les sys-
> tèmes symboliques tout en les utilisant. Ce n'est pas seulement dans le
> jeu des symboles que le sujet est constitué.[38]

This means that motivations arising from a specific situation intervene between reality and its conceptualization; this situation gives rise
to "conceptual needs." Thus, practices that constitute the subject find
their symbolic representation in discourse rather than language
proper. In this sense, discursive symbols are rationalities that interact
with practices; they inspire or adapt to them according to what is at
stake. When one questions the reasoning behind translations and the
transformations they cause the linguistic material to undergo, one sees
the consensual establishment of specific relations between language
and identity through cooptations and exclusions. These are coexten-
sive with social practices motivated by the quest for identity—ethnocentric practices excluding alterities perceived as destabilizing agents
of heterogeneity. In short, in the particular historical situation analyzed here, the rapport between language and identity is a power relation that reproduces, within the theatrical institution, the frameworks
of legitimization and delegitimization that a new *"québécois"* elite is
installing in society.

Notes

1. "Le discours social: tout ce qui se dit et s'écrit dans un état de société;
   tout ce qui s'imprime, tout ce qui se parle publiquement ou se représente
   aujourd'hui dans les média électroniques. Tout ce qui se narre et s'argu-
   mente, si l'on pose que *narrer* et *argumenter* sont les deux grands modes
   de mise en discours. Ou plutôt appelons 'discours social' non pas ce *tout*
   empirique, cacophonique à la fois et redondant, mais les systèmes
   génériques, les répertoires topiques, les règles d'enchaînement d'énoncés
   qui, dans une société donnée, organisent le dicible—le narrable et l'opin-
   able—et assurent la division du travail discursif" (Marc Angenot, *1889.
   Un état du discours social* [Montréal: Le Préambule, 1989], 13). Unless
   otherwise indicated, all translations are ours.
2. This process is part of the new translation studies paradigm derived
   from the theory of the polysystem. See Itamar Even-Zohar, ed.,
   Polysystemic Studies, Poetics Today 11(1) (1990). See also Gideon
   Toury, *In Search of a Theory of Translation* (Tel Aviv: The Porter
   Institute for Semiotic and Structural Studies, 1980).

3. Michel Tremblay, *Les Belles-Sœurs* (Montréal: Leméac, 1972), 94.

4. Michel Garneau (tr.), *Macbeth* (Montréal: VLB Editeur, 1978), 120-21. In the original scene, the two characters, long separated by exile, do not recognize each other immediately; they have become *strangers to each other.* In the *québécois* version, more emphasis is placed than in the original dialogue on *loss of native identity,* and its replacement with a foreign identity. Because of the pattern of cuts made by the translator in the text surrounding the excerpt quoted, "virer en étranges" is clearly understood by the listener as "to become a stranger in one's own land," in other words, "to be assimilated." For a detailed analysis of this translation, see the chapter entitled "Shakespeare, poète nationaliste québécois: la traduction perlocutoire" in A. Brisset, *Sociocritique de la traduction. Théâtre et altérité au Québec* (Montréal: Éditions Balzac-Le Préambule, coll. "L'Univers des discours," 1990).

5. Jean-Claude Germain, "Du Décor et des costumes" (préface), *Les Faux Brillants de Félix-Gabriel Marchand* (Montréal: VLB Editeur, 1977), 8.

6. Jean-Claude Germain, *Le Buffet impromptu ou la nôsse chez les propriétaires de bungalow,* adapted from Bertolt Brecht's *Die Kleinbürgerhochzeit* (Montréal: École nationale de théâtre manuscript, 1976).

7. Jean-Claude Germain, *Diguidi, diguidi, ha! ha! ha!* and *Si les Sansoucis s'en soucient, ces Sansoucis-ci s'en soucieront-ils? Bien parler, c'est se respecter!* (Montréal: VLB Editeur, 1972), back cover.

8. Chekhov, *Oncle Vania,* tr. by Michel Tremblay with the cooperation of Kim Yaroshevskaya (Montréal: Leméac, 1983), 18–21.

9. Chekhov, *Les Trois Sœurs,* tr. by Robert Lalonde (Montréal: École nationale de théâtre, manuscript), 3–5. Gisèle, the eldest of the three Côté sisters, is first a teacher, then a headmistress.

10. Bertolt Brecht, "La bonne âme de Setchouan," tr. by Gilbert Turp (Montreal: École nationale de théâtre, manuscript).

11. Rudel Tessier, "Afterword," in Gratien Gélinas, *Hier les enfants dansaient* (Montréal: Leméac, 1968), 151–52.

12. Michel Bélair, *Le Nouveau théâtre québécois* (Montréal: Leméac, 1973), 42.

13. This also applies to the paratext and commentaries that accompany lexicographic works on the "*québécois* language" or the "*Québécois* of today."

14. Monique Mercure on the *québécois* translation of *Mère Courage* by Gilbert Turp. Quoted by Pierre MacDuff, "Monique Mercure/Mère Courage," *En Scène* 2(2) (1984): 14.

15. Gilles Marsolais, "Traduire et Monter *Mademoiselle Julie,*" *Cahiers de la Nouvelle Compagnie Théâtrale* 11(2) (1977): 12. Emphasis

mine. Gilles Marsolais's retranslation follows Boris Vian's version extremely closely, but "unburdens" it of its poetic qualities. More striking yet is the resemblance between the *québécois* version of *Uncle Vania* by Michel Tremblay and the translation by Elsa Triolet. C.f. A. Brisset, *Sociocritique de la traduction*, 301–2.

16. These translations have become just as unstageable in France, but the publishers who hold exclusive rights are blocking retranslations. The new translations done with contemporary stage directions in mind remain more or less clandestine; see for example *Désir sous les ormes*, directed by Matthias Langhoff in a remarkably inventive sociolectic translation by Françoise Morvan.

17. Michèle Lalonde, *Défense et illustration de la langue québécoise* (Paris: Seghers-Laffont, 1979), coll. "Change." Translation by Rosalind Gill and Roger Gannon.

18. Gaston Miron, *L'Homme rapaillé* (Montreal: Presses de l'Université de Montréal, 1970), 111–12, emphasis his. Clear traces of the theme of *bilingualism associated with madness* are found in recent writings, such as the libretto of the opera *Nelligan* by Michel Tremblay. One sees the shift from what Miron denounces, the dissolution of one language in another, toward bilingualism itself. In this case, otherness is presented as *intrinsically* harmful. The Other must be blocked off in order to guarantee the unity and homogeneity of the subject.

19. Ibid., 110.

20. Ibid., 112.

21. Henri Gobard, *L'Aliénation linguistique. Analyse tétraglossique* (Paris: Flammarion, 1976), 34.

22. Sinclair Robinson and Donald Smith, *Manuel pratique du français canadien* (Toronto: Macmillan, 1973). This "manual," designed for anglophone students, is aimed at demonstrating that Canadian French is a language distinct from French in France, in the sense that it possesses, like any other language, the ability to express the entire range of subjects relevant to humanity (Introduction, i). Arranged in three columns, the manual highlights the *gaps* in "the French of France," making them up if necessary, guided by the same principle of differentiation as that which prevailed in the graphic codification of the *québécois* language in theatrical translations and creations.

23. Miron, *L'Homme rapaillé*, 119.

24. Ibid., 119.

25. Jean-Claude Germain, preface to *A Canadian Play / Une plaie canadienne* (Montréal: VLB Editeur, 1983), 23.

26. Program of the Théâtre de la Manufacture, October-December, 1978.

27. Johann-Gottlieb Fichte, *Addresses to the German Nation* (New York: Harper & Row, 1968), 48, 55, 57–58.

28. Miron, *L'Homme rapaillé*, 118.

29. Lalonde, *Défense*, 12.
30. Miron, *L'Homme rapaillé*, 117–18. Emphasis mine.
31. Lalonde, *Défense*, 43–44.
32. Bélair, *Le Nouveau théâtre québécois*, 62. Today these images have disturbing connotations. They have given way to an apologia for intermingling, even though this new discourse rubs shoulders with the old in an ambiguous manner. It is striking to see notions of "disparity" or "heterogeneity" surface in social discourse to absolutely disqualify intermixtures of alterity, for example a cast of actors of different nationalities for the same film or, more fundamentally, during the constitutional debate, the delegitimizing multi-ethnicity of "Canada outside Quebec" deprived *ipso facto* of identity. Likewise, the *topos* of "openness to the world" and "universality" coexists in contradictory fashion within people who, in the same breath, proclaims a radical break from the nearest alternative, "the rest of Canada."
33. Miron, *L'Homme rapaillé*, 118.
34. Wilhelm von Humboldt, "Man's Intrinsic Humanity: His Language," in *Humanist Without Portfolio,* tr. by Marianne Cowan (Detroit: Wayne State University Press, 1963), 245.
35. In the *Addresses to the German Nation,* a series of speeches made in reaction to the Napoleonic conquests, the rapport between language and nation does not involve the ethnic factor. This aspect would more than a century later be grafted onto the messianism which, however, emanates from the Addresses.
36. W. von Humboldt, *Werke* (Berlin: Walter de Gruyter, 1968), 4:24. Our emphasis.
37. Ibid., 33.
38. Michel Foucault, *Un parcours philosophique. Au-delà de l'objectivité et de la subjectivité* (Paris: Gallimard, 1984), 344.

From "Homespun" to "Awesome":
Translated Quebec Theater in Toronto

Jane Koustas

❖ ❖ ❖ ❖ ❖ ❖ ❖ ❖ ❖ ❖ ❖ ❖ ❖ ❖ ❖ ❖ ❖ ❖ ❖ ❖

In an article describing the 1986–88 Canadian theater scene, Alan Filewood, noting Toronto's keen interest in Quebec theater, concludes, "Montréal seemed closer than it had in years."[1] His comment underlines the importance and extent of exchange between Canada's two largest theater communities and suggests that this was a new development: Toronto audiences had had the opportunity to see Quebec theater in translation for several decades but it was not until the 1980s that Quebec productions in Toronto fostered a greater understanding of the "Other" culture and a feeling of proximity. The present study considers critical response to professional Toronto productions of translated Quebec theater from 1951 to 1988 and concludes that despite its long history, theater transfer did not draw the communities closer until very recently. This article argues that theater exchange failed to bridge the "two solitudes" not because of a shortage of productions, for indeed Quebec theater became "a staple of the Toronto season,"[2] but because of the perspective from which Quebec plays were viewed and reviewed.

Until the arrival of Michel Tremblay on the Toronto English theater circuit in 1972, an average of only one Quebec play in translation was staged a year, Gélinas and Languirand being the most popular playwrights. However, from 1972 to 1980 Toronto audiences had the opportunity to see usually two, if not three, professional productions, at least one of these being a Tremblay play. The 1980s witnessed not only an increase in the number of plays staged but the introduction of many new playwrights representing a wider range of theater practice. This study argues that until the arrival of theater resulting from the Quiet Revolution known as the nouveau théâtre québécois,[3] introduced to Toronto by Jean-Claude Germain, Jean Barbeau, and Michel Tremblay, Toronto critics illustrated, though somewhat patronizingly, sensitivity to plays' origins: productions were identified as "Quebec plays." With the introduction of *joual*, which posed more complex translation problems, and of the social and political issues associated with the "nouveau theatre québécois," which demanded a greater understanding of a radically different Quebec, critics were unsympathetic toward a play's Quebecness or *québécitude*; indeed this seemed to work against the play, rendering it too remote for the Toronto audience. Response to recent and more universal Quebec theater suggests a less defensive, more open attitude which is not centered on specific cultural questions and on the English/French Canada conflict.

In 1972, in his review article of *Forever Yours Marie-Lou*, Herbert Whittaker, the eminent *Globe and Mail* theater critic, urged Toronto audiences to attend French-Canadian plays in translation in order "to learn, to know its [Quebec's] differences, to understand Quebec's backgrounds and motivations."[4] He was, however, idealistic. While the popularity of Quebec theater in Toronto could suggest a genuine curiosity about Quebec culture and an appreciation of its theater, and, indeed, more Quebec literature is translated during periods of tension between French and English Canada (there was for example a marked increased in the early 1970s following the October Crisis,[5] translating the "Other" culture is not necessarily a sign of interest and esteem as Annie Brisset illustrates. It frequently results, instead, in the appropriation of the "Other" and the claiming of its literature as one's own. Brisset accuses Quebec theater translators and companies, for example, of eliminating or downplaying the alterity of non-Quebec theater in their translations, adaptations, parodies, or reappropriations of foreign works. Citing the following definition by Antoine Berman, she concludes that Quebec theater is essentially ethnocentric:

> Ethnocentrique signifera ici: qui ramène tout à sa propre culture, à ses normes et valeurs et considère ce qui est situé en dehors de celle-ci— l'Etranger—comme négatif ou tout juste bon à être annexé, adapté, pour accroître la richesse de cette culture.[6]

A toi pour toujours ta Marie-Lou, 1983. Photograph by André Le Coz.

Such cultural exploitation is not new in the Canadian literary tradition for, as E. D. Blodgett points out,[7] English Canada too has a long history of claiming the "Other," that is French-Canadian and *québécois* authors, as its own. Similarly, Robert Wallace, although enthusiastic about the popularity of translated Quebec theater,[8] accuses the Toronto theater community of ethnocentrism; it either dismisses or appropriates work that is culturally different. He states:

> Indeed my general concern with the reception of *québécois* plays in Toronto originates with my discomfort over the attitudes with which they often appear to be approached, not just by the critics who review them but also by the companies that produce them. In a word, I would typify these attitudes as Toronto-centric, adding to the historical complaint. . .that Toronto's artistic institutions suffer from an arrogance that leads them either to appropriate or dismiss whatever appears to them as genuinely different.[9]

Like Brisset then, Wallace argues that ethnocentrism interferes with genuine exchange. It is in the light of Wallace's and Brisset's studies that this article examines the tradition of translated Quebec theater in Toronto based on the critical response to these plays.[10] Although reviews are, as Wallace states, the "subjective reactions of individuals whose perceptions are often not shared by others,"[11] a study of the criticism, rather than of the translated text, situates the play in a particular social context, treating it as a form of social discourse which is clearly anchored in and greatly influenced by the target culture. Translated drama is, after all, like all translations, a "discourse in the sense that it is a linguistic event produced by a subject within a specific historic context."[12] This article studies the extent to which critics accept, reject, appropriate, or respect Quebec theater and its *québécitude*.

Before their experience with Quebec drama's new voices of the 1980s, whose plays were avowedly less nationalistic, theater critics exhibited ethnocentrism as described by Brisset and Wallace in two ways. First, little attention was paid to the importance of the mediation of translation and to the question of place, thus severing the play from its origins. Wallace suggests that critics, as well as those participating in and/or attending the production avail themselves of a knowledge of place in order to understand the play's "context of time and place."[13] They need also to recognize the importance of the translation process and the "degree to which the translation alters the original and creates, in a sense, a new play."[14] Critics generally ignored the plays' origins and the importance of the translator, frequently crediting the latter only when he or she rendered the work more familiar.

Those same critics demonstrated in a second way their reluctance to recognize, appreciate or respect the society in and for which the play was written: their interpretations do not reflect what current criticism has identified as the plays' central issues but rather what the critics themselves wished to believe about Quebec. In his article on the English Canadian interpretation of Roch Carrier's novels, Pierre Hébert labels this tendency to extract only the ideas that conform to one's prejudices about Quebecers the "Krieghoff syndrome."[15] A popular nineteenth century painter, Krieghoff produced numerous paintings of French-Canadian life showing the *habitants* as jovial but decidedly unruly, undisciplined, and overly exuberant. This unfavorable portrayal sold tremendously well to English Canadians who preferred to see Quebecers in this light and, indeed, a Krieghoff painting was recently chosen for the cover of *The French Canadian Experience*, published in 1979.[16] Commenting on Krieghoff's success, Barry Lord states: "Isn't that just like them? We can hear the British buyer chuckling."[17] Hébert maintains that Carrier's tremendous success in English Canada, unparalleled in Quebec, is due to his Krieghoff-like portrayal of Quebecers which, intended as caricatures,[18] were interpreted by English Canadians as totally realistic. Hébert states:

> . . . Or, ce que j'appellerais le syndrome Krieghoff, c'est justement cette perpetuation du mythe selon lequel le Canadien français est jovial, animé, certes mais aussi grossier, anarchique, irrespecteux des conventions, insubordonné. . . .[19]

A similar attitude is prevalent in Toronto's critical response to Quebec theater from the 1950s to the early 1980s. Indeed, in his review of *La Guerre, Yes Sir!*, staged at the Stratford Festival, Herbert Whittaker remarked, "What he [Carrier] set out to show his audience was their [Quebecers] stupidity, ignorance and superstition."[20]

Toronto has always welcomed Quebec theater enthusiastically, albeit often in a "wrong-headed" fashion.[21] It did, for example, "throw out the red carpet"[22] to Gratien Gélinas and his production of

Tit-Coq (Royal Alexandra Theatre, 8-13 January, 12-17 March 1951). Gélinas, author/director/star, was honored with a doctorate and the sensational opening night, "a theatrical event about as rare as a blizzard in July"[23] concluded with "one of the most gala events of the winter season."[24] Although this suggests that the Toronto public "indicated its appreciation of the significance of this theatrical opening,"[25] reviewers showed little understanding of or appreciation for the social issues addressed in *Tit-Coq,* described as "an unpretentious effort, an earnest, straightforward even naive drama"[26] by a playwright who "understands *his* (emphasis added) country well."[27] No mention was made of the conscription crisis nor, more importantly, of the significance of Tit Coq's bastard origins, recognized by scholars to be "symbolic of Quebec itself, symbolic of a shared alienation."[28] A "down-to-earth piece of homespun" about a "simple trusting little soldier who found his big love before shipping overseas," "a tender and pathetic story of *one* man's (emphasis added) insecurity," "the same tearful source used by soap-opera writers,"[29] *Tit-Coq,* much like Krieghoff's paintings, only confirmed Torontonians' notion of the narrowness of a Catholic society and seemed very much "wrenched out of the soil of Quebec."[30] Some critics were also clearly uncomfortable with the traces of *québécitude* unintentionally present in the performance: the play was performed in English by the original cast, thus producing "crude, picturesque accents"[31] that were "at times very difficult to understand."[32] No mention was made of the translator or of the translation.

In their reviews of Gélinas' subsequent Toronto production, *Bousille and the Just* (Royal Alexandra, 16-20 January 1962), critics demonstrated the same tendency to emphasize that which conformed to their vision of quaint, rural Quebec while dismissing the larger questions addressed by the play. "An awkwardly constructed, ineptly staged and performed melodrama,"[33] which took "a hard look at hypocrisy as it flourishes in [his] native Quebec,"[34] *Bousille* said little to Toronto critics about social injustice in general, or about discontent in Quebec society on the eve of the Quiet Revolution. Only one critic commented on the "stilted and somewhat antiquated translation," but omitted the translator's name. He added that the "things that make the play worthwhile can only be effective in the native tongue and idiom,"[35] but did not specify what these things were nor how the translator failed to convey them.[36]

While Gélinas, in both the pre- and post-Tremblay years, received considerable attention in Toronto, being at one point "the most honoured man in Canadian theatre,"[37] Marcel Dubé, sometimes identified as the "father" of Quebec theater, was largely ignored. *The Time of the Lilacs* (Royal Alexandra, 28 October-1 November 1958), his only Toronto production, received little critical attention. Described as "gently sentimental,"[38] the play drew only a neutral review. While he noted Ken Johnstone's "questionable translation," Whittaker did not explain why it was problematic nor how this affected the play. More significantly, other Dubé works, *Zone* and *Le Retour des oies blanches* for example, which offer images of a greatly troubled, less Catholic and traditional Quebec were never staged in Toronto.

Given its coolness toward the very popular Dubé, Toronto's interest in the less well-known, more avant-garde Jacques Languirand is all the more surprising. Languirand staged three plays in Toronto, *The Partition* and *Departures* (Central Library Theatre, from 17 February 1966) and *Man Inc.,* produced for the grand opening of the Saint Lawrence Centre (from 16 February 1970). While all plays received mixed reviews, Languirand's theater, and the author himself, generated considerable critical interest. In his review of the first two plays, Whittaker compared Languirand's work to the author describing both as "humorous and unexpected."[39] *The Departures*, "a blithe tragedy without answers"[40] was more successful and "far more satisfying and complex"[41] than *Partition,* a "poorly translated, two finger exercise."[42] The translator's name was not mentioned nor were specific translation problems discussed, but both Nathan Cohen and Whittaker identified Languirand as a "Montreal dramatist" whose approach, according to Cohen, was "partly scornful, partly sympathetic and romantic in a specifically French Canadian intellectual way."[43] Although the critic does not explain what was specifically French Canadian nor how this differed from an English Canadian approach, his comment suggests that Languirand's somewhat avant-garde and experimental work[44] was, indeed, too remote for a Toronto audience that preferred a more "homespun" vision of Quebec. Reviews of *Man Inc.* stressed almost exclusively the play's technical dazzle rather than its content or Languirand's Quebec origins.

Toronto critics were divided over Jean Basile's *The Drummer Boy* (Royal Alexandra Theatre, 17 January–4 February 1968) which presents a disturbing and thus less palatable picture of old Quebec. The story of the rape of an eleven-year-old girl and the abuse of the young, accused soldier, it was both lauded as "a significant debut [for Theatre Toronto]"[45] and condemned as an "insult"[46] and "spluttering jumble, a French Canadian version of Billy Budd."[47] Only Whittaker noted that something may have been "lost in the translation" in this "occasionally jarring version,"[48] but he did not specify the nature of the loss.

Toronto's introduction to *joual* in translation and to a new Quebec theater which spoke of a different, post Quiet Revolution society was with Jean-Claude Germain's *Notes from Quebec* (Théâtre Passe Muraille, from 7 May 1970). Toronto critics were clearly unreceptive to this new experience. The play was condemned as "sophomoric and amateurish"[49] and labelled an "absurdist soap opera."[50] It was primarily its *québécitude* that worked against it. Judged to have lost "some pertinence in the translation"[51] and "impact in its uprooting from Quebec to Toronto,"[52] the play, the understanding of which relies on the audience's appreciation of a modern, nationalistic Quebec, was "over the head"[53] of at least one, if not all, of the critics. Dubarry Campeau was also offended by Germain's, or the translator's, use of four-letter words. The translator's name was not mentioned.

The negative reaction elicited by a play's *québécitude* and political intent, as well as by the use of *joual,* is even more evident in Jean Barbeau's Toronto experience. Critics saw in *Manon Lastcall* and *The Way of Lacross* (W.W. Theatre Productions, Poor Alex, 1-27 May 1972) "one hit, one miss."[54] *Manon Lastcall* was little more than "a tiresome farce"[55] that "misfired."[56] However, *The Way of Lacross,* though "not an entirely successful play,"[57] did illustrate "Barbeau's positive grip on dramatic craftsmanship."[58] More significant is the observation that "the play suffer[ed] from being aimed specifically at a Quebec audience,"[59] thus rendering the social criticism irrelevant. The jokes on Parisian French in *Manon Lastcall,* for example, did not "come across"[60] and critics (and according to them, the audience) were particularly insensitive to the political message of both plays: Lacross' final outburst "fell flat."[61] Searching for the reasons for Lacross' arrest and apparently unaware that the play was based on the actual arraignment of a political demonstrator, Whittaker commented that the "play's accusatory drive [was] weakened."[62] Although noting the play's use of "a quality closely identified with

Quebec's separatist pangs," Whittaker, as did most other critics, failed to acknowledge or explain the significance of the October Crisis as the play's political background. Only Urjo Kareda[63] was sensitive to both the linguistic and cultural problems involved in transporting this new type of theater and to the Toronto audience's difficulty in understanding or appreciation. He pointed out the importance of "the sound of language,"[64] stating that "Barbeau uses words with exceptional muscularity and vigour." He noted as well the importance of "words that contain other words much as social structures contain other social structures" and the failure of the "self-deprecating and listless" translation to convey this. Kareda further commented on the difference between the original and English versions, which ran at the same time, arguing that the latter suffered because of the "wilful obliteration of the ceremonial [religious] nature of the play"—dropped because it could have proved to be "too remote" for the Toronto audience. Kareda recognized as well the importance of cultural difference or the question of place in Barbeau's work and suggested as well that translating and transposing such plays could be a "troublesome point."

Given this initial negative reaction to the deliberately nationalistic *nouveau théâtre québécois*, and to a Quebec that was no longer quaint and familiar, Michel Tremblay's tremendous success[65] is all the more remarkable. Recognized as "a writer of apparent power and tremendous drive"[66] after his first production *Forever Yours Marie-Lou* (Tarragon Theatre, 14 November–10 December 1972), he was soon "the darling of the critics and the chosen one of the Toronto theatre scene."[67] However, the critical reaction to his work suggests that the Toronto theater community was not responding to Tremblay, the ardent Quebec nationalist, whose "theatre is intimately linked to the world he describes,"[68] the Plateau Mont-Royal, but rather to a "Toronto's favourite *Canadian* (emphasis added) playwright"[69] who was talking more universally about "deceptions and the need for them, and the loss of them and comfort in misery. About *any* (emphasis added) life in fact."[70] Tremblay's success cannot be attributed to his ability to convey in popular language and to a sympathetic and informed audience the sentiments and concerns of post Quiet Revolution and October Crisis separatist Quebec nor to the fact that "when you're up to your ass in mud, any kind of solid ground is solid joy."[71] His popularity is instead due to the Toronto public's and theater critics' ability and willingness to interpret Tremblay's message as solely universal at the expense of its *québécitude*. Charles Pope stated:

> . . .no other Canadian dramatist has succeeded so completely in creating startling, in terms of psychological insights as well as shock tactics and [sic] original theatre that is inherently Canadian without being provincial to the point of being incomprehensible to a non-Canadian audience.[72]

Pope's assessment confirms Wallace's observation that Toronto's theater institutions, like their Quebec counterparts studied by Brisset, need either to appropriate or dismiss work that is culturally different. A study of the critical response to Tremblay indicates that the political, Quebec message was ignored or condemned as being "too remote," while the universal elements were appropriated.

Marie Lou's return to Toronto (Theatre Plus, St. Lawrence Centre, 4-21 June 1975) was described as a "riveting performance."[73] The almost unanimously positive reaction[74] suggests that the Toronto audience "had more of an opportunity to study his [Tremblay's] style enabling it to spot the surging currents beneath the dazzling movement of the actor stream,"[75] but critics failed to identify the theme of Quebecers' shared degradation and alienation present in all of the Plateau Mont-Royal plays.[76] *Marie-Lou*, like subsequent Tremblay productions, succeeded despite, not because of, its Quebec origins. The product of a "church-ridden state," the play was deemed to have lost some "courage" either through "transplant or translation."[77] It could, however, "reach beyond its point of origin"[78] and "flourish without a political analysis."[79] The *Star* critic further downplayed the play's and Tremblay's Quebec origins by stating: "Tremblay himself would say that he is a Quebec playwright, not Canadian, but never mind."[80]

After Tremblay's sensational return to Toronto with *Les Belles-Sœurs* (St. Lawrence Centre Repertory Theatre Company, 31 March–28 April 1973), a "milestone play, a high point for the St. Lawrence Centre,"[81] critics commented more directly on Toronto's tolerance of *québécitude*. Kareda urged the crowds lined up at *Move Over Mrs. Markham*, "a shoddy British import" to cross the physical and cultural intersection and to "go next door" to see the "10,000 times more entertaining" Tremblay play, but questioned the Toronto theatergoers' ability to "jump across the [cultural] intersection."[82] Whittaker referred as well to "a kind of mute edged condescension indelibly WASP."[83] Observing that it was not clear whether the audience who stood and cheered at the end of the play did so to show their praise for the production or their respect for the national anthem with which it ends, David McCaughna suggested that the audience's support was indeed ambiguous.[84] Despite their enthusiasm, critics once again failed to comment on the play's political message. For example, stating that there was a risk of losing the political angle in the translation[85] and that "*Les Belles-Sœurs* [was] a play about Quebec, about false promises and political exchange catalogues," Kareda nonetheless identified it as a "Canadian play."[86] He praised its universality, observing that the production "takes that singularly perspective vision of a specific social world and transforms it to take in the rhythms of all our individual fantasies."[87] Only Myron Galloway, the *Montreal Star* critic who described the Toronto production as a "massacre," expressed awareness of the importance of the play's *québécitude* and the failure of the Toronto staging to convey this; he wrote: "the play has nothing to say if the French-Canadian flavour is missing." Thus, in the St. Lawrence Centre production, "which [had] no more to do with Montreal than it [did] with Hong Kong," the play "in no way came across."[88]

It is in its response to Tremblay's greatest Toronto hit, *Hosanna,* that the Toronto theater community most clearly demonstrated its need to dismiss a play's alterity and political, Quebec message and, instead, to appropriate the play and playwright.[89] A resounding success when it first opened at the Tarragon Theatre (15 May–1 June 1974), *Hosanna* continued to draw Toronto crowds in four subsequent productions (Global Village Theatre 6 September–4 October 1974, Toronto Workshop Productions, 13 January–14 February 1977, NDWT Theatre, 11-12 March 1980, Tarragon, 17 May–28 June 1987) and also ran at the Bijou Theatre on Broadway. However, while Toronto enthusiastically recognized the merits of this "shimmering production,"[90] which was "a heart-pounding tour de force,"[91] and a "landmark"[92] after which "Canadian theatre [was] not quite the same,[93] it was also quick to claim Tremblay as its own at the expense of his theater's political drive and *québécitude*. Like all of Tremblay's plays, *Hosanna* contains a political message. As Tremblay himself stated:

> I do not mean that they [Hosanna and Cuirette] are Quebec symbols
> or images of Quebec. But their problems with the wider society are polit-
> ical problems. Because they are the fringe group in society, this society in
> a way hates them. But they want to be happy and they want to be some-
> body. Hosanna is a man who always wanted to be a woman. This
> woman always wanted to be Elizabeth Taylor in *Cleopatra*. In other
> words, this Québécois always wanted to be an English actress in an
> American movie about an Egyptian myth in a movie shot in Spain. In a
> way, that is a typically Québécois problem. For the past 300 years we
> were not taught that we were not people, so we were dreaming about
> somebody else instead of ourselves. So *Hosanna* is a political play.[94]

Based on the critics' comments, the political aspect was largely missed.
The play was, instead, seen as an exploration of the "poetics of
love,"[95] a "study of deception and humiliation and the loss of
dreams,"[96] a "sensitive delineation of a homosexual relationship,"[97] or
a "classic study of homosexual revenge"[98] by "the Canadian theatre's
most compassionate poet of *individual* (emphasis added) isolation."[99]
Those critics who did recognize an attempt at a political message
downplayed it claiming that such an allegory was "far-fetched"[100] or
that "there was no inkling of such an idea to be found in the play no
matter how hard one looked for signs."[101] More relevant to this study
is McCaughna's comment that although Tremblay is "a very political
writer and all of his plays have dealt in one way or another with the
condition of Quebec society, it does not hit home that this is a play
which has a great deal to do with Quebec."[102] Clearly even those critics aware of the political message refused to acknowledge its importance; they chose instead to ignore the play's philosophical sources.

Tremblay did not always have the same resounding success in
Toronto and critical comments suggest that the other plays' *québécitude* did work against them rendering them too remote. Furthermore,
translations and translators were acknowledged only when they rendered the work more familiar. *En pièces détachées* (New Theatre, 5
March–15 April 1974), "rather disgustingly re-titled *Montreal Smoked
Meat*"[103] was criticized for being merely a repetition of "more
Montreal misery."[104] Whittaker questioned the Toronto audience's
willingness to accept Montreal's "squalid side" instead of the "quaint,
charming, historic vision of Montreal to which [we] have been exposed
in the past."[105] *Bonjour là, Bonjour* (Tarragon Theatre, 1 February–16

March 1975) drew mixed reviews but, according to one critic, the translation, "void of the rough joual," was able to "serve the Ontario audience well" since the English version was "in no way a reproduction of the Quebec original."[106] *Saint Carmen of the Main* (Tarragon Theatre, 11 January–26 February 1978) seemed "curiously uprooted," its "spirit" being lost on the Toronto audience.[107] Freeman also accused the translation of not conveying the play's political fable. A *New York Times* critic found the play touching, but dismissed the political vision as "preposterous," while not explaining what the message really was.[108] Critics did not comment on the political message of other Tremblay plays, *Surprise, Surprise* (Toronto Arts Productions, St. Lawrence Centre, 22 October–8 November 1975), which generated a limited but positive response, *La Duchesse de Langeais* (22 May–28 June 1980)[109] a "left-over from the primal scream of gay lib,"[110] and *The Impromptu of Outremont* (Tarragon Theatre, 22 May–28 June 1980) Toronto's first glimpse at Tremblay's interpretation of the life of the upper classes.

Although the success of this distinctly Quebec nationalist playwright might initially suggest an openness to the "Other," reviews thus indicate that he triumphed as a Canadian, not Quebec, playwright due primarily to the universality, not *québécitude,* of his plays. Furthermore, the negative reaction elicited by the distinctive Quebec flavor and subject of the theater of Roland Lepage, Anne Hébert, Michel Garneau, Jovette Marchessault, and Roch Carrier, staged during the same period, suggests a rejection of the unfamiliar and a reluctance to accept and interpret the importance of place when this ceased to be "homespun." Considered less universal, thus not appropriable, these plays could not compete with Tremblay's "Canadian" theater. Anne Hébert's *Le Temps sauvage* (Firehall Theatre, 23 November–9 December 1972) was described as merely a "symbolic analysis of Quebec's problems."[111] Michel Garneau's *Four to Four* (Tarragon, 30 March–28 April 1974) suffered from dealing solely with "Quebec women"[112] whose background was too "exotic in an Ontario setting."[113] Roland Lepage's *Le Temps d'une vie* (Tarragon, 13 May–25 June 1978), though recognized for its literary merit, also suffered from its regional subject matter. It was merely "a lyrical look at simple habitant life,"[114] an exploration of the "rural roots of French Canada,"[115] which dealt essentially with "the soul of Quebec."[116] Commenting on the play's limited subject matter "my problem and one I suspect I will share with others," Bryan Johnson questioned the Toronto's public's "burning interest in a lyrical epic about one woman's life in rural Quebec."[117] The "magic" of Jovette Marchessault's *The Saga of the Wet Hens* (Tarragon, 18 February–19 March 1982) was lost due in part to a "poor translation of shameless literary pretention"[118] but primarily due to cultural differences; the numerous allusions to the authors depicted as well as to the Catholic church as the key oppressor were too remote for the Toronto audience.[119] Despite the critic's assessment, the play was a box office success, suggesting that, faced with the larger question of feminism, far more central to the play than nationalism, Torontonians were in fact able to bridge the cultural gap and accept the play's inherent alterity. The "otherness" of Roch Carrier's *Celestial Bicycle* (Tarragon, 1 April–1 May 1982) clearly worked against it. The play, which illustrates Carrier's fantastical side, was essentially "lost in a smoke screen."[120] Toronto's cool response to this Quebec hit was attributed to the language barrier "which never seemed more inseparable"[121] and once again to the cultural gap; it simply "did not work with the anglophone sensibility."[122] Overshadowed by Tremblay, these authors, whose work relied on an understanding of its *québécitude,* and who spoke of a Quebec radically different from that portrayed by previous more homespun plays, could not flourish in an ethnocentric climate.

The cycle of the *Belles-Sœurs* ended in 1977.[123] Three years later, a lag for which translation time could account, after the Black Cat Cabaret's unsuccessful production of *La Duchesse,* Tremblay's domination of the Toronto theater scene ended. However, while Toronto's "darling" wrote novels, theatergoers sampled a much more diversified, radically different Quebec theater and did so in a somewhat less ethnocentric way. Review articles suggest that in the 1980s critics and audiences were more able to "cross the cultural intersection"; critics identified playwrights as *Québécois*, rather than Canadian, no longer appropriating the "Other" and ceased to dismiss or ignore their work on the pretext that it was too remote or culturally different. Furthermore, more attention was paid to the play's origins. As Wallace argues,[124] they continued to confuse the translation with the original commenting, for example, on the translator's style as if it were the playwright's, but the critics also acknowledged the translator and translation more frequently, hence recognizing both the importance of the play's place and language of origin. Thus, although the

Toronto theater community continued to produce and review Quebec in a somewhat "wrong-headed" fashion, a change of attitude, insufficient as it may have been, is nonetheless perceptible and can be attributed to changes within both theater communities. First, both Quebec and Toronto theaters exhibited greater openness to and interest in a wide variety of theater from all over Canada and the world; Montreal hosted the Festival des Amériques, Quebec held the Quinzaine Internationale and Toronto staged the du Maurier and Quay Works festivals. Referring to the 1986–88 period, Alan Filewood notes, "This was the period when English Canadians discovered the new wave of imagistic performances in Quebec; at the same time, *québécois* artists discovered the audience beyond their borders."[125] He observes as well that Toronto audiences saw more productions from Quebec than they did from other parts of the country. Diane Pavlovic, commenting on the same period, likewise emphasizes the importance of the theater festivals in Quebec which illustrate "l'ouverture de [notre] pratique théâtrale à celles qui viennent d'ailleurs."[126]

It is not just Toronto's new attitude to Quebec theater that led to increased openness. The introduction of the "new wave of imagistic performances," and of other new theater directions as well as less nationalistic authors greatly facilitated transfer from Montreal to Toronto. Quebec plays survived translation and transportation more easily because they were less Quebec-centred and perhaps would have appealed more than earlier productions even had the audience remained Toronto-centric. In addition to experimenting with new forms of theater resulting from the integration of various media into performance, such as dance, video, and pyrotechnics, Quebec playwrights steered theater in entirely new directions. As Pavlovic states, the nationalist issue, so central to the theater of Barbeau, Germain, and Tremblay, was replaced by a greatly diversified response to broader, universal questions of the human condition:

> Dans les années 1970, le projet théâtral coïncidait avec un projet de société: les artistes semblaient investis d'une mission et servaient volontiers la cause du nationalisme, de l'indépendance. . . . Avec la fin des grandes causes, la fonction proprement politique du théâtre a connu un recul certain. . . . N'étant plus réunies dans un même projet, les démarches artistiques sont éparpillées et proposent, chacune de son côté, des métaphores plus générales sur la condition humaine.[127]

Toronto showed its appreciation of a less folkloric and provincial the-ater[128] responding to Quebec plays as a total theater experience, rather than as a lesson on the "two solitudes."

One of the greatest successes in the history of Quebec theater, the Théâtre des Voyagments' *Broue* (co-written by Claude Meunier, Michel Côté, Marcel Gauthier, Marc Messier, Jean-Pierre Plante, Francine Ruel, and Louis Saia), translated as *Brew* (Centrestage Company, 29 September–29 October 1983), took English Canada by storm. Although the authors, who claimed to be "not that interested in nationalism any more,"[129] based these series of sketches on a specifically Quebec event, the closing of the men-only *tavernes*, they reached a much wider audience, cutting "across Canada's bilingual blood" in their portrait of "men together of any nation."[130] Critics and public clearly welcomed the signal that "Quebec theatre [was] beginning to recover the comic sense lost during the 1960s when the-atre artists [here] decided it was important for them to express the province's social and political realities."[131] *Brew's* successful cross-Canada tour indicated to the theater community that, as Jean-Claude Lesperance, a theater producer, remarked, "There doesn't seem to exist any barrier between English and French now. Where one per-forms is no longer a political question."[132]

Bachelor, another collective production co-authored as well by Louis Saia and Louise Roy and translated as *Single* by Michel Sinelnikoff (Toronto Free Theatre, November 1983) did not fare as well. However, Toronto critics, while noting that it was from Quebec, blamed the failure on an "insensitive director" and a "grotesque translation"[133] and a "performance as contrived as the monologue"[134] rather than on any cultural differences. Indeed the story, based on the empty life of a single woman controlled by con-sumerism and the pursuit of selfish pleasures, was "a script for everyone."[135]

While *Brew* introduced Toronto to more universal, cross-cultural Quebec theater, the play's format remained traditional and it was not until the arrival of Robert Lepage that Toronto experienced the totally new directions in which Lepage, Gilles Maheu, and others were leading Quebec theater. Lepage, later to become the director of the National Arts Centre French Theater, first appeared in Toronto with the Théâtre Repère production of *Circulations* (Canadian Rep Theatre, 11-22 February 1985). One critic was quick to recognize

Lepage's talent and the power of the "riveting aural and visual poetry"[136] used by Lepage as well as by other new playwrights who were "stretching and twisting the language of theater into bizarre and fascinating shapes,"[137] but another saw in this bilingual production, which combined various sound effects with music, theater and mime "a multi-media mish-mash" signifying "very little."[138] It was not until his latter productions of *The Dragon's Trilogy* (du Maurier World Stage, from 31 May 1986 and Factory Theatre, 18-28 May 1988), *Tectonic Plates* (du Maurier World Stage from 3 June 1988) and *Vinci* (du Maurier Quay Works, from 20 January 1988) that Lepage's "theatrical mastery"[139] was unanimously acknowledged. Sending "shock waves" through the Anglophone community now "forced to recognize the extent of the remarkable theatrical explosion in Quebec,"[140] Lepage introduced Toronto to a new form of theater. Recognized as one of the most "important shows" when it first opened in the World Stage Festival at Harbourfront (1986) and "a must" for anyone wanting to know "the direction of the most exciting theatre in Quebec,"[141] *The Dragon's Trilogy,* a trilingual English, French, Chinese production, was in fact "legendary"[142] by the time it returned two years later. "A lyrical epic about the meeting of cultures" which illustrated "imagistic theatre at its best,"[143] it electrified both audiences and the international press appealing to "different audiences with different tastes and expectations."[144] Lepage "came and conquered"[145] once again with *Vinci,* and "grabbed the audience hard and never lost [his] grip"[146] with *Tectonic Plates*. While critics readily identified Lepage as Quebec's "enfant terrible,"[147] the playwright's and the plays' origins clearly did not interfere with the comprehension and appreciation of these imagistic, dream-like, multimedia, multilingual, and multicultural theater pieces which earned Lepage international recognition.

However, as Wallace suggests,[148] Toronto was not entirely ready for Gilles Maheu's totally non-textual theater pieces. *Le Rail* (23-28 October 1986), staged as part of the Brecht festival, recognized as "stunning" but "murky"[149] received little critical attention. *Hamlet-Machine* (du Maurier World Stage, 10 June 1988) was not appreciated by critics who displayed what Paul Leonard and Wallace identify as a typical English-Canadian preoccupation with the text and uneasiness with its absence; they would "still doggedly insist that the performance event is best regarded as primarily an expression of a transcendent meaning—the script."[150] Predisposed against totally imagistic theater, they described *Hamlet-Machine* as "pretention"[151] and "self-indulgent, intellectual bulltwaddel."[152] As Wallace notes, however,[153] their extreme negativity suggests, as did Hebert Whittaker in his review of *Marie-Lou*,[154] that their "response. . .was hedged by an element of curiosity and envy" for critics did recognize Maheu's talent, "his command of stage imagery" and the "awesome" physical discipline of his performers,"[155] which resulted in "breathtaking," "superbly done" productions.[156]

Demonstrating reserved enthusiasm about this innovative theater, Toronto maintained its interest in more traditional plays and its faithfulness to old favorites. Michel Tremblay once again wooed and won the Toronto audience with *Albertine in Five Times* (Tarragon, 9 April–11 May 1985).[157] Significantly, it was a new style play, "symptomatic of the Quebec writer's increased introspection"[158] that earned mixed reviews, being described as both "pure theatrical magic,"[159] "soporific,"[160] and "hard to grasp."[161] Seeking to "speak of all women in all times of their lives,"[162] this play introduced Toronto to a far less political Tremblay who recognized his change of direction, stating, ". . .instead of judging society I was beginning to ask *myself* questions."[163] Similarly, his later production and critical success, *The Real World* (Tarragon, 15 May–26 June 1988), was "a gripping look at parallel realities"[164] by "a master craftsman now exploring an intensely personal phase in his artistic career"[165] and thus "a far cry" from his earlier, more political productions.[166] Critical response to revivals of *Bonjour là, Bonjour* (Toronto Centre Stage, 25 November–20 December 1986) and *Hosanna* (Tarragon, 17 May–28 June 1987), both considered classics, indicated a greater appreciation for and understanding of his earlier work. Controversial and comparatively unsuccessful when if first opened, *Bonjour là, Bonjour* was welcomed as a "highlight,"[167] although the same critic judged the performance to be a "disappointment."[168] Another praised it as a "modest masterpiece."[169] Overcoming their sensitivity to the incest issue, blamed in part for the first production's failure,[170] theatergoers had "realized in spite of their Toronto reserve that they had been given something unexpectedly fine."[171] *Hosanna*'s political message, no longer such a sensitive point in post Referendum Canada, was now readily acknowledged by the theater community: Richard Monette, the star of the previous productions now turned director, noted, "The central metaphor is about being yourself, with the political implication that Quebec should be what she is."[172] Toronto's understanding of Tremblay, who admitted that he felt before that he was being treated "as a nice neighbour,"[173] had clearly evolved.

The Toronto theater community did not limit itself to the sensational new nor to the revival of the old: equally as impressive as the number of Quebec plays staged in Toronto in this period is the diversity of the productions. Feminist, gay and, lesbian companies, Buddies in Bad Times and Nightwood Theatre, responded quickly to the homosexual currents in Quebec theater although their productions were not always critical successes. Jovette Marchessault's *The Edge of the Earth is Too Near, Violette Leduc*[174] (Nightwood Theatre, 14 May–1 June 1986) did not draw good reviews, due in part to a poor translation. One critic clearly recognized the importance of this by commenting on Susanne de Lotbinière Harwood's "overwrought translation,"[175] but another confused it with the original text. He stated that "when it comes to use of language it is difficult to determine where Leduc leaves off and Marchessault begins,"[176] ignoring de Lotbinière's intermediary role. The Buddies in Bad Times production of Normand Chaurette's *Provincetown Playhouse, July 1919* (3-21 December 1986), was described as a "compelling work,"[177] but once again the critic collapsed the work of the playwright and the translator, William Boulet, commenting on the "evocative" writing without distinguishing between the two versions. Tarragon's production of *Being at Home with Claude* (Tarragon, 29 March–10 May 1987) generated a much greater, more enthusiastic critical response, earning for author René-Daniel Dubois the reputation of "Toronto's playwright of the hour."[178] As in their comments on Marchessault's and Chaurette's work, all Toronto critics identified Dubois as a Quebec playwright, but his origins did not interfere with the reception of his work for like Meunier, Lepage, the new Tremblay, Marchessault, and Chaurette, Dubois was not writing to a Quebec audience about the Quebec question.[179] As Linda Gaboriau, his translator, stated, "Dubois is one of a new trend of Quebec playwrights who are more North American, more internationalist in their interests than those who came before."[180] Toronto's "first glimpse of the power and the passion of a major new voice from Quebec"[181] was, in fact, a doubleheader including *Pericles Prince of Tyre by William*

Shakespeare (Theatre Passe Muraille, 9-26 April 1987) written in English.

Other new Quebec voices did not enjoy Dubois' success but the poor critical response is not necessarily attributable to the public's nor to the critics' ethnocentrism. Like Dubois', these writers' message was more universal than *Québécois* and the plays' Quebec origins, while acknowledged by the critics, were neither central to their interpretation nor responsible for their failure. René Gingras' award-winning *Syncope,* translated as *Breaks* by Linda Gaboriau (Toronto Free Theatre, 6-24 January 1988), according to both *Star*[182] and *Globe and Mail*[183] critics, suffered from bad direction, poor acting, and a clumsy translation. Critics illustrated a keen awareness of the importance of language in Gingras' work and of the difficulty in translating "the poetic quality of Quebec theatre, the exuberant use of language."[184] That the critics blamed linguistic, rather than cultural barriers suggests greater openness: the play and its message were not deemed to be too remote; the text was, instead, difficult to translate. In the Toronto Free Theatre's staging of Marie Laberge's *L'Homme Gris,* translated by Rina Fraticelli (Toronto Free Theatre, 2 March–3 April 1988), the poor critical response was not attributable to the translation or to the production: the play itself, a "static yet intense drama"[185] was judged to be repetitious[186] and too much like a "long sermon on how not to be a parent."[187] Although the reviews were sometimes negative, both Gingras and Laberge drew considerable critical attention, indicating the theater community's awareness of their importance.

In May 1988 the Factory Lab theatre began an exchange program with the Centre d'Essai des Auteurs Dramatiques of Montréal. The initiation of this joint translation project, entitled "Interact," indicated that genuine exchange between Canada's largest theater communities, the absence of which both Wallace and Brisset had lamented, was becoming a reality. The reading of Linda Gaboriau's translation of Michel Marc Bouchard's *Les Feluettes,* retitled *Lilies* (Factory Lab Theatre, 20 May 1988) was, according to Robert Wallace, "an historical occasion"[188] to which the audience responded with an emotional generosity rare in his considerable experience of Toronto theater.[189] Toronto welcomed "the excitement and diversity of the theatre being produced in Quebec" (Factory Lab Press Release) and, as Robert Nunn observes in an article that is somewhat of an update of Brisset's study, Montreal too was showing greater openness to English Canadian and, indeed, to all "foreign" theater. He states:

> . . .there is the unprecedented opening of Quebec to the rest of the world, no less evident in the arts than in industry and commerce. That is, there is a two-way communication between Quebec and the rest of the world. . . . In this new atmosphere, the ideologically-driven necessity to ignore this looming other no longer applies: the Montreal press can notice with gratification that *québécois* plays in translation are popular in Toronto; there is no reason not to read, translate and produce English-Canadian scripts.[190]

This article has attempted to trace the evolution of a similar attitude in Toronto. Once viewed somewhat patronizingly, much like Krieghoff's paintings, Quebec theater in translation, with the arrival of Tremblay, received genuine recognition, but from a perspective that went partially against the spirit of the plays; the central issue of nationalism and Quebec's struggle for identity was ignored. The arrival of new voices such as Claude Meunier, Gilles Maheu, Robert Lepage, René-Daniel Dubois signalled new directions in Quebec drama. Deliberately more universal, this theater was frequently well received in Toronto from a perspective that coincided more closely with its original intent. Critics acknowledged the translator more frequently, though not always favorably, thus demonstrating a better understanding of the difficulties of theater transfer and increased respect for the play's origins. Theater in translation was finally becoming a reliable "vehicle through which cultures travel"[191] without the misdirection, rerouting, detours, and frequent losses that plagued previous transfers.

Notes

1. Alan Filewood, "Diversity in Deficits: Theatre in Canada 1986–1988," *Canada on Stage* (Toronto: PACTS Communications Centre, 1991), xiv.
2. Robert Wallace, *Producing Marginality: Theatre and Criticism in Canada* (Saskatoon: Fifth House Publishers, 1990), 216.
3. Michel Bélair, *Le Nouveau Théâtre québécois* (Montreal: Leméac, 1973).

4. Herbert Whittaker, *Globe and Mail*, 24 November 1972.

5. David Homel, "Dans les deux sens (la traduction littéraire au Canada)," *Liberté* 205. 35. 1 (1993): 133.

6. Annie Brisset, *Sociocritique de la traduction: Théâtre et altérité au Québec* (Montréal: Éditions Balzac-Le Préambule, coll. "L'Univers des discours," 1990), 111.

7. D. Blodgett. "How Do You Say Gabrielle Roy?" *Translation in Canadian Literature* (Ottawa: University of Ottawa Press, 1983), 13–35.

8. Wallace, *Producing Marginality*, 216.

9. Ibid., 220.

10. This article will discuss only professional productions of translated plays staged in Toronto. See as well: Mariel O'Neil-Karch and Pierre Paul Karch, "Le théâtre québécois à Toronto," *Revue d'histoire littéraire du Québec, le Théâtre* (Ottawa: Editions de l'Université d'Ottawa, 1984), 99–107.

11. Wallace, *Producing Marginality*, 217.

12. Paul St. Pierre, "Translation as a Discourse of History," *Traduction, Terminologie, Rédaction* 6(1) (1993): 51.

13. Wallace, *Producing Marginality*, 218.

14. Ibid., 221.

15. Pierre Hébert, "La Réception des romans de Roch Carrier au Québec et au Canada anglais ou le syndrome de Krieghoff," *Le Roman Contemporaire au Québec (1960–1985)* (Montréal: Fides, 1992), 211.

16. Gaston Saint Pierre, *The French Canadian Experience* (Toronto: Macmillan, 1979).

17. Barry Lord, *The History of Painting in Canada* (Toronto: NC Press, 1974), 47.

18. Hébert, "La Réception," 201.

19. Ibid., 212.

20. Herbert Whittaker, *Globe and Mail*, 5 August 1972.

21. Wallace, *Producing Marginality*, 217.

22. J. Karr, *Toronto Star*, 9 January 1951.

23. Ibid.

24. Herbert Whittaker, *Globe and Mail*, 9 January 1951.

25. Ibid., 8 January 1951.

26. Ibid., 10 April 1951.

27. Ibid., 9 January 1951.

28. Jonathan M. Weiss, *French-Canadian Theater* (Boston: Twayne, 1986), 11.

29. Karr, *Toronto Star*, 9 January 1951.

30. Whittaker, *Globe and Mail*, 9 January 1951.

31. Ibid.

32. Karr, *Toronto Star,* 9 January 1951.
33. Nathan Cohen, *Toronto Star,* 16 January 1962.
34. Whittaker, *Globe and Mail,* 16 January 1962.
35. Cohen, *Toronto Star,* 16 January 1962.
36. Another Gélinas play, *Mortier* (Factory Lab Theatre, 6–21 December 1972) received little critical attention and, as part of a short play festival that became a "killing marathon," was described as only a "dreary marriage game" (U. Kareda, *Star,* 7 December 1972).
37. Whittaker, *Globe and Mail,* 16 January 1962.
38. Ibid., 28 October 1958.
39. Ibid., 17 February 1966.
40. Ibid., 18 February 1966.
41. Ronald Evans, *Telegram,* 8 February 1966.
42. Ibid.
43. Cohen, *Toronto Star,* 18 February 1966.
44. Weiss, *French-Canadian Theater,* 21–22.
45. Whittaker, *Globe and Mail,* 18 January 1968.
46. McKenzie Porter, *Telegram,* 22 January 1968.
47. Cohen, *Toronto Star,* 18 January 1968.
48. Whittaker, *Globe and Mail,* 18 January 1968.
49. D. Rubin, *Toronto Star,* 8 May 1970.
50. Whittaker, *Globe and Mail,* 8 May 1970.
51. Ibid.
52. Rubin, *Toronto Star,* 8 May 1970.
53. Dubary Campeau, *Telegram,* 8 May 1970.
54. Whittaker, *Globe and Mail,* 12 May 1972.
55. U. Kareda, *Toronto Star,* 12 May 1972.
56. Whittaker, *Globe and Mail,* 12 May 1972.
57. Ibid.
58. Kareda, *Toronto Star,* 12 May 1972.
59. Grace Richardson, *That's Show Business,* 9 June 1972.
60. Ibid.
61. Ibid.
62. Whittaker, *Globe and Mail,* 12 May 1972.
63. Kareda, *Toronto Star,* 12 May 1972.
64. See Robert Wallace, "Towards an Understanding of Theatrical Difference," *Canadian Theatre Review* 55 (Summer 1988): 9.
65. Tremblay's success has been the subject of numerous studies. See for example: Paula J. Dancy, "Tremblay at Tarragon, 1972–1981: The Plays, the Productions and the Critics," Master's Thesis, University of Guelph, 1985; Renate Usmiani, *Michel Tremblay* (Vancouver: Douglas and MacIntyre, 1982); Renate Usmiani, "Tremblay Opus: Unity in Diversity," *Canadian Theatre Review* 24 (Fall 1979): 12–25; Renate Usmiani, "Where to Begin the Accusation," *Canadian Theatre*

Review 24 (Fall 1979): 26–38; Renate Usmiani, "Discovering the Nuance," *Canadian Theatre Review* 24 (Fall 1979): 39–41.

66. Whittaker, *Globe and Mail,* 15 November 1972.
67. Ed Bean, *Varsity,* 29 September 1974.
68. Weiss, *French-Canadian Theater,* 27.
69. Kareda, *Toronto Star,* 5 June 1975.
70. Whittaker, *Globe and Mail,* 15 May 1974.
71. Bean, *Varsity,* 20 September 1974.
72. Charles Pope, *Scene Changes,* January 1977.
73. George Anthony, *Toronto Sun,* 6 April 1975.
74. U. Kareda found that Theatre Plus had made "a minus of Tremblay" (*Star,* 5 June 1975).
75. Whittaker, *Globe and Mail,* 5 June 1975.
76. Weiss, *French-Canadian Theater,* 27–48.
77. Whittaker, *Globe and Mail,* 1975.
78. Whittaker, *Globe and Mail,* 1972.
79. Kareda, *Toronto Star,* 15 May 1972.
80. Ibid, 15 June 1975
81. Whittaker, *Globe and Mail,* 4 March 1973.
82. Kareda, *Toronto Star,* 7 March 1973.
83. Whittaker, *Globe and Mail,* 4 March 1973.
84. David McCaughna, *Toronto Citizen,* 20 April 1973.
85. Kareda, *Toronto Star,* 26 March 1973.
86. Ibid., 4 April 1973.
87. Ibid.
88. Myron Gallaway, *Montreal Star,* 4 April 1973.
89. Sections of the discussion of *Hosanna* have appeared previously in J. Koustas, "'*Hosanna* in Toronto' 'Tour de force' or 'Détour de traduction?'". *Traduction, Terminologie, Rédaction* 2 (2) (1989): 129–39.
90. Kareda, *Toronto Star,* 16 May 1974.
91. Whittaker, *Globe and Mail,* 16 May 1974.
92. Gina Mallet, *Toronto Star,* 14 January 1977.
93. David Ossea, *Varsity,* 21 January 1977.
94. Geraldine Anthony, ed., *Stage Voices: Twelve Canadian Playwrights Talk about Their Lives and Work* (Toronto: Doubleday Canada), 283.
95. Agnes Kruchio, *Excalibur,* 19 September 1974.
96. Kareda, *Toronto Star,* 16 May 1974.
97. McCaughna, *Motion,* July/August 1974.
98. Anthony, *Toronto Sun,* 13 September 1974.
99. Kareda, *Toronto Star,* 16 May 1974.
100. Pope, *Scene Changes,* January 1977.
101. John Herbert, *Onion,* 15 February 1977.

102. McCaughna, *Motion*, July/August 1974.
103. Kareda, *Toronto Star*, 8 March 1974.
104. McCaughna, *Toronto Citizen*, 29 March 1974.
105. Whittaker, *Globe and Mail*, 8 March 1974.
106. Ibid., 3 February 1975.
107. B. Freeman, *Toronto Star*, 15 January 1978.
108. Richard Eder, *New York Times*, 2 February 1978.
109. According to M. O'Neil Karch and P.P. Karch the play had been pro-
     duced previously at the Tarragon Theatre (25–26 January 1976)
     along with *Johnny Mango and his Astonishing Dogs*, but no reviews
     could be located.
110. Kaspars Dzeguze, *Sun*, June 1980.
111. Kareda, *Star*, 27 November 1972.
112. McCaughna, *Toronto Citizen*, 12 March 1974.
113. Whittaker, *Globe and Mail*, 7 April 1974.
114. J. Erdelyi, *Ottawa Citizen*, 15 April 1978.
115. Freeman, *Star*, 15 April 1978.
116. Jamie Porter, *Calgary Herald*, 30 April 1978.
117. Bryan Johnson, *Globe and Mail*, 15 May 1978.
118. Mallet, *Toronto Star*, 19 February 1982.
119. N. Harris, *Globe and Mail*, 20 February 1982.
120. Mallet, *Toronto Star*, 2 April 1982.
121. Mallet, *Star*, 2 April 1982.
122. Ray Conlogue, *Globe and Mail*, 2 April 1982.
123. Weiss, *French-Canadian Theater*, 151.
124. Wallace, *Producing Marginality*, 213–43.
125. Filewood, "Diversity in Deficits," xiv.
126. Diane Pavolic and Lorraine Carmelain, "Le Québec des années 1980:
     éclectisme et exotisme," *Canada on Stage* (Toronto: PACTS
     Communications Centre, 1991), xxxii.
127. Ibid., xxx.
128. Ibid., xxxii.
129. *Calgary Herald*, 20 October 1982.
130. Lloyd Dykk, *Vancouver Sun*, 31 December 1982.
131. Brian Brennan, Montreal, *Calgary Herald*, 20 October 1982.
132. Marianne Ackerman, *Globe and Mail*, 27 October 1982.
133. Mallet, *Toronto Star*, 14 November 1983.
134. Conlogue, *Globe and Mail*, 15 November 1983.
135. Maureen Peterson, *Montreal Gazette*, 2 December 1983.
136. Matthew Fraser, *Globe and Mail*, 1 March 1985.
137. Ibid.
138. Crew, *Toronto Star*, 28 February 1985.
139. Filewood, "Diversity in Deficits," xv.
140. Ibid., xiv.

141. Conlogue, *Globe and Mail,* 3 June 1986.
142. Press Release, The Factory Theater, 18 April 1988.
143. Crew, *Toronto Star,* 19 May 1988.
144. Vit Wagner, *Toronto Star,* 13 May 1988.
145. Crew, *Toronto Star,* 20 January 1988.
146. Groen, *Globe and Mail,* 7 June 1988.
147. Mallet, *Toronto Magazine,* May 1988.
148. Wallace, *Producing Marginality,* 226.
149. Crew, *Toronto Star,* 24 October 1986.
150. Paul Leonard, "Critical Questioning," *Canadian Theatre Review* 57 (Winter 1988): 6.
151. Conlogue, *Globe and Mail,* June 1988.
152. Crew, *Toronto Star,* 12 June 1988.
153. Wallace, *Producing Marginality,* 227.
154. Whittaker, *Globe and Mail,* 15 November 1972.
155. Conlogue, *Globe and Mail,* 13 June 1988.
156. Crew, *Toronto Star,* 24 October 1986.
157. An earlier production of *Remember Me* (Canadian Rep Theatre, January 1985) was cancelled.
158. Conlogue, *Globe and Mail,* 10 April 1985.
159. Crew, *Toronto Star,* 10 April 1985.
160. Conlogue, *Globe and Mail,* 10 April 1985.
161. Ibid., 20 May 1985.
162. Margaret Penman, *Toronto Star,* 5 May 1985.
163. Quoted by R. Crew, *Toronto Star,* 31 May 1988.
164. Conlogue, *Globe and Mail,* 26 April 1988.
165. Crew, *Toronto Star,* 25 May 1988.
166. Ibid., 21 May 1988.
167. Ibid., 11 March 1986.
168. Ibid., 28 November 1986.
169. Conlogue, *Globe and Mail,* 28 November 1986.
170. Paula Dancy, "Tremblay at Tarragon 1972–1981: The Plays, the Productions and the Critics" (Master's Thesis, University of Guelph, 1985), 93.
171. Conlogue, *Globe and Mail,* 28 November 1986.
172. Crew, *Toronto Star,* 22 April 1987.
173. Ibid., 21 May 1988.
174. Marchessault's work was staged, as well as part of the Factory Lab Theatre's Brave New Works' series for which there were no reviews. These include *Night Cows* (March–April 1983) and *The Edge of the World is Too Near, Violette Leduc* (April 1985).
175. Conlogue, *Globe and Mail,* 17 May 1986.
176. Henry Mietkiewicz, *Toronto Star,* 20 May 1986.
177. Crew, *Toronto Star,* 7 December 1986.

178. Ackerman, *Montreal Gazette,* 5 May 1987.
179. Robert Wallace points out the critics misconstrued the setting and ignored the importance of the social and historical context (1967) but did not let this interfere with their appreciation of the play (Wallace, *Producing Marginality,* 229).
180. Linda Gaboriau, *Maclean's,* 27 April 1987, 61.
181. Crew, *Toronto Star,* 8 April 1987.
182. Ibid., 18 January 1988.
183. Conlogue, *Globe and Mail,* 9 January 1988.
184. Ibid., 2 January 1988.
185. Wagner, *Toronto Star,* 26 February 1988.
186. Conlogue, *Globe and Mail,* 3 March 1988.
187. Crew, *Toronto Star,* 3 March 1988.
188. Wallace, *Producing Marginality,* 213.
189. Ibid., 216.
190. Robert Nunn, "Cognita: Has Quebec Discovered English Canadian Plays?" *Theatrum* (June/July/August 1991): 17.
191. David Homel and Sherry Simon, *Mapping Literature* (Montreal: Vèhicule Press, 1988), 9.

The Language of Theater

Lucie Robert

Recent studies have tended to emphasize the various stage-related aspects of theater, concentrating on what has become known as "theatricality,"[1] a concept used to pinpoint the specificity of theater as compared to other artistic forms. In so doing, these studies have tended to set aside the traditional text-centered analysis of theater. There is no intent here to criticize such a perspective, which I believe has made possible a considerable number of significant studies. Compared to other stage-produced cultural forms, however, theater has specific characteristics, among which speech is particularly relevant.

Speech takes many forms in theater. The answer to questions such as "Who is speaking?" and "To whom?" usually distinguishes between two main forms of speech: dialogue and didascaly.[2] Dialogue is first and foremost the interaction of characters through language. As such it is one of the many ways to describe a social space, that is, a sphere framed precisely by various relationships. Didascaly is also "stage-direction," based on the assumption that it is mainly directed toward the actors and the director of a staged play. However, theater history has shown that the relation between these two forms of speech is more complex than it seems at first, and that in many ways didascalies may be considered, in a published play at least, a form of narrative voice somewhat similar to that found in a novel, and which is used to facilitate the *reading* of theater.[3] Although this may appear a secondary issue in the study of stage-produced theater, it is essential when considering the dramatic text or play.

Why, it might be asked, would anyone give consideration to a published play? Is it not simply part of a larger entity called Theater, and not even the main part? Is it not merely just a prelude to the work of the actor and director? The text is not theater; it is related to it in many obvious ways, but the two constitute distinct realities. Although a literary reading of drama is still possible, it has to be seen in the context of the study of theater as an autonomous form of expression. Plays are still published nowadays, not so much for actors as for readers; they are studied as a component of the literary canon. They are often all that is left of theater or all that is made available to those who do not live in cities or close to an active theatrical milieu.

Certainly, among all components of theatrical activity, texts represent the most important link to linguistic practices. Drama is language, if nothing else. Moreover, texts are written in a specific national language, which lies at the heart of a national identity; hence, drama functions as the main link between theater and national identity. Thus, to write anything of value about "Quebec drama" one has to take language (and text) seriously.

So the question addressed here is twofold: what does drama say that cannot be said through other means of expression? More specifically, what is the role of dramatic language in Quebec?

The issues of language in Quebec drama have been many and they have gone far beyond the much discussed question of *joual*. From language to speech, the system analyzed by Ferdinand de Saussure has been used in every possible way by dramatists and playwrights; it has been carnivalized, ridiculed, hybridized as Mikhaïl Bakhtine has shown it could be; seized, gendered and transformed by women; written, uttered, oralized for stage representation, and then de-oralized and re-written for publication; even brandished for political purposes. Theater was not the only stage for these sometimes quite radical demonstrations but, since drama is a speech act of its own, it did carry a few particular messages forward. The new dramaturgical canon thus created became hegemonic,[4] and contributed significantly to the institution of a new national identity.

❖ ❖ ❖

Looking Back

Language is by no means a recent issue in Quebec drama. It is the oldest of all, and for many reasons. First, because language, along with law and religion, has been a problem of national and political survival from the moment the British Empire took over the French colony in North America in 1763. As a newly conquered part of the Empire, the colony was supposed to accept its institutions: English common law, the English language, and the Anglican religion. So the very first aim of the Empire in its new colony was to "unfrenchify" it (as they said at the time) and to have all British subjects, old and new, speak the same language, obey the same law, and believe the same creed. While we all know this did not happen, why it did not happen is anybody's guess. Resistance was certainly a part of it, as was the fact that the linguistic unity of New France was already half a century old[5] when the British arrived, a fact that made major change more difficult and hazardous.

The private use of a specific language and religion is one thing, however, and the public recognition of a political right, as happened with the Quebec Act (1774), is another. Why the British Empire went against all precedent in allowing the French people of Quebec to retain their own law, religion, and language—something it would not consider in Ireland or Australia, and even less in Acadia, where the French Catholic population was deported in 1755—is much too complex an issue to be discussed here,[6] but the fact is that this happened. The "public sphere,"[7] which had no real existence under the French Regime, opened itself to the French population of Quebec: newspapers, addresses, memoirs, and parliamentary discourse were among the media people learned to use. As for theater, which, as Jürgen Habermas has shown, may be considered a main anchor of the eighteenth-century "public sphere" in Europe, it was no different in Quebec, except that this role was filled much longer here than anywhere else.

In fact, theater was a stronghold of liberal resistance to the Catholic Church throughout the nineteenth century. From the moment, circa 1840, when the Catholic church took over part of the public sphere and declared itself the symbol of the Franco-Catholic resistance to materialism brought about by industrialization, Protestantism, modernism, and other so-called "devils," theater became somewhat of an act of courage: professional actors were harassed, sometimes excommunicated; no female actress was tolerated on stage; repertory had to be chosen within very strict moral boundaries and touring companies were criticized and eventually condemned. The bourgeoisie of Montreal and Quebec, to be sure, never much followed the Church guidelines on this matter, and the French public attended local representations. Although the Catholic Church could never completely stop theatrical activity, it did succeed in making things difficult for everyone.

So it is not only as a metaphor, borrowed from the pragmatics of John Searle (1969), that, in Quebec history, theater has been a speech act. In fact, it was the first speech act of Quebec literature and its very first subject was precisely that of language. Anglomania, as it was called, was the subject of one of the first original plays in Quebec after 1763. Its author, Joseph Quesnel, had already written and staged a few operettas in the years prior, but this first dramatic text, entitled *L'Anglomanie ou le Dîner à l'anglaise* and usually dated 1803, is, as Leonard Doucette describes it, "a short verse-comedy that ridicules the attempt by some members of French-Canadian society to adopt British manners, customs, and speech."[8]

The subject was to be the topical content of many more plays during the nineteenth-century, among which Pierre Petitclair's *La Donation* (1842), Félix-Gabriel Marchand's *Fatenville* (1869), and Louis Fréchette's celebrated *Félix Poutré* (1862).[9] All are satirical comedies, written mostly in classical French, with traditional features borrowed from playwrights in the Molière tradition. Most presented characters belonging to the upper classes, *seigneurs,* or bourgeois. A typical plot is based on Molière's *Le Bourgeois gentilhomme*, where the main character's social ambitions cause him to adopt upper-class manners, language, and customs, with the difference that in those days there were two upper classes, one French and the other of British descent. This condition led to the first attempts to organize systematically, in writing, the various levels of the French language: upper-class characters speak a classical language or an English-tainted version of it, whereas lower-class characters speak a popular, idiomatic form of French or an English-tainted version of it. That makes for four levels of language, each belonging to a particular group of characters.

In this context, Louis Fréchette's *Félix Poutré* possesses a revolutionary aspect similar to the plays of his model, Beaumarchais, for

Fréchette's main character was what then seemed to be a true hero of the 1837–38 rebellions. Not only was his play the first to take the revolt of the "Patriotes" as a reference, but Fréchette was one of the first playwrights to make a main character of an illiterate peasant. The plot may be summarized as follows: after the ill-fated rebellions, Félix Poutré was arrested and stood with other convicts ready either to be deported to Jamaica or Australia, or hanged for treason. He cleverly played the fool to regain his freedom, at times laughing so hard at British institutions, including the monarchy, that nobody could believe a sane man in his situation would risk his life by doing so. He was thus set free by reason of insanity.

Language plays an important role in this plot. In opposition to the main character and his idiomatic, popular form of French are upper-class characters (judge, priest, doctor, jailer) who use a formal language. Poutré subverts and ridicules all uses of language by these upper class characters, be it French, English, or Latin. In so doing, he accomplishes through language what the patriots had failed to accomplish with arms on the battlefield, i.e., to defeat the British. History would later show that the real Poutré was actually a police informant, but at the time Fréchette's play was written and produced, the story, with its disrespect for British institutions, including language, created one of the greatest theatrical successes in Quebec theater history.

The expression "popular language," that I have used so far, requires a bit more explanation. In the context of Quebec theater, "popular language" applies only to the special effect created by playwrights who, like some novelists in their dialogues,[10] make use of some elements of realism to create what is usually called "local color." It describes a particular form of language hybridization in which a writer tries to imitate the language of lower-class laborers and peasants of suburban or rural Quebec. In so doing, they pick up a few (usually very few) significant traits from the spoken language, translate them into a written form, and make a somewhat systematic use of them. Of course, no amount of "color" could effectively re-create in written form the real language of the lower classes. In novels, the separation between the levels of language remained absolute and the popular language was restricted to dialogues. Only a few words from rural folklore could be tolerated in the narration, to create the "couleur locale" effect, and only provided they were well underlined.[11]

Consequently, novels in the nineteenth century used a very conservative, literary form of language, except in some dialogues. The objective was to protect the true French language from external assaults, whether by the English language or by the uneducated use of French they said was characteristic of popular classes. Playwrights did not share as great a role in this folklorization process as the novelists, but they did contribute to the identification of significant linguistic particularisms and to their translation into writing. Although they did not always make use of language as topical content, most nineteenth-century playwrights worked on the linguistic material, including those who wrote adaptations of folktales for the amateur stage of the classical colleges. Thus, looking back to nineteenth-century Quebec drama, one has to understand the historical inscription of the use of language in all aspects of social life, including the part that concerns us here: literature and drama.

The nineteenth century was especially concerned with the language issue, although it took a while before it was called a "language" issue, as Franco-Catholic conservatives tended to mix language with religion and other so-called "national interests." They later accepted Confederation, the new constitution of 1867, in the belief that a federation would allow each member to establish its own laws, its own independent state apparatus, and to answer its specific institutional needs in its own way. The nineteenth-century political leaders believed cultural aspects of a nation could exist independently of the economic sphere. Of course, they could not foresee what would become of all the elements, some unknown at the time, that would eventually form the basis of a permanent jurisdictional struggle between federal and provincial governments; and, thus, show the ideal basis of Confederation to be illusory.

Hopes were high in 1867, however, and beliefs seemed well founded, so the political aspects of linguistic conflict tended to fade out of literature and drama. New aesthetic preoccupations took over, and drama was written according to then well-established literary canons: realism, naturalism, or the avant-garde. From the end of the nineteenth century to the mid-1950s, drama was of little symbolic importance within Quebec culture: most contemporary plays were written for the amateur stage and they represented historical and traditional examples of "national" life. Most professionally staged plays imitated canonical aesthetics, borrowed from either French vaudeville and melodrama or the successful contemporary American movies which, from the turn of the century, were beginning to flood the Canadian and Quebec market. Local settings were predominant in these adaptations or "palimpsests," as Gérard Genette (1982) would call them. However, language was not an important issue on the stage, although some dramatists would write plays in the nineteenth-century tradition and have their lower-class characters use a more popular form of language. Only when actors from the burlesque tradition, who used to perform in English because the producers believed the public to be mostly Anglophone, reverted to French in the middle of a play, in order to prove them wrong, did the theater become the stage for a new linguistic "coup."[12]

From "Popular" to *Joual*

Our exploration of nineteenth-century and early twentieth-century Quebec drama should demonstrate that the use of popular language is by no means an extraordinary phenomenon. One can see that it is rooted in the very beginning of the history of Quebec drama; but until a rather recent period, the use of popular language in theater was hardly discussed, so natural did it seem. Beginning in the 1960s, however, popular language, or *joual,* became the centerpiece of Quebec theatre, and its use became self-conscious.

No one really agrees on what *joual* is. For some, as Jean-Paul Desbiens who created the word from the mispronunciation of *cheval* (horse), in his famous pamphlet, *Les Insolences du frère Untel* (1960), *joual* is a spoken language, derived from French, but showing the speaker's evident lack of linguistic sophistication. He saw it as a poor man's language, as the sign of oppression and of neglect. A few years later, sociolinguists would sometimes use the same term non-pejoratively to designate the dialect spoken by the East-end Montreal working class. However, this narrow geographical and social location of *joual* made it virtually impossible to use the word, unless one was ready to give a name to all other dialects and regional versions of the French language spoken in Quebec. The fact is, and this is the definition on which I will base the following arguments, the term *joual* was created by the intellectual, literary class. It was used mostly to describe an "improper" use of the French language of whatever kind

115

(notwithstanding geographical and social variations), and it has since become mostly a literary form of language. Hence, *joual* is less a language than a literary style.

What is really at stake here? Let us backtrack a little. For over a century, Quebec writers were aware of three different issues concerning language:

1) With time, the French language spoken in Quebec had become a little different from the mother tongue, spoken in France, but not enough to become an autonomous language. The poet Octave Crémazie was very conscious of this fact in 1866 when he wrote, in a letter to his friend and mentor Henri-Raymond Casgrain, that it would be much easier for a Quebec writer to make it on the French literary scene if he were to speak some exotic tongue such as "huron" or another Indian dialect. At the time, Quebec writers still wrote largely for a French audience, for it is only in the twentieth century that the idea of an autonomous Quebec literary institution would come into being.

2) Through the development of higher education, differences between upper- and lower-class French became more apparent in the areas of vocabulary, accent, and diction. This phenomenon was first visible around 1850 when the fast-growing elementary school population expanded to include most children, and the even faster-growing population of classical colleges enrolled more and more young men from illiterate families. A similar phenomenon occurred again in the 1960s at the beginning of the "Quiet Revolution," when the private, expensive, Classical College was replaced by a public college known as the CÉGEP.[13] Post-secondary education went from being the privilege of the few to the right of the many, most of whom could never have afforded any kind of secondary education. Such fast-developing innovation in instruction created a generation gap within both families and society in general. As a consequence, linguistic differences became apparent and would be explored subsequently in the works of writers belonging both to the newer and the older generations.

3) As already stated, from the moment the British empire took possession of the French colony, the political and public status of the French language became problematic. Although the manner in which it was experienced changed with time, the language problem itself remained and it was permanently linked to other institutional

116

problems such as civil law and religion. It took time, but language eventually replaced religion as the major nationalist issue, becoming the primary vehicle of modern Quebec nationalism, or, more precisely, modern, secular Quebec nationalism. The first signs of this progression had appeared in the 1930s, just before World War II, but the language issue would become the main issue in Quebec politics following the 1960s.

These were the circumstances when, in 1968, Éloi de Grandmont decided to adapt for the Montreal stage George Bernard Shaw's *Pygmalion* using Quebec popular speech rather than "Parisian argot." Why such a decision was made and approved by the Théâtre du Nouveau Monde, already becoming at the time a major theatrical institution of Quebec, is still a matter of discussion. The choice of this particular play was in itself a point of interest, however, for one cannot fail to notice that it is a dramatization of the problem of language and class. Popular language is opposed to a more educated way of speaking, and this opposition is coupled with two others concerning "good" and "bad" taste or manners, as well as the tension between a male and a female character. As we have already seen, the first two of these oppositions has been dramatized extensively in Quebec drama, whereas the male-female opposition raises still another language-related issue.

The French sociologist Pierre Bourdieu (1982) has shown the importance of the idea of "exchange" in the linguistic situation, and, one must admit, scholars have tended to forget that language is first and foremost a relationship among people, and that speech is verbal intercourse. There is no use to language without the exchange of words, and this is precisely the point of the Shaw play. The male and female characters exchange their wor(l)ds in such a way that love becomes a metaphor of the linguistic exchange. Of course, one cannot fail to notice that the exchange is not symmetrical, but then again Bourdieu has shown that symmetry is rarely achieved, and that linguistic exchange is regulated by social norms and rules, things usually designated by words such as manners, authority, etiquette, and so on. That language was an object of value to be exchanged between two characters was at the time quite new. However, it was precisely at that moment that language had become a political issue in Quebec theater and drama.

Grandmont's never published translation of Shaw's play stirred the literary world, not as much as some other plays would in the following twenty-five years, but significantly nonetheless. Not only was language propelled to the front of the stage, although the love story surrounding the whole issue would give it a more conventional organization (the female character being traditionally expected to give way in such a setting and marriage, and the happy ending being another traditional way of dissolving the conflict) but, and most importantly at the time, popular Quebec French was being used as a language of translation. Developing Ferdinand de Saussure's hypothesis,[14] Annie Brisset (1990) has convincingly shown how important translation is in the legitimation of a particular dialect as a language in its own right. Éloi de Grandmont's *Pygmalion* was a *new* translation, written to *replace* a more traditional French translation, with *joual* taking over *Parisian argot* as the target language. The recognition of Quebec's popular use of French language, as a *legitimate* language of translation, was the newest idea put forward by Grandmont's work.

How different is *joual* from the nineteenth-century popular forms of French used either in novels or dramatic texts? It is difficult to answer precisely this question, for there are as many forms of *joual* as there are playwrights, and there were as many forms of popular language as there were lower-class characters in nineteenth-century literature. A few dominant lexical and morphological characteristics can be detected: *joual* is mostly an urban working-class language, that is to say that it is not only an abstract linguistic system of its own. It is always used in reference to a particular social context. Lexical references are mostly work-place and city-oriented and a dictionary of *joual* would contain many English words, or words adapted from English. It would also point to a few morphological and grammatical particularisms. The nineteenth-century popular forms were more often archaisms belonging to the vocabulary of rural life, commerce and navigation. As a literary style, *joual* is first and foremost a form deriving its originality from the exigencies of a written language. The devices most often used are the graphic elision of some letters or syllables ("j'parl'" for "je parle"), the inscription of accents into the written word ("Urope" for "Europe"), and the use of idiosyncratic blasphemy.

For the most part, however, obvious differences are referential: *joual* is a violent language making an extensive use of blasphemy and harsh sonorities. It is used to refer to what a better-educated audience might call "kitsch" aesthetics or maybe a "kitsch" way-of-life. In its very use, *joual* designates a particular way of life and a social class. It is used in place of a description to identify the typical features of a character.[15] *Joual* was originally written or spoken to shock the audience and, at first, audiences were in fact shocked. The more it was used on stage, however, the more it became difficult to obtain a shock effect, with the result that the *joual* had to become even more violent. Thus, in reading plays from different periods, one can detect varying levels of intensity. Jean Barbeau's use of *joual,* for example, is more extensive and harsher than that of Michel Tremblay. The 1971 edition of the latter's celebrated *Belles-Sœurs*, first published in 1968, is an even better case in point, however, for in this second version, Tremblay emphasizes the graphical features of *joual,* adding along the way new linguistic detail in the form of crossword puzzles, slogans, and puns.

It would be an understatement to affirm that the 1968 stage-production of Tremblay's *Belles-Sœurs* made a strong impression on Montreal's Théâtre du Rideau-Vert audience. It shook the theater establishment to its roots! Tremblay's play was an event, perceived as such immediately by audiences, critics, and other playwrights. History has confirmed this impression and credits Tremblay's play for having changed permanently the theater scene in Quebec. What was it that stirred such an uproar? Language was certainly part of it: it was in fact the part most immediately perceived by everyone. The day following the first performance, newspapers were filled with articles on the language of the play, not only reviews or essays written by critics, but also letters from the public. Words such as "vulgar," "disgusting," and "outrageous" marked the torrent of critical reaction. Some letters also complained that women were using this language and that the working-class characters did not exhibit the conventional thought and expression that usually made them acceptable to a better-educated and somewhat "snobbish" theatrical audience.

In theater criticism, *joual* has usually been invoked to explain the early rejection of *Belles-Sœurs* by audiences and critics, but recent studies show that language was only part of it. The 1980 stage-production of Tremblay's *L'Impromptu d'Outremont,* a play that also makes use of familiar language to depict a bourgeois family, did not attract as much negative attention, in part because Tremblay's style

Les Belles-Sœurs, 1971. Photograph by Daniel Kieffer.

was by then familiar, in part because, like the Molière *Impromptu,* the play dealt mainly with aesthetic problems. However, there may be still another more important reason: each time I expose a student audience to excerpts from both plays in order to compare their reactions, they never fail to react negatively to Germaine Lauzon's first act monologue, while at the same time showing little concern for any part of *L'Impromptu.* Over time, I have become convinced that two extralinguistic elements are actually responsible for their response. First, Germaine Lauzon's dream house, as described in a Green Stamp catalog, is pictured by everyone as being in the worst possible taste, but she still aspires to it, as it is out of the reach of her means. Secondly, she describes these objects with words that are often misspelled and mispronounced, thus adding a certain darkly comic aspect to the play. Both elements reveal a poorly educated woman whose wishes one can hardly begin to qualify with the expression "bad taste" and, even worse, a woman who despises our own taste, our own life, and says so openly, over and over. These two elements, popular language *and* the massacre of good taste, are the very essence of *joual.*

Another landmark play in the history of *joual,* Denise Boucher's *Les Fées ont soif,* was first produced in 1978, ten years after Tremblay's *Belles-Sœurs,* and well after the outcry over *joual* had waned. What was it then that stirred the public and the critics to the point where protesters gathered in front of the theater before each night's performance and Quebec's minister of justice had to lift a ban, imposed by a lower-court judge, on the distribution of the published play? One may point to the fact that Boucher's play belongs to the radical feminist movement. However, this is not the only reason; by then, many such plays, such as *La Nef des sorcières* (1976), had been produced in the Montreal theaters.

Admittedly, the subject of Boucher's play was in itself iconoclastic: three classic images of women, the mother, the prostitute, and the Virgin Mary, are put together on stage to form a strange new trinity. Again, the language is what was most criticized. Although Boucher's language in this play is still to be analyzed, a few observations can be made. Boucher makes liberal use of profanity, usually degrading women. In French, these are not known as "four-letter words," but some belong to the same sexually oriented paradigm. Most of them, some of the more popular ones, usually relate to the degradation of women; others belong to the religious vocabulary. When Boucher

121

stages women as mothers, sexual objects, and religious symbols, she literally makes a character out of a swear word, and creates a trinity using this crude, sometimes filthy language, reversing it, turning it inside out, to denounce what it does not say about women through the literal use of what it does say. It is like a slap in the face, the audience has its own language thrown back at it, along with the political implications. From this perspective, Boucher's play is *joual* at its zenith; and, in this respect, it has never yet been surpassed. Nor has the violence of the audience's reaction!

The main point about the use of *joual* is that it allowed dramatists to stage characters from popular classes with their own aesthetics and language. Previously, playwrights might create popular-class characters, but these characters rarely used their own language, aspiring rather to a higher-class aesthetic, as in George Bernard Shaw's *Pygmalion.* The use of *joual* allowed dramatists to avoid what would have been otherwise long descriptions or narrations which always disturb the dynamics of theater. Henceforth, on the Quebec stage, whether *joual* or classical French was used, language was it own description. It pointed toward entire cultural universes, some of them unknown to the audiences, but which no longer needed explanation: language became part of the décor, of the stage setting, and was certainly as effective. While bringing about those changes, *joual* also unleashed a radical critique of what became known as "literary theater," i.e., a form of drama written as literature.

Literary language in Quebec drama has not followed the traditional path of hybridization: where *joual* is concerned at least, languages tend toward polarization and monolinguism, and characters tend to be circumscribed by their own language. So the "choc des langues,"[16] the language struggle, has become a subject of drama in itself. Nowhere is that more apparent than in anglophone, Montreal playwright David Fennario's *Balconville.* Although the dramatist has to cheat a little, for no audience can be presumed sufficiently bilingual to understand slang versions of both English and French, the play stages a working-class backyard war between an English-speaking and a French-speaking family. The characters understand and speak both languages, although the second language is not entirely mastered, but they come to refuse to speak the same language in conversation and, as a consequence, stop speaking to each other at all. Subsequently, each raises its flag in a provocative way, a Canadian maple leaf for the English-speaking family, and a Quebec *fleur-de-lys* for the French-speaking family. Finally, when fire engulfs the neighborhood, the two men refuse to make amends or to help each other, and both houses, flags flying, burn to the ground.

Like Michel Tremblay, David Fennario makes use of language to create particular characters and to picture a working-class setting. However, and here is a main difference between the two, Fennario does not make great use of the opposition between more- or less-educated uses of the same national language. He opposes lower-class versions of two national languages, thus creating a setting in which nationalism becomes a red herring, an illusionary problem, masking the fact that both families belong to the working-class and are exploited in the same North American historical context.

In the last analysis, the language of the theater has become a metaphor, a universal metaphor for struggles of all kinds. It has replaced class differences as the main obstacle to communication, friendship, and love. In many ways, the language struggle encompasses all others. It absorbs them, thus allowing Quebec playwrights, through the manipulation of language, to develop their own conception of Quebec society. In Quebec Francophone drama (more rarely in English-language drama), *joual* is not only the speech of the working class, nor was it ever intended to be. It is the speech of the whole Quebec people.

After *Joual*

Many things changed after the *Parti québécois* came to power in 1976, or so it seemed, for the appearance of change was, in some cases, stronger than the reality itself. Bill 101, adopted in 1977, made French the official language of Quebec and created the Office de la langue française, an agency responsible for developing an original Quebec linguistic norm. Although the decision resolved many of the "language issues," it had the effect of bringing other issues to the surface.

Although French still needed defending (in a North American context where the small French population is surrounded by more than 200 million Anglophones), its use had now been secured by a political and legal apparatus. While the English population of Quebec thought of itself as belonging to a majority on the North American continent and in Canada, it had become a minority within the new political entity of Quebec. Politically defeated, economically drained as a community (many individuals have left the province, although having suffered no concrete loss), English-Quebecers (the name itself was new) were no longer perceived as a threat. Also, because Bill 101 placed newly arrived immigrant children and young people in the French school system, it was a primary impetus for a multiracial and multicultural Quebec population. The difficulty of integrating these immigrant communities quickly replaced a bilateral linguistic struggle as the main "language issue" of the 1980s and 1990s. Playwrights such as the Francophone Marco Micone or the Anglophone Vittorio Rossi staged good examples of this "new" linguistic struggle in their respective studies of the Montreal Italian community.[17]

Once the *Parti québécois* came to power, it jettisoned most of its leftist economic policies. At the same time, a string of economic crises in the 1970s and 1980s produced political solutions unfavorable to the working-class, thus marking the end of populist nationalism. *Parti québécois* leaders, after René Lévesque resigned as the Quebec Premier, confirmed this turn to rightist economy-oriented policies, by discarding writers and artists as "dreamers" and "romantics," thereby separating the literary and political spheres. Many critics noticed an immediate change of subject and rhetoric in literature and theater after the 1976 election. Populism was out. The social division of language along class lines had led to a more individually oriented, self-reflexive style of writing.

As far as literary institutions were concerned, the 1970s saw the establishment of a linguistic norm from within the province. From the start, the Office de la langue française had been seen as an efficient body of people making reasonable decisions leading to the creation of an autonomous French language in Quebec. Although the first task of the Office involved the "Francization" of specialized work-place vocabularies, it did address urgent—and more politically oriented—problems, such as the feminization of language. In the course of its work, the Office has made a few strange decisions, even some blunders, but on the whole it succeeded in establishing a respectful relationship with comparable French and other European organizations and has even become a world leader in its field. In a way, one may say that the international success of the Office has made the fight for linguistic supremacy obsolete. The creation of the Office de la langue française has institutionalized, and thus brought under control, long-standing linguistic controversies.

These transformations of the domestic political context made writers more aware of the international literary scene. They encountered some success abroad and even south of the border. Books and plays have been translated and sold or staged everywhere with success. However, as language is the main tool of playwrights and writers, French readers and audiences are still the main target of export. In the 1970s, Michel Tremblay's plays were staged in *joual* with no particular difficulty—indeed with great success—all over Europe, whereas, in 1986, Marie Laberge's *L'Homme gris* was translated "from the *joual*" before being staged for a Parisian audience.

The days of *joual* are now largely gone. In every play published by the Montreal-based publishing house Les Herbes Rouges, an editor's note now says that language has been "normalized" according to the conventions of written language to ensure the "readability" of the play. That is not to say that language has lost its appeal as the topic of drama. On the contrary, two centuries of tradition have left an indelible mark. As in Hélène Pednault's *La Déposition* (1989) or Michel Garneau's *Les Guerriers* (1989), the language issues have gone beyond the opposition of literary form to theatrical speech.

Pednault is a well-known Quebec feminist and her play belongs to a new feminist trend of literary works attempting to establish a new gender-based social contract. Produced and published in 1989, it stages a confrontation between a male and a female character through the use of language. Both have to give an interpretation of a particular event, the death of the woman's mother. At the beginning of the play, the female character makes an extensive use of language to narrate and explain the event. She admits to murder and is ready to bear all consequences. The male character refuses to believe her story and, after having let her speak, he takes over and has her renounce her particular interpretation of the event. He then suggests that this death may be the consequence not of murder, but of euthanasia, which is not, at least morally, the same thing. The fact that the man is the police inspector in charge of the case is, of course, very relevant, for this inscribes an institutional power into the relationship. Although this play depicts the traditional hegemony of the male, it does so for an unusual purpose, i.e., in order to arrive at the truth, to force out the true expression of the female self. The structure of speech in the play is very effective in carrying out this project. One can hear or read the changes: with time, the woman's speech goes from voluble to sparse and finally to silence, whereas the man's speech moves in quite the opposite way.[18]

The second example is a pacifist play by Michel Garneau. In *Les Guerriers,* Garneau, who is also a well-known poet, writes against all attempts to make war appear ordinary and acceptable. In the play, advertisers search for a slogan for the latest public relations campaign of the Canadian army. They have to top the successful "There's no life like it!," and, through a derisory selection, they come up with the somewhat unbelievable "We are in the Yellow pages." (It is important to realize that these two slogans were part of actual ad campaigns and were seen, sometimes criticized, by millions of Canadians.) In his play, Garneau make a vibrant plea against the banalization of extraordinary events through language and cultural products, here, the idea that war is an employer just like any other, and more generally against linguistic compromise. To help make his point, he opposes literary to ordinary language, has his main character die (after all, war kills) and, in the published version, writes his stage-directions in verse. The result is quite arresting.

I have chosen these two examples to illustrate my point that Quebec politics are not limited to nationalism and that they embrace other more universally shared preoccupations. In the same manner, the language of Quebec's theater cannot be centered simply on the question of *joual,* however important this question has been. Other language issues (issues of power or gender, for example) previously in the background have begun to surface recently.

There can be no closure, nor definitive conclusion, to this historical reading of the role and status of language in Quebec drama and theater. However, there are two final points that should be emphasized. First, drama is language in a social and political setting: it portrays characters speaking, whether to other characters or an audience is of a secondary importance here. The very simple act of speaking was theorized as a "speech act." Drama bears the same characteristics and functions as this theoretical concept. Speaking, on a Quebec theatrical stage, was an interlocutory act: it did play (and still plays) an important role in the public recognition of the French language, and of the particular form of the French language spoken in Quebec. It is no accident that we find the most acute difficulties in theatrical language occurring at the very moments when Quebec politics were in crisis: that is, toward the beginning of the nineteenth century, around the time of the Confederation debates, and during the Quiet Revolution of the 1960s.

The second point is that drama is defined as language in action. Contrary to the novel, in which the story is told directly through narration, drama must communicate indirectly via dialogue. Therefore, to find speech to be precisely the object of the subject's quest is not surprising. Form reflects content, and most plays can be read in part as metaphors of the playwright's struggle with his own language. Quebec drama is no exception, although this individual struggle has so far been largely taken over by a political one. For most of Quebec's history, nationalism channeled the language issue. As of the 1970s, however, other political issues have tended to inform the use of linguistic devices. Some dramatists, such as Michel Garneau, have exploited this trend by creating, for the published version of his play *Les Guerriers,* a conflicting relation between dialogue and didascalies. There is no reason to believe that the language issue will disappear from the Quebec stage, but new forms and new subjects are to be expected. Among those new subjects, some, like the commodification of language and multiculturalism, have already been put forward. Others are still to come.

Notes

1. On "theatricality," a concept created by Roland Barthes, see in particular Josette Féral, "La Théâtralite," *Poétique* 75 (September 1988): 347-61. I have discussed more extensively the limits of the concept of theatricality in Lucie Robert, "Le Statut littéraire de la dramaturgie," in *La Littérarité*, edited by Louise Milot and Fernand Roy (Sainte-Foy: Presses de l'Université Laval, 1991) and "Toward a History of Quebec Drama," *Poetics Today* 12(4) (winter 1991): 747-67.
2. On didascaly, I share Jeannette Laillou Savona's point of view. See her "Didascalies as Speech Act," *Modern Drama* 25(1) (March 1982): 25-35 (translated from the French by Fiona Strachan) and "Narration et actes de parole dans le texte dramatique," *Études littéraires* 13(3) (December 1980): 471-93.

3. See Savona, "Didascalies as Speech Act."
4. See Annie Brisset, *Sociocritique de la traduction: Théâtre et altérité au Québec* (Montréal: Éditions Balzac-Le Préambule, coll. "L'Univers des discours," 1990) and Lucie Robert, "The New Québec Theatre," in *Canadian Canons: Essays in Literary Value*, edited by Robert Leeker (Toronto: University of Toronto Press, 1991).
5. And this is one century before the linguistic unity of France was completed. See on this subject Philippe Barbaud, *Le Choc des patois en Nouvelle-France: Un Essai sur la francisation du Canada* (Sillery: Presses de l'Université du Québec, 1984) and Renée Balibar, *L'Institution du français: Essai sur le colinguisme des Carolingiens à la République* (Paris: Presses Universitaires de France, 1985).
6. For a start, see Danièle Noël, *Les Questions de langue au Québec, 1759–1850: Étude revue pour le Conseil de la langue française* (Quebec: Éditeur Officiel, 1990).
7. I am using this concept as developed in Jürgen Habermas, *Strukturwandel der Öffentlichkeit: Untersuchungen zu einer Kategorie der bürgerlichen Gesellschaft* (Neuwied: Hermann Luchterhand Verlag, 1962). Translated. into French from German by Marc B. de Launay, *L'Espace public: Archéologie de la publicité comme dimension constitutive de la société bourgeoise* (Paris: Payot, 1986). About the development of this public sphere in Quebec's history, see Maurice Lemire, ed., *La Vie littéraire au Québec 1763–1805,* vol. 1. (Québec: Presses de l'Université Laval, 1991).
8. See Doucette's entry on Joseph Quesnel in the *Oxford Companion to Canadian Theatre*, gen. ed. Wiliam Toye (Toronto: Oxford University Press, 1983), 451.
9. Further analysis of these plays will be included in Maurice Lemire, ed., *La Vie littéraire au Québec, 1840-1869,* vol. 3. (Québec: Presses de l'Université Laval, 1995).
10. On dialogues in the novel see Gillian Lane-Mercier, "Pour Un Statut sémiotique du dialogue romanesque," *Versus* 54 (September–December 1989): 3–20 and "Pour Une Analyse du dialogue romanesque," *Poétique* 81 (February 1990): 43–62.
11. On this subject, see Javier Garcia Méndez, *La Dimension hylique du roman* (Montréal: Le Préambule, 1990) and Marie-Andrée Beaudet, *Langue et littérature au Québec 1895–1914: L'Impact de la situation linguistique sur la formation du champ littérairé Essai* (Montréal: L'Hexagone, 1991).
12. On this and the place of burlesque tradition in Quebec theater history, see Chantal Hébert, *Le Burlesque au Québec: Un divertissement populaire* (Montréal: Hurtubise HMH, 1981).
13. CÉGEP stands for "Collège d'enseignement général et professionnel." Created in 1968, CÉGEPs took over the last years of the classical

college's program. It is somewhat close to the American community colleges. However, CÉGEP offers, after high school, a two-year general program for those who intend to go to the university or a three-year terminal professional course. On the place of language and literary teaching in these colleges, see Joseph Melançon, Clément Moisan, and Max Roy, eds. *La Littérature au Cégep (1968–1978): Le Statut de la littérature dans l'enseignement collégial* (Québec: Nuit Blanche Éditeur, 1993).

14. Saussure's hypothesis was that some dialects such as Portugese and Dutch have become languages of their own because they had a literature. Ferdinand de Saussure, *Cours de linguistique générale*. New edition with an introduction by Tullio de Mauro (Paris: Payot, [1916] 1982), 278. See also Annie Brisset, *Sociocritique de la traduction: Théâtre et altérité au Québec* (Montréal: Éditions Balzac-Le Préambule, coll. "L'Univers des discours," 1990).

15. On the relation between description and sociolect, see Mendéz, *La Dimension hylique du roman.*

16. The expression is taken from Guy Bouthillier and Jean Meynaud, eds., *Le Choc des langues au Québec, 1760–1970* (Montréal: Les Presses de l'Université du Québec, 1972) and has also been used in Barbaud, *Le Choc des patois en Nouvelle-France.*

17. See for example Marco Micone, *Gens du silence* (Montréal: Québec/Amérique, 1982). and Vittorio Rossi, *Scarpone* (Montréal: Nu-Age Editions, 1990).

18. On contemporary Quebec feminist drama, see Lucie Robert, "Changing the Subject: A Readin of Contemporary Feminist Drama," in *Women on the Canadian Stage: The Legacy of Hrotsvit,* edited by Rita Much (Winnipeg: Blizzard Publishing, 1992).

Quebec Theater in the Postmodern Period: A Theatrical Institution in the Shadow of the Mass Media[1]

Gilbert David

> Dans l'organisation de la société, aucune oeuvre d'art ne peut se soustraire à son appartenance à la culture, mais il n'en est aucune, si elle est plus qu'un produit industriel, qui n'oppose à la culture un geste de refus: cette démarche par laquelle elle est devenue oeuvre d'art.
>
> T. W. Adorno (1951)[2]

> Lieux privilégiés de la culture et de la civilisation, le cabaret, l'église et le théâtre jouent un rôle de moins en moins important dans la société québécoise par la raison que ces lieux furent traditionnellement des lieux étrangers, des zones d'influence au service du catholicisme romain, dans le cas de l'église; de la culture française et universelle, dans le cas du théâtre; de l'*american way of life* dans le cas du cabaret. Tant et aussi longtemps que le théâtre n'aura pas trouvé sa polarisation et sa motivation créatrice en lui-même, tant et aussi longtemps qu'il n'aura pas assumé sa condition québécoise avec ses hauts, ses bas et ses incohérences, tant et aussi longtemps qu'il ne sera pas le reflet de ce qui s'écrit *ici* et *maintenant,* le théâtre restera un phénomène artistique marginal dont l'importance ira en décroissant.
>
> Jean-Claude Germain (1970)[3]

Since the 1930s, the number of theatrical companies in Quebec has increased dramatically, engendering a proliferation of theatrical activities of considerable socio-esthetic diversification. At the same time the theater truly established itself as an institution.[4] This essay will attempt to describe the principal components of that institution, and

131

to put these in perspective with respect to both the underlying socio-cultural situation and the internal tensions that clarify its relatively autonomous dynamic.

From a strictly quantitative point of view, a good idea of the size and speed of this change can be had by underlining the fact that there were hardly more than two or three stable theaters concurrently producing plays in Montreal between 1930 and 1945—a few more if the Francophone *burlequer*[5] troupes are included. Since the beginning of the 1980s, however, more than a hundred professional companies were on the roster, in all categories—large, medium, and small, and of every type—children's and youth repertories, creation theaters, multidisciplinary or experimental theater, puppets, etc.—throughout Quebec, and even more if we add the commercial theaters that play mostly during the summer in the various holiday resorts. This growth is all the more remarkable as 60 percent of Quebec's population of three million was already urbanized in the 1930s; the Montreal region alone accounted for a million individuals. In the 1960s, the number of regularly active Montreal theaters was less than a dozen, but during the 1970s and the following decade, the number of theatrical organizations and the volume of productions increased dramatically—in part as a result of the demographic growth of the postwar baby boom.[6]

This all-out growth, today held in check by a serious recession, appears to be inseparable from the cultural and social changes that have affected Quebec, especially since the Great Depression of the 1930s. Following close on the heels of the general improvement in the standard of living in the 1950s, and of the democratization of education in the 1960s, the theater after 1945 became little by little an important factor in the culture of Quebec. Since 1980, however, the economic situation of non-commercial theaters[7] on the whole has become alarming. There are accordingly a certain number of problems concerning the allocation of government subsidies (stagnant if not diminishing), in a context in which the theater finds itself obliged to establish priorities, without which almost all theaters risk suffocation in the short term. There are great risks of a decline in the quality of theatrical productions in the absence of serious consideration of resolving the contradictory objectives within an artistic milieu which is encountering serious obstacles in this difficult politico-economic period.

Current Obstacles

From a historical point of view, the structuring of the theater as an institution in Quebec occurred because of the initiatives of theater practitioners, of the state, or a combination of the two, with or without consensus among members of the profession. The first sign that actors expected to gain the respect of producers and that they intended to resolve the basic conditions of employment goes back to the founding of the Union des Artistes in 1937. This is still the only corporate organization with authority to negotiate contracts with the various theater producers. It was radio, with its numerous soap operas, that in the 1930s gave actors their livelihood since they had few opportunities to practice their profession in theaters during the Depression. Things would slowly change, thanks to certain pioneers who would throw themselves body and soul into theatrical activities that bore the stamp of an eclectic pragmatism designed to win over an audience. Before 1955, there was almost no public financial support for the theater; only box-office receipts determined the future of a company. Gradually, and especially beginning in the 1960s, public authorities at the municipal, provincial, and federal levels (Montreal, Quebec, Canada) have followed the lead of other Western market-economy societies in creating organizations (art councils, a ministry of cultural affairs, for example) whose responsibility has been to grant funds to producers of symbolic goods—among them theatrical companies—while obtaining at the very least that such beneficiaries had the legal status of non-profit companies.

The criteria for awards remained flexible (some might say vague), in the absence of a cultural policy seeking a rigorous delineation of the public-interest objectives of Quebec society. One thing is certain: public funds from all sources and dedicated to the arts in Canada have remained well short of the percentages allocated to such activities in the national budgets of developed societies such as France or Germany.[8] Repeated struggles by *québécois* artists to obtain a significant percentage of governmental budgets have essentially encountered outright refusals. Continuing neo-liberal attacks on the welfare state in Quebec and elsewhere in the West have sought to turn the area of cultural practices over to the laws of the marketplace; this line of reasoning has undoubtedly put pressure on politicians whose education generally leaves them insensitive to the role of art in the so-called developed societies.

Artists regularly stand together when it comes to demanding an overall increase of funds—a stance that allows them to play the "victim" of a tight-fisted regime. Otherwise, they often remain divided as to the regulatory role of the state in the complex dynamics of a postmodern[9] society like Quebec. This and the fragility of societal consensus about the priorities of state functions in artistic matters have had the result of removing responsibility from the artists, bureaucrats, decision-makers, and citizens who should agree for the common good on the rules of the game and on adequate levels of support demanded by the living presence of art in a society that considers itself enlightened. Repeatedly shunted from pious vows to vague promises, artists have become eternal *Didis* and *Gogos*. To pass their time, they form committees, call meetings, hold conventions, make recommendations, and in general assembly vote for the same list of recommendations approved in the past. This ritual may have a cathartic effect on those who are engaged in it, but it has in no way concretely changed the status of the theaters. It is difficult to see how this situation will change as long as careful reflection has not brought artists to look beyond the contradictions that sap the strength of the theater. Contrary to what the theatrical milieu of Quebec would have us believe, the very desirable injection of new state funds into the dramatic arts would not by itself resolve the question of the cultural and social goals of public assistance to this sector.

Early Development: An Inventory

To understand the contradictions that currently plague the theater in Quebec, we must take note of competing practices, molded historically by the establishment of various sorts of peer recognition, as well as the presence of various means of defining success that influence the fate of artists and theatrical troupes.[10] Before making this analysis, we should note that the current limited-production situation,[11] which has regrouped all non-profit theatrical groups, is noteworthy for the youth and the mobility of its members. The oldest, Le Théâtre du Rideau Vert, was founded in 1948. Most other companies mounting original works are less than twenty years old. It should be further pointed out that as of 1970, the field was considerably widened by the influx of a number of creation collectives, although there were also remarkable fluctuations in the composition of the field because of the unusually high failure rate of new companies, even those that had managed to survive for ten years.

There are two other factors that weigh heavily on the play of competing creative forces. The art theater (of repertory or creation) hires artists and designers on a contractual basis for the length of the production (on average, no more than twenty to thirty shows).[12] The status of the freelancers in the theater is characterized by low pay and a very unstable level of employability according to the availability of productions. Freelancers are extremely dependent on other sources of income, especially income from the composite sector of television drama, advertising and dubbing, as well as in specialized teaching any of the six schools[13] that train candidates for the various stage-related occupations. Furthermore, the pyramid of subsidy levels of companies seems to have been greatly flattened, considering the nature of their obligations[14] and the fixed costs and administrative expenses that they must assume. We are led to wonder if public aid does not discriminate significantly between the various producers in terms of responsibility and artistic accomplishment, and if assistance has come to be based on accounting principles of profit-and-loss. One production thus becomes as valid as the next, and all theatrical enterprise is then evaluated with reference to a rigid technocratic model that is quite insensitive to organizational individuality, to the originality of the artistic process and to the influence of each of these factors, despite official rhetoric to the contrary. All are then judged according to the lowest common denominator.

As far as artistic practice is concerned, and without attempting to name each of the regularly subsidized companies, we can still get an idea of the overall major trends in theatrical production since 1980.

There are about ten major companies that are at the top of the public subsidy pyramid. These have long been characterized as "institutions," not without some misunderstandings of the implications of such a term. Their respective mandates have remained fairly nebulous, particularly with respect to their programming. It appears these producers, who receive approximately one half of the public funds devoted to the theater, do not share the same artistic standards. Many inconsistent if not mediocre productions blight this sector of theatrical activity; this has not prevented several from obtaining the approval of a middle-class audience. La Compagnie Jean-Duceppe (1973), for example, supported by some 20,000 of the most faithful subscribers, offers season after season of routine programs that frequently present plays from the Anglo-American repertory of dramatic comedy; it occasionally spices up its program with slightly more hard-hitting plays, usually staged and played in a superficial manner but acted by well-known television stars. The formula has paid off, with uneven results.

At the opposite pole from this production-line treatment of theater (which is mixed with a populism priding itself on a sold-out house) is the Théâtre du Nouveau Monde (TNM) (1951) which has always set for itself higher standards consistent with the production of distinguished works from the worldwide theater repertory, including some from the national repertory. Some people criticize this company for no longer creating new plays—something it did regularly before the recent period with which this essay deals. This does not take into account the fact that, for the major companies taken as a whole, creation does not seem to be a priority, to the detriment of an entire generation of authors who have to be content with having their plays staged by companies with modest budgets. Despite its reliance on well-known works, the situation of the TNM has remained precarious because of the resounding failure of several productions that had been put in the hands of mediocre directors. This in a context where an inventive and more masterful theatricality was being exhibited elsewhere. The difficulties of the TNM have naturally resulted in fluctuating audience levels. Nevertheless, the Company continues to play the role of artistic benchmark in the exercise of the different stage-related occupations. For the same reason, it is the object of great expectations, and its partial successes are therefore seldom forgiven.

Between these two poles—the one oriented toward American-style entertainment, the other toward the European tradition of high-art theaters—are other companies that have been at the mercy of weak, sometimes incompetent direction, with no obvious master plan other than the production of their share of plays: this is the case with the Théâtre du Trident (1971) in Quebec, of the Théâtre du Rideau Vert (1948) in Montreal, and of the Théâtre Populaire du Québec (TPQ) (1963), which is based in Montreal although it has the mandate of touring throughout the Province of Quebec. The TPQ, incidentally, has long been the only company to assume the responsibility of taking theater across the province. In recent years, it crossed paths with other large and medium-sized companies that offer diversified programs outside the urban centers. Regional companies, moreover, which remain vulnerable in the absence of a genuine policy of decentralization, look askance at the growing presence of productions out of Montreal that sometimes undermine their efforts at establishing their own dramatic centers worthy of the name.

Three other Montreal companies in this first category manage in various ways to escape from the insufficient resources that we have been discussing. The Théâtre de Quat'Sous (1955), a tiny theater with just 150 seats, has a justly excellent reputation acquired through the production of a bold and eclectic program supported by high standards of production. The Nouvelle Compagnie Théâtrale (1964)—whose principal mandate is to play before secondary-school students—has had more ups than downs because of a careful selection of plays and a brilliant choice of directors to stage them. Finally, the Théâtre d'Aujourd'hui (1968), with its recent acquisition of a well-furnished theater, alone carries the banner of national dramaturgy (creation and repertory). It does so with great conviction if with unequal success. Nevertheless its very existence—however recent—is a recognition of the diversity of the *québécois* dramatic imagination, even if this company is not the only one to offer a stage to local authors. Since 1965, the latter have availed themselves of the services of a support organization, the Centre d'Essai des Auteurs Dramatiques, which offers workshops and public readings. It also works to bring unpublished texts to the attention of national producers, and to promote the national repertory abroad.

Following this group of large companies are the so-called medium-sized companies.[15] Most of the thirty-odd active companies in Quebec (the majority based in Montreal) are at this intermediate level of subsidy, which does not imply that all are subsidized equally. This sector of theatrical activities is the most diversified from the standpoint of aesthetic approaches, yet at the same time the most shaky in its financial stability, if we take into account the great risks that their creators take.

Let us now consider the case of the companies which, despite promising beginnings in the 1970s, have, in a manner of speaking, lost their soul in the 1980s. The foremost in this category is the Théâtre Parminou (1973). It was founded with the goal of looking critically at society, but fell back on facile formulas while practicing a *théâtre de commande,* confusing service to the community with artistic independence. This company was therefore not able to further its original objectives of social activism. It should be pointed out that the politically and socially engaged theater, so active in the 1970s, has not flourished with the increasing complexity of social stakes and the relative weakening of leftist ideologies in the 1980s. Curiously, Brechtian dramaturgy and experimentation seem to have had little noticeable effect on the companies that lay claim to politically committed theatrical practices, whether twenty years ago or more recently.

In another vein, the management of the Place des Arts—a five-theater center in downtown Montreal—has just announced that the tiny Théâtre du Café de la Place (1978) will close for budgetary reasons. This theater embodied the idea of a dramaturgy of *"petites formes,"* a form of austerity in the interest of an intimist encounter between audience and play. The company primarily staged texts of contemporary foreign authors (among them, Beckett, Duras, and Bernhard). In most cases, however, the productions were somewhat bourgeois in approach, with stars and billing *à la parisienne.* More often than not, despite a careful selection of plays, true theater was sacrificed to fashionable celebration.

Upheavals came from elsewhere. Among the medium-sized companies that made their mark in the 1980s, there are two noticeable trends. The first concerns companies led by stage directors who devoted themselves to experimentation: Gilles Maheu with Carbone 14 (1975), Gabriel Arcand and Téo Spychalski at La Veillée (1973), Jean-Pierre Ronfard and Robert Gravel at the Nouveau Théâtre Expérimental (1975), Jean Asselin with Omnibus (1970), Monique Rioux and Daniel Meilleur at the Deux Mondes (1973), and Robert Lepage at the Théâtre Repère (1980). These companies together contributed greatly to the renewal of a language of the stage. For the most part, they continue to spearhead theatrical creativity, but not without constituting a threat to the preeminent place that authors like Michel Tremblay and numerous others had begun to hold as of the early 1970s.

The second trend includes companies that have flirted with new as well as repertory texts. These companies have emphasized staging as an entirely autonomous undertaking: Lorraine Pintal at La Rallonge (1973), René Richard Cyr and Claude Poissant at the Théâtre Petit à Petit (1978), Alice Ronfard and Louise Laprade at l'Espace GO

(1979), Serge Denoncourt at the Opsis (1986), Paula de Vasconcelos with Pigeons International (1986), and Denis Marleau at the Théâtre Ubu (1982). These directors reinvented theatrical codes and forms by impressing their strong personalities on plays they directed with these companies or elsewhere.[16]

Additionally, venues such as La Licorne (1976), the Fred-Barry (1977), the Espace La Veillée (1985), l'Espace GO (1986), the Théâtre La Chapelle (1990) in Montréal, or Le Périscope (1985) in Quebec, appeared to serve as springboards for young companies, without excluding the possibility of having one or more groups in residence at the same time. The formula has had the merit of offering relatively well-equipped stages to emerging stage directors, although their administrations have not escaped the hazards of programming that depended on the subsidizing of projects; in this area, many were called, but few were chosen.

During these years, other medium-sized companies, including those that were established outside Montreal, across the province and, with the exception of the Théâtre Repère, in Quebec City, exhibited a certain disarray when faced with seething creativity emanating from Montreal. The abrasive action of experimental groups and of talented and aggressive directors could not fail to create a certain alienation in the face of the appropriation by one and another of a consistent theatricality, suffused with a new questioning of play and space and the relationships of text to staging.

At the bottom of the ladder of subsidized companies, there are several groups that stand out for their dynamism, which may be tinged with a certain anti-establishment, even anarchist, spirit. Author-directors—the hyphen is important—like Dominic Champagne with the Théâtre Il Va Sans Dire (1984), Jean-Frédéric Messier with Momentum (1988), and Michel Monty with Trans-Théâtre (1991), appear determined to favor less formalistic approaches than do the majority of their elders. Their careers will certainly bear watching in the future.

An Institutional Structure Lacking in Artistic Criteria

The vitality of the theater in the 1980s was unfortunately not accompanied by a State consolidation of the companies that had taken the lead. It may not be surprising that a gloomy mood, tinged with bitterness, now infects the ranks of producers. The relative newness of theatrical practice in Quebec has been detrimental to obtaining necessary funds, without which those dedicated to dramatic creation are poorly remunerated compared to what the powerful television marketplace can offer. From this there arises a prejudicial distortion of the autonomy of the theater and dramatic creation, to the extent that it can be stated that television now practices a kind of economic and ideological control over theater.

The theater as art is thus confronted with a form of short-term public assistance, without clear rules and with no other evaluation procedures than the regular, sometimes evasive, evaluation of peers— who are called to sit on so-called consulting committees or on art councils and who are reluctant to make judgments. The cultural bureaucracy acts with extreme caution, rather than steadfastness, at all three levels of government; in the long run, this course of action constitutes an abdication of responsibility. It is subject to political pressure, to the forces of bureaucratic inertia, and to the blusterings of prominent actors and vociferous directors. This complex situation in which arbitrary struggles against inconsistency results in disoriented theatrical practices and leads toward paralyzing cynicism, imprudent thrift, and ridiculously subjective claims. For the *Québécois* theatrical milieu is, all in all, eminently tribal, the last vestige of a socio-cultural tradition at one and the same time ultra-nationalist, overly sensitive, and conservative, if not frankly anti-intellectual. The least that can be said is that the art of the theater has little chance of progressing under such conditions.

There exist, nevertheless, pockets of resistance to the flattening of values and artistic objectives. The most important strategy, sometimes suspected by disgruntled individuals of renewing the old alienation of the colonized French-Canadian, consists in finding support abroad for artistic processes that would have little chance of surviving locally because the creators can count only on a relatively limited adventurous segment of the public. Since 1980, a dozen or so *québécois* companies have thus regularly taken to touring outside the country, accepting the more or less prestigious invitations they received when their operating subsidies were insufficient. They have improved their lot somewhat by finding supplemental assistance through various governmental programs dedicated to the diffusion of Quebec culture and, of course, thanks to box office revenues thus generated. Concurrent with the arrival of foreign tour groups, the establishment of three biennial international theater festivals (one in Quebec in 1984; two in Montreal: one in 1985, and one, dedicated to youth theater, in 1990)[17] contributed to combining a knowledgeable public of professionals, critics, and spectators, and unusual, if not provocative works.

From this point of view, the 1980s may have jostled a number of certainties in the domain of theater. In the 1970s, if a man of the theater like Jean-Claude Germain had been able to sum up in a quip ("Nous faisons le meilleur théâtre québécois au monde") the general feeling of self-satisfaction with respect to the liberating careers of artisans amidst the abundance of dramatic creation and experimentation in the theater, we must recognize that during the following decade, this nationalistic fervor gave place to more individualized approaches centered on the mastery of staging and scenography. It would be an exaggeration to conclude that dramatic writing had been devalued, although directors were more and more ready and willing to take center stage.

There is no doubt that dramaturgy, despite the appearance of talented authors—René-Daniel Dubois, Normand Chaurette, Michel Marc Bouchard, to mention the three most important—has experienced difficulty in imposing its tempo on the current situation in the theater, which is dominated by directors able to highlight new dimensions of contemporary reality.

Some directors have acquired important positions as artistic directors of major theaters. It follows that the nascent stardom of these directors has engendered a probably irreversible dynamic, according to which the "Text," formerly central, has had to give way to staging insofar as the latter harbors new visual and performance potential. There is also a recognizable, typically modernistic tendency that favors a more or less radical formalism through an arrangement of concepts, images, and figures. This arrangement is often detached from the discursive thrust of dramatic writing. Theater practice has been marked for the past fifteen-odd years by a voluntarist appropriation of modern codes of theatricality, along the path opened by Appia and Craig, rather than on the route taken by Brecht.

It would be fitting to refine this statement by pointing out that theatrical creation has experienced a number of disturbances, both in dramatic and in scenic writing. If we were forced to choose a reference figure to delineate the galaxy of productions that have given an innovating boost to the theatrical activity of the 1980s, we might suggest the figure of two-faced Janus: Pirandello (for the deconstruction of the bourgeois drama) and Artaud (for his inclusion of the ecstatic body and of the unconscious in the theatrical imagination).[18] These two faces, in varying proportion, have projected their anxious vision onto a number of dramatic texts and productions which, against a background of disintegrating traditional values and a fascination with the devices and myths of mass culture, have participated in what must be called, for lack of a better term, the postmodern condition.

What more can be said? Nearing the end of this century, the *québécois* theater is faced with a dilemma: caught between an octopus-like bureaucratic apparatus and the comfortable seduction of the mass media, the art of the theater seems to have no real choice. The same conditions may prevail elsewhere in the West but nowhere perhaps so heavily as in Francophone Quebec, itself a minority on the North-American continent. By trying to compete with the products of the *Kulturindustrie,* the theater risks losing what makes it a true *espace de résistance* to dehumanization and the siren calls of consumerism. The pressing task of stage creators is to defend the time of the theater, the time regained for craftsman-like preparation and for the necessary stages of reflection, which never need give way to expedient solutions and to the demands of productivity. In Quebec, the theatrical milieu must, now more than ever, identify a practicable path between the technocratic discourse of the State (with its penchant for claiming that everything is of equal value) and the necessities of art, or risk discouraging its vital forces and then collapsing.

In the quotation that begins this article, Jean-Claude Germain is completely unaware of the existence of television, as if the *québécois* theater had until then escaped its clutches, and that it had had as its only rivals, in the inner recesses of our national history, the offshoots of the church and the cabaret (not to mention the French theatrical model, the rejection of which corresponded to a need for emancipation, nourished by our love-hatred relationship with the Hexagon). In fact, television appears today, in all its imposing domination of public space, like the new church of postmodern times, and it offers itself, by subjecting all reality to the norms of the *société du spectacle* (Guy Debord), like an immense but soulless cabaret. To remain vibrant and alive, at least in Quebec, the theater has no other choice than to fight, with its own means, both this church and this cabaret.

Notes

1. Translated by Leonard Rahilly, Michigan State University. Our thanks as well to Colette Tougas for her help in reading proofs of this article.
2. Theodor Adorno, *Minima Moralia, Réflexions sur la vie mutilée* (translation from the German by Eliane Kaufholz and Jean-René Ladmiral [Paris: Payot, 1991], 199).
3. "C'est pas Mozart, c'est le Shakespeare québécois qu'on assassine," a text that appeared first in *L'Illettré* in 1970 and later in the *Cahiers de théâtre JEU*, no. 7 (Montréal: Editions Quinze, 1978), 13–14.
4. It is impossible within the confines of this text to analyze the preceding period (1880-1930), which we are tempted without further discussion to call pre-institutional, even if we see at that time the emergence of professional theater in French. Indeed, it is not enough that there be regular theatrical offerings along professional lines (themselves needing definition) for it to appear that there is an institutional structuring (in the modern sense) of this activity. I hope that this text will lead to an understanding that the institutionalization of the theater is inseparable from the struggles toward the greatest possible artistic autonomy of the practitioners concerned, which requires the latter to put in place mechanisms, on the one hand, to ensure the continuity of their activities, and on the other, to keep at bay or destroy the external forces that unfailingly put pressures on their production. At the same time, "actors" are led to specify within themselves the ins and outs of dramatic art from criteria and principles that are the constant topic of debates, and that impose a dynamic quality on the field of theater practice.
5. The burlesque theater, a Montreal variant of an American type of variety show, enjoyed widespread success among the working class and a part of the middle class until the arrival of television at the beginning of the fifties. Between 1930 and 1945 all professional theatrical production in Quebec, in French and in English, took place in Montreal, then considered a Canadian metropolis. Nevertheless, there was at the time in Quebec, Montreal included, an abundance of amateurs groups. In this essay, I will speak only of theatrical activities in French.
6. The Francophone population is currently about 80 percent of the 6.7 million inhabitants of Quebec, half of which lives in greater Montreal and its suburbs.

7. There are no state theaters in Quebec and each of the non-profit theaters is a private company that depends on a board of directors, on which the artistic director normally sits.

8. To give an idea of the assistance given to the theater in Quebec, I quote the following sums from Josette Féral, *La Culture contre l'art* (Sillery, Québec: Presses de l'Université du Québec, 1990). For the fiscal year 1987–88, the Canada Council awarded $4.6 million to theater companies in Quebec, while the provincial government gave them $5 million and the Conseil des Arts de la Communauté urbaine de Montréal contributed a meager $1.2 million, for a grand total of $10.8 million (granted, in round numbers, to about a hundred beneficiaries in all categories). Since that time, with inflation factored in, this level of assistance has hardly risen, and in present-day dollar figures, it would seem, according to reliable sources, that state support overall has diminished, even though the *québécois* government has doubled its aid to the theater from 1989 to 1990 to $10 million.

9. The postmodern paradigm sees itself as an indicator of the profound disturbances that have touched Western societies on the cultural level, Quebec especially, after the appearance of television at the beginning of the 1950s. But postmodernism obviously goes beyond this phenomenon without depriving it of its importance.

10. The institutional structuring of the theatrical sector was done according to the budgetary size of the enterprises, or their target audiences (the young, for example). The reader will find appended a chronological table of the organizations that criss-cross the theatrical activities of the various companies. Among these, the Conseil québécois du théâtre plays the role of super authority which seeks, not altogether successfully, to preserve the solidarity of all theater groups in the face of the cultural policies of the governments. As for definitions of success, room must be given to the ascending curve of distinctions (by critics, by theater audiences called upon to give their preferences, and soon by members of the profession in academia). But we suspect that this does not exhaust the sources of recognition of artistic merit by peers (juries granting subsidies to companies, individual grants) or by the intermediary of selection to international festivals, etc. Referring only to the stormy relations in the last five years between a significant number of subsidized theaters and the critics, whose association has existed after a fashion since 1984, it is easy to understand that both groups are sensitive to the unveiling of the artistic and socio-cultural stakes imbedded in contemporary theatrical activity, both in Quebec and abroad. Finally, the impact of private and state-owned television, radio, and large-circulation magazines on the theater cannot be ignored, even though no study has yet been made on the effects of the mass media on both theater and its audiences.

11. To sketch out the tensions in the field of theatrical production in Quebec, I refer to the heuristic hypotheses of the sociologist Pierre Bourdieu (*Réponses*, avec Loïc J. D. Wacquant [Paris: Seuil, 1982]). Needless to say, I do not intend here to go deeply into the subject, nor to apply the method of the French sociologist to the letter, but rather to put forth some ideas to clarify the institutional functioning of a particular national sector of theater production.

12. In fact, the great majority of theatrical productions does not exceed thirty shows in a normal season, and very few attract ten thousand or more spectators. Nevertheless, it is not unusual that shows created by the youth-theater companies, all of which tour, receive more than 100 performances.

13. There are two Conservatoires d'art dramatique, one in Montreal (since 1955), the other in Quebec (since 1958); the Ecole nationale de théâtre du Canada, established in Montreal in 1960, offers two parallel training programs, one in French and one in English; finally, two professional *collèges* have offered, respectively since 1968 and 1969, special training that leads to the workplace. To these five schools, we should add the Francophone programs for the *baccalauréat* and the *maîtrise en art dramatique* that is offered by the Université du Québec à Montréal.

14. A company like the Théâtre du Nouveau Monde (1951), for example, has five productions per season in Montreal, for which it pays all plant costs. For the 1992-93 season, the TNM received from public sources $1.55 million (which covers half of its operating costs), which in absolute figures makes it the most subsidized theatrical company in Quebec. These figures alone are deceptive because they do not take into account the nature of the technical and esthetic requirements that this company faces in its productions, which are mostly dedicated to the classical repertory.

15. In this group must be included several companies from the childhood-youth sector, among which are several troupes of puppeteers. I will confine my remarks to the medium-sized companies whose activities are primarily limited to what is commonly called the *grand public,* which does not always exclude the young.

16. A number of these directors, from various backgrounds, have been invited to work in the major companies and even to direct them, as was the case with Brigitte Haentjens, who had come from a medium-sized company in French-speaking Ontario. In comparison, other important directors, such as André Brassard, Olivier Reichenbach, Guillermo de Andrea, Daniel Roussel, Michèle Magny, and Yves Desgagnés, have practiced their art almost exclusively with established theaters. Even if we cannot outline here the evolution of production in the 1980s, it would be unjust to exclude the significant contributions

of other directors in the redefinition of the theatrical language; we should mention here at least the names of Alexandre Hausvater, Jacques Lessard, Michel Nadeau, Martine Beaulne, and Gregory Hlady, knowing that this list is all too limited.

17. This is the Carrefour international de théâtre de Québec (1992), which took over from the now-defunct Quinzaine internationale de théâtre de Québec (1984); the Festival de théâtre des Amériques (1985) and the Rendez-vous international de théâtre jeune public (1990) in Montreal.

18. It is a matter of pointing out a connection and, above all, a recognizable intertextuality ("intertheatricality"), but not of claiming direct or unmediated influences. This being said, in Artaud's case, it would be rather easy to discover the impact of his writings on *avant-garde* theater practices in Quebec as early as the 1940s.

Appendix

The Development of Institutionalized Francophone Theater in Quebec

FORMATION	PRODUCTION	LEGITIMATION		
		ENDOGENOUS	EXOGENOUS	
		Organizations	Diffusion	Recognition
1930–1965				
	Semi-Professional Theaters (e.g., Les Compagnons de St-Laurent, 1937-52)	Union des Artistes (1937)		
	Private Theaters (e.g., revuiste G. Gélinas, 1938-46)			
	Private Subsidized Theaters (not for profit) (e.g., Rideau Vert, 1948 TNM, 1951)		CBFT (1951)	
Conservatoire d'Art dramatique (Montréal, 1955; Québec, 1958)			Festival de Montréal (1954–64)	
				CAM (1955)
	Beginning of Summer Theater (1957)			CAC (1957)
		Association canadienne du théâtre d'amateurs (1958–72)		

FORMATION	PRODUCTION	LEGITIMATION		
		ENDOGENOUS	EXOGENOUS	
		Organizations	Diffusion	Recognition
1930–1965				
	Comédie-Canadienne (1958–71)			
École nationale de théâtre (1960)				
				MAC (1961)
Théâtre Populaire de Québec (1963)				
	Association des directeurs de théâtre (1964–84)			
	Nouvelle Compagnie Théâtre (1964)			
1965–1992				
		CEAD (1965)		
	Creation Collectives (1964–80)		Festival-carrefour/Jeune Théâtre (1967–85)	
Option théâtre Lionel Goulx (1968)			Radio-Québec (1968)	
Option théâtre de St-Hyacinthe (1969)				
UQAM (bac. en théâtre, 1969)				
	AQJT (1972–86)			Jeune Théâtre (1972–79)
			Festival international de théâtre jeune public du Québec (AQJT, 1974–85)	
				SQET (SHTQ) (1976) Cahiers de théâtre Jeu (1976)

FORMATION	PRODUCTION	LEGITIMATION		
		ENDOGENOUS	EXOGENOUS	
		Organizations	Diffusion	Recognition
1965–1992				
		UNEQ (1977)		Pratiques théâtrales (1977–84)
	100 Active Theater Companies (around 1980 and after)			
		AQM (1981)		
		CQT (1983)		
		APASQ (1984)	MAQTEJ (1984)	
			Quinzaine international de théâtre de Québec (1984–91)	
		AQCT (1984)		
		TAI (1985)	Prix de la critique (1985)	
		TUEJ (1985)	Festival de théâtre des Amériques (1985)	L'Annuaire théâtral (1985)
		APTP(1968)		
		AQTA (1986)		
Conseil supérieur de la formation en art dramatique (1989)		ACT (1989)		Veilleurs de nuit (1989–92)
ACT (1989)				
			Rendez-vous international de théâtre jeune public (1990)	
			Les Vingt Jours du théâtre à risque (1990)	
		AQAD (1991)		
			Carrefour international de théâtre de Québec 1992)	
		Académie que´- bécoise du théâtre (1993)		CALQ (1993)

Abbreviations

ACT	Association des compagnies de théâtre
APASQ	Association des professionnels des arts de la scène du Québec
APTP	Association des producteurs de théâtre professionel
AQAD	Association québécoise des auteurs dramatiques
AQCT	Association québécoise des critiques de théâtre
AQJT	Association québécoise du jeune théâtre
AQM	Association québécoise des marionnettistes
AQTA	Association québécoise du théâtre amateur
CAC	Conseil des arts du Canada
CALQ	Conseil des arts et des lettres du Québec
CAM/CACUM	Conseil des arts de Montréal, puis Conseil des arts de la Communauté urbaine de Montréal (1980)
CBFT	Société Radio-Canada (chaîne télévisée d'État, canal francophone)
CEAD	Centre des auteurs dramatiques
CQT	Conseil québécois du théâtre
MAC	Ministère des Affaires culturelles du Québec (devenu ministère de la Culture en 1993)
MAQTEJ	Maison québécoise du théâtre pour l'enfance et la jeunesse
SQET	Société québécoise d'études théâtrales (fondée sous le nom de Société d'histoire du théâtre au Québec)
TAI	Théâtres Associés inc.
TUEJ	Théâtres unis enfance jeunesse inc.
UNEQ	Union des écrivains québécois

Experimental Theater in Quebec: Some Descriptive Terms[1]

Gilles Girard

❖ ❖ ❖ ❖ ❖ ❖ ❖ ❖ ❖ ❖ ❖ ❖ ❖ ❖ ❖ ❖ ❖ ❖ ❖

Of 134 theaters in Quebec forty-six give "experimental theater[2]" as their principal (or one of their principal) areas of endeavor. This observation illustrates why this theatrical movement can no longer be considered marginal. Admittedly, if one looks more closely at these numbers, several of the theaters profess this orientation a bit too readily while other companies, not so designated currently (Théâtre Ubu, Groupe de la Veillée), deserve consideration as experimental theaters. It remains that this tendency toward theatrical experimentation is quite significant by reason of the quality of its questioning and its attempts to explore and innovate. By refusing to subjugate its activity to an aesthetic of realism, by breaking with the so-called "traditional" theater's mimetic preoccupations, the experimental theater gives itself free rein to explore its resources and adjust its focus on theatricality.

Experimental theater takes itself as its object of investigation and subjects each of its component parts to experimentation, but with a critical eye that strives to be both liberating and innovative. Here, we shall briefly examine and illustrate a few of the descriptive terms which, when combined, present a (partial[3]) portrait of this kind of theater: fable, spatial-temporal settings, status of the character, thematics, use of signs, theater of image, theatrical objects, and role of the spectator.

Fable, Time, Space

The traditional fable selects and structures episodes of action according to a temporal order (story) or a logical order (plot). The sequence of events begins with an exposition (the initial inventory of informative data), passes through certain obstacles that thwart the proposed projects and is resolved with a denouement. The experimental theater overturns this organization of the fictional narrative and, replacing its linear development based on a logical or chronological order, freely juxtaposes fragments of fiction by association, producing images that progress at times according to the velleity of the imaginary. In Jean-Pierre Ronfard's *Le Titanic*[4] a stunning choreography unfurls, flinging together, pell-mell, a bizarre list of guests, present or alluded to: among others, Isadora Duncan, Sarah Bernhardt, Adolf Hitler, Charlie Chaplin, Greta Garbo, Mother Teresa, Al Capone . . . and all the passenger-spectators dining at table on the bridge. However, the organic coherence of the action or the consistency of the characters is of little importance here, since it is the configuration of the signs that reveals the mythic meaning. The image of the Titanic is intended to be a metonymic reduction of our Civilization of Progress, humanity's great dream henceforth made concrete thanks to the limitless ability of science and technology to overwhelm nature. In the belly of this unsinkable phantom vessel, a twentieth-century Noah's Ark, "image et support" for our hallucinations, seemingly as "Eternal as God the Father Himself and the British Empire," there ferments an abundance of themes subject to a Grotowskian dialectic of fascination/transgression, apology/irony: voyages toward hope and the desire for love, glory, beauty, power; caprices of blind destiny; or the inevitability of death. The linear story is fragmented here into a series of pointed segments, which the active spectator associates, reconstructing creatively the contours of the piece of fiction that he makes his own. The disarticulated epic made up of brief *tableaux* reminds us that the apocalyptic night of 14 April 1912 is renewed at each individual's death, all destinies are aborted, and our ribs also "appelle l'iceberg qui forge son couteau dans les cavernes glacées du Nord."[5]

The breaking down of the walls between spatial and temporal data allows for a dialog among "great minds" and the institution of immediate and original dialectical relationships between characters from

Le Titanic, 1985. Photograph by Ives Dubé.

any time or any place. The denunciation of the presumptive logic of a diachronic organization of history allows for the short-circuiting of the apparently imperative relation between causes and effects. The abolition of time and geographic divisions provides a transverse and synchronic view of a cultural space. This space is reactualized in the moment of a fiction in which everything can collapse on itself and constitute a radical and subversive way of rethinking myths here and now. This process carries us above and beyond the historical catastrophe to the uncertain frontiers of this modern myth of the "Titan," a place teeming with outsized dreams.

No longer predetermined and framed as in a "classical" play, the spatial-temporal settings explode and play supplely with space, which has been compressed or dilated in all directions, or with time, which is condensed or enlarged (the fifteen-hour staging of Ronfard's *Vie et Mort du Roi Boiteux*), time that accelerates, bogs down, vanishes in an ellipse, or simply ceases.

153

The Status of the Character, Thematics

A unit of significance bearing a name, a character is composed of a unified set of differential features that constitute him in the fictional paradigm; he possesses a participatory role which constitutes him in the fictional syntagma. In naturalist theater the actor who assumes a role bases his portrayal on a minute reconstruction of these distinctive features. The experimental theater can depsychologize and desocialize the character, eliminate the psychic and socio-political data in order to convey instead metaphysical questions, dreams, symbols, or incursions into the unconscious archetypes and myths. The anarchic theater of Ronfard scours away symbols engraved in our collective unconscious and myths, both ancient (*The Thousand and One Nights*) and modern (Mao Tse Tung. . . , Marilyn).

Liberated from its mimetic function, theater can realize itself as an object of experimentation, put itself on stage, thematize itself, even do its own autopsy, thereby leading to theater in the theater, and theater on the theater and the other arts. Authors, actors, and spectators see themselves as integrated into the fiction in this specular and self-referential theater. Along the lines of Usevolod Meyerhold, the stage becomes conscious of itself and its conventions, contemplates itself, and delivers up its secrets. Its traditional foundation is challenged; sacrosanct illusion is denounced while the theater divides itself into fiction and discourse upon the fiction which it reveals, not in a Brechtian perspective of distanced social criticism but to purely esthetic or philosophical ends ("All the world's a stage"). In this way the theater shows itself to be theater by showing its very interworkings, by producing a metatheatrical discourse. Ronfard's *Don Quixote* blandishes its fiction and reveals the artifice of its own creation. The charm of illusion is replaced by the pleasure of witnessing the construction/deconstruction of conventions: theater in the theater, *commedia dell'arte*, puppet shows, the set constructed like a "large blank page," some costumes anachronistic and others of the period; Rossinante is replaced by a 1900s bicycle, and a "big wheel" tricycle serves as Sancho's donkey. These signs of spectacle, in place of signs of fiction, unmask conventions and locate the spectator's pleasure in the "ludere" (playing) rather that in the "illudere" (deceiving). Far from erasing all visible traces of the production out of a concern for realism and illusion—they are in fact made obvious—the esthetic and

154

ideological conventions or presuppositions are knowingly caricatured. This process, whereby the theater places itself or another art on stage, is favored by experimental theater but is not exclusive to it; the device is in fact often used in more conventional types of *québécois* theater, such as Michel Tremblay's *Le Vrai Monde?*, Jean Barbeau's *Théâtre de la maintenance,* and Michel Marc Bouchard's *Les Feluettes ou la répétition d'un drame romantique.*

The Use of Signs

This metatheatrical discourse, through which convention is accepted and displayed and where the play of the imaginary is presented as such, is also manifested in the presentation of signs that do not come on stage as finished products but can display themselves as they are being created. It is before our astonished eyes that the protagonist of Robert Lepage's[6] *Vinci,* using shaving cream, transforms his head, that of a young photographer, into the head of Leonardo da Vinci. Having been taken into the confidence of the *metteur en scène* and being a witness to the construction of the sign, the spectator feels a complicity with the creative process and adds his participation to that of the players.

The principle of the mobility of the theatrical sign[7] that allows, for example, lighting to replace stage sets, or gestures to replace speech or a prop, is used even more systematically. In this principle of the interchangeability of means of expression lies all the inventive genius of a Robert Lepage, who is a magician of this reciprocal substitution of the languages of the stage. A blind tour guide on the Piazza del Duomo in Florence in *Vinci,* the character's own body becomes sacred and stands as the analogical substitute for the cathedral. This metonymic equivalent of the flesh and the spirit excellently replaces, by its eloquent economy of means, any pretentious scenographic effort to faithfully reproduce the holy place.

The "polyphonie informationelle" or "épaisseur de signes" referred to by Roland Barthes[8] in defining the theater at the level of performance no longer presents itself in the usual way, with the text monopolizing meaning and constituting the inevitable point of convergence of the other signs. Henceforth, the hierarchy of signs possesses a variable geometry, with each play determining the order of priority of

Vinci, 1986. Photograph by Robert Laliberté.

each of the systems of signs in the whole of the play as within each of its parts. *Le Dortoir* by Carbone 14 plunges into a phantasmagorical universe using dance. Bernard Bonnier's sound background structures *L'Anti-Monde de Ionesco* directed by Jacques Lessard of the Théâtre Repère.

The inventory of signs used greatly transcends the traditional stock of theatrical signs and it becomes necessary to borrow from the other arts and from the world of computers. Being multidisciplinary the theater integrates the resources of dance, painting, sculpture, and literature, in addition to audio-visual techniques, the synthesizer, cinema, and television projections. This new alchemy of signs provides a hybrid translation of the oneiric world in *Le Dortoir* by Carbone 14, fusing dance, theater, music, and poetry. There is an astonishing compression of genres in *En attendant* staged by the Théâtre Repère in which the very refined Japanese drawing, *sumi-e*, western music, and the sign language of the hearing-impaired are brought together. The direction by Michel Nadeau of *Le Bord extrême* is founded on Ingmar Bergman's *Det Sjunde Inseglet* and integrates the resources of cinema, photography and holography.

This kaleidoscopic theater freed from the constraints of text and fable strives to subsume the referential universe to a visual translation of its images: the videographic images of Carbone 14 in a disquieting *Marat-Sade,* images of the unconscious in the oneiric *tableaux* of *Rail,* or an eerie W*ork in Progress* directed by Gilles Maheu. The theater leaves behind the familiar ground of the cerebral and the precise meaning of signs for the adventure of free associations, the patches of darkness in the past, the underground corridors of the dream, and the phantasmagoric landscapes. Better than the delimiting territory of words, the imprecise and fleeting contours of the image can do justice to these nebulous and murky universes. One can imagine the innovations to come in the theater with the use of the techniques of virtual reality, not to mention the transformation/deformation of images using computer software, developed by Soft Image of Montreal, which has been used in video (*Steam* by Peter Gabriel) and in cinematographic language (*Jurassic Park* by Steven Spielberg).

Having lost its hegemonic status in the configuration of signs, text is treated like a malleable material that one can modify more or less freely: adaptations, cuts, additions, permutations of segments, as well as dialogues that metamorphose into narration. The text remains

Hamlet-Machine, 1987. Photograph by Yves Dubé.

open to change and becomes a *work in progress,* each major stage of which is offered to the public as a tentative step in the long labor of elaborating signs. Lepage's *La Trilogie des dragons* offers three levels of his dramaturgical and theatrical writing in versions lasting ninety minutes, three and six hours, and in productions that change with each performance. Lepage intervenes sometimes just an hour before a performance to suggest an important change, thereby adding to its verve. The play refuses to yield to definitive closure and therefore presents the dynamism of a living organism.

The technique of collage also operates by bringing together, in an arbitrary fashion, disparate elements that clash upon their unexpected juxtaposition. Disputing the supposed logical organization of the world, the text and the performance juxtapose elements with no logical connection: Denis Marleau, Friedhelm Lach and the Théâtre Ubu—whose name itself is quite evocative—offers the collage-theater *Merz Opera* based on the work by Kurt Schwitters. In the prologue, a quartet of speakers enumerates simultaneously in several languages, a series of numbers, and later do a musical interlude based on as fanciful series of letters whose content is voided: "Ziiuu ennze ziiuu nnnnkrrmüüüü." The subversive letterism violates the law of syntax and the surrealistic crumbling of the letters creates a new linguistic code, counting on the sonorous virtualities of the signifier. The Théâtre Ubu transforms speech into an amazing musical score and exploits with great virtuosity a vast range of vocal possibilities.

This awareness of the musicality of speech and the preoccupation with internationalism of the *québécois* experimental theater leads innovators to integrate various languages into the same play. This is the case in *Hamlet-Machine* directed by Gilles Maheu, which juxtaposes French, English, and German just as Lepage has frequently done: French-English-Italian in *Vinci*, French-English-Chinese in *La Trilogie des dragons*, French-English-Mohawk in *Alanienouidet*.

Work on the signifier does not leave out its connotative potential, and research on forms can be bound with a study of the content. That is the sort of revealing exercise that Jeanne Bovet tackles in her article "The symbolism of speech in *Vinci*" in which she concludes as follows:

> L'analyse des effets produits par la dimension sonore de l'énonciation permet donc de dégager certains réseaux symboliques dans *Vinci*. L'opposition articulation forte-articulation faible concrétise des oppositions conceptuelles telles raison-émotion, vérité universelle-doute intime. L'opposition rythme marqué-arythmie symbolise une opposition entre la superficialité et la profondeur. L'évolution de ces oppositions sonores à travers la pièce va de pair avec la progression de Philippe dans sa recherche de l'absolu. Il y a là une très nette volonté de dégager la parole de sa simple fonction de restitution orale du texte, pour exploiter son potentiel symbolique spécifique et la faire participer, au même titre que les autres langages scéniques, à l'élaboration du sens.[9]

The Theatrical Object

Experimentation can take place at the very genesis of theatrical creation. Unlike the case of traditional theater, the creative procedures of the Théâtre Repère, or of Lepage in particular, do not originate from some concept, feeling, or abstract theme; they are a gaze upon some object and the progressive decoding of its language. The object functions as a trigger whose polysemy takes over gradually. A Leonardo da Vinci sketch in a London museum, used as the premise for *Sainte Anne, la Vierge et l'Enfant*, serves as the initial impulse on the road to the creation of *Vinci*.

Objects are also utilized for their metaphorical value: a simple little electric train illustrates a recurrent theme in the play; "l'arte è un veicolo." The object is retained as a representative sampling of reality; its metonymic qualities allow the participation of the audience, which completes the mental picture based on a few reference points; the silhouette of a driver's cap suffices to convey the image of a guide on a London bus.

The object is also polyvalent, being infinite in its virtualities and allowing multiple readings. It changes functions and metamorphoses before our astonished and delighted eyes: in *Vinci*, the most rigidly and supremely practical object, a tape measure, changes itself successively into a panoply of artistic forms: pyramids, the Great Wall of China, a work by Picasso, a radio, a cinema, a television, etc. At a gesture or at a word, the magic, the "transubstantiation," occurs. Everything is anything. All that is needed is an effort of imagination by the creator and the spectator.

In Lepage's *Plaques tectoniques,* stacks of books of varying heights by a pond—near a couple on a park bench with Gershwin's music playing—metamorphose into skyscrapers evocative of the skyline of New York, recreating the most memorable scene from Woody Allen's *Manhattan*.

The object finds it global meaning in a network of analogies illustrated under different appearances throughout the play. By way of illustration, the image of the wall is at the center of the problematic in *Polygraphe* by the same Lepage. The lie detector is an instrument trying to break through the wall separating lies from truth. This image is found throughout the play: a wall situated between reality and fiction and being questioned by art; a wall between the personal drama that occurred in Quebec (the murder of a young actress) and the historical drama symbolized by the Berlin Wall; an affective wall separating individuals and already laid down in the very structure of the heart which the septum divides in two; and the city of Berlin whose shape evokes the shape of a heart. We see that the image spreads out in all directions and weaves an anaphoric network of calls and references. The same sort of phenomenon occurs in *Plaques tectoniques*. The drifting of the Earth's crust between the Americas and Europe and Africa—whose shapes interlock if brought together, proof of their original union—constitutes the central metaphor of this work: drifting and degeneration at the level of the belly, between fine cuisine *à la* Brillat-Savarin and North American *fast food*; sexual drifting, where one must distinguish between gender and sex, and where a feminine personality is susceptible of being associated with masculinity in this era of hermaphrodism; the drifting of affective tectonic plates as in the case of the girl from Quebec drowning her heartsickness in Venice; and artistic drifting where a canvas showing at first Chopin and George Sand was cut in two and the halves sent to two different continents. The image thus woven in different garbs maintains the organic coherence of the play.

The Spectator

Experimental theater enlarges the mandate of the spectators, who are no longer content to subjugate themselves to the giddiness of illusion, attractiveness of identification and chills of emotion; nor are they content to use their ability to distance themselves or to deny signs. Psychological and ideological circuits continue to link stage and audience, whatever the shape or the nature of their rapport. Signs and the images make demands on all the senses (*Projet pour un bouleversement des sens ou Visions exotiques de Maria Chaplin* by Pierre A. Larocque), however, and work their way into the deepest strata of the unconscious mind. Limited in size, the public is nearer the source of stimuli, the connection is closer, and the relationship more intimate. The spectacle breaks the perceptive automatisms, renews the approach to space, objects and sound; it breaks codes, disorients and destabilizes: the welcoming and the individual attention given to the members of the audience, the seating within the theater according to the constraints of the story, the mobility of the spectator, the modified positions assumed by the spectators (they lie about voluptuously on cushions enjoying the scent of perfumes and snacking on tidbits in Ronfard's *Mille et Une Nuits*; spectators as movie screens in *Le Bord extrême* by the Théâtre du Repère). In the midst of this new configuration of signs, the spectator targets his attention or allows it to wander, makes connections, decodes meaning; he becomes lost when the trail is tangled and the customary channel markers are removed, but his senses are alive and his imagination awakened, his overall activity is increased. To his role of decoder of meaning, the spectator adds the role of maker of meaning. His activity is to discover meaning, construct it or become lost, to vibrate emotionally, to discover new ways of perceiving, to bring all his senses alive, to allow his imagination to be impregnated with images and associate them freely, and to participate in the creative process (Théâtre sans détour in the tradition of the theater of Augusto Boal; the Théâtre Niveau Parking and the co-creation by the audience in *Passion "fast-food"*). In short, there is a distinct widening of the palette of possibilities for participation by the audience in theatrical communication.

The experimental theater is constantly pushing the frontiers of what is possible with its multidisciplinary discourse, all the while orienting, in the case of a given company, its field of experimentation to a more restricted area, for example the area of body movement, stage settings, or rapport with the audience. This systematic questioning prevents this theater from becoming sclerotic, from resting on its laurels and from using recipes that would annihilate creative effort and originality. The number and diversity of companies working at this cutting edge are a token of the dynamism of the *québécois* theater as a whole, which also profits from it.

Of all the currents that have invigorated the *québécois* theater over the last two decades, the direction that has been the most consistently innovative—by its very nature—and aesthetically stimulating has called itself experimental theater. Paradoxically, the theater that best represents Quebec, the theater that has been most illustrious on the international scene (Robert Lepage, Carbone 14) is the theater that has done most to cast aside its mimetic function and socio-political frame of reference in order better to serve the cause of pure theatricality.

Notes

1. Translated by E. Dean Detrich, Michigan State University.
2. According to a count made as a part of a study conducted by the Conseil québéois du théâtre, "auprès de toutes les compagnies professionnelles du Québec, et ce jusqu'au 31 août 1989." *Répertoire théâtral du Québec, 1989-1990* (Montréal: *Les Cahiers de théâtre Jeu,* 1989). On the theater of research or experimentation see, among others: "Vous avez dit expérimental?," *Les Cahiers de théâtre Jeu* n° 52, 1989.3; n° 44, «Théâtre et technologies», 1987.3; n° 42, «*Vinci,* Robert Lepage», 1987.1; n° 45, «*La Trilogie des dragons,* Théâtre Repère», 1987.4. André G. Bourassa,«Vers la modernité de la scène québécoise. Influences des grands courants du théâtre français au Québec (1898-1948)», *Pratiques théâtrales,* automne 1981, n° 13 et «Vers la modernité de la scène québécoise (II). Les contre-courants, 1901-41», ibid., hiver-printemps 1982, n° 14-15. Bernard Andrès, «Notes sur l'expérimentation théâtrale au Québec», *Théâtre québécois: tendances actuelles,* n° sous la direction de G.Girard, *Études littéraires,* vol.18 n° 3, hiver 1985, 15-49.
3. Excluded from this discussion, among other topics, are data on space, body movement, background sound and lighting, all of which require specific studies.
4. Cf. Gilles Girard, "Le Théâtre de Ronfard ou l'opération démythification," *Québec français* 69 (March 1988): 70–74.
5. Jean-Pierre Ronfard, *Le Titanic* (Montréal: Leméac, 1986), 80.
6. Cf. Gilles Girard, "Du théâtre de Robert Lepage: quelques points de repère," *Québec français* 89 (Spring 1993): 95–96.
7. Jindrich Honzl, "La Mobilité du signe théâtral," *Travail théâtral* 4 (1971): 5–20.
8. Roland Barthes, "Littérature et signification," *Essais critiques* (Paris: Seuil, 1964), 258.
9. Jeanne Bovet, "Les Dix Ans de Repère," *L'Annuaire théâtral* 8 (4th trimester 1990): 102.

A Theater of "La Répétition"[1]

Guy Teissier

RÉPÉTITION

*redite, retour de la même expression/*action de répéter ce qu'un autre a dit/*reproduction/*action d'essayer ce qu'on doit exécuter en public./*Le Petit Littré*
*le fait d'être dit, exprimé plusieurs fois/*emploi répété d'un élément/*le fait de recommencer une action, un processus/*action de reproduire; ce qui est reproduit/*séance de travail ayant pour but de mettre au point les divers éléments d'un spectacle/*Le Petit Robert*

En langage théâtral: action de travailler avant la représentation/en langage courant: acte de recommencer quelque chose, de redire un mot, une phrase.

The 1960s and 1970s

During the 1960s and the 1970s, *québécois* theater revived a number of great theatrical texts, usually classic French plays, which became fashionable in Quebec after being rewritten to coincide with contemporary taste and preoccupations.

With *Hamlet, prince du Québec*, written in Montreal in January of 1968, Robert Gurik reinterpreted Shakespeare's tragedy in the light of *québécois* politics.[2] The Hamlet of this play, as the author himself puts it:

c'est le Québec avec toutes ses hésitations, avec sa soif d'action et de liberté, corseté par cent ans d'inaction. Autour de lui se meuvent les masques de personnages qui conduisent sa destinée. Le Roi, l'anglo-phonie qui tient les rênes du pouvoir politique et économique, la Reine, cette Eglise qui dans notre histoire a accepté tous les compromis; le premier ministre, instrument exécutif du Roi.[3]

Laurent Mailhot adds: "Hamlet, c'est à la fois l'ancien Québec et le nouveau, le Québec réel et le Québec possible, ce 'pays incertain' dont parlait Jacques Ferron," and referring to this same play, concludes, "Il [*Hamlet*] est autre chose qu'une parodie littéraire. Il s'agit plutôt d'un pastiche historique, d'une satire et sur certains points, d'une politique-fiction prophétique."[4]

Similarly, in his *Cid maghané*, Réjean Ducharme did not simply parody Corneille; rather, he held a mirror up to contemporary Quebec society.[5] When Antoine Maillet wrote her *Bourgeois gentle-man*,[6] she did more than base her work on Molière. Situations from Molière's *Bourgeois gentilhomme* are substantially transposed to the Quebec context of the 1940s (and to a lesser extent the seventies) in order to ridicule the Anglophile pretensions of certain members of the bourgeoisie. "Pas trop vite. . . More tea? the bridge last night, the pussy, how is the puddle? Ah! que c'est joli les mots d'amour en anglais. Apprenez-moi surtout à bien prononcer, pour qu'on ne soupçonne pas sainte-Pétronille à mon accent."[7]

By choosing to reprise masterpieces from the classical repertory,[8] these writers sought the assistance of well-known plots to highlight the unique situation of a Quebec caught up in the dramatic changes of the Quiet Revolution. Aside from the shock effect initially produced by these transpositions, which did much to excite spectator curiosity, and the obvious humor excited by the discovery of an already-known work in its *québécois* metamorphosis, these texts are never really preoccupied with their status as revivals, also known as hypertext. They function at the first level of theatricality, with no metatextual reflection at the interior of the play—that is with one very important but atypical exception.

Le Théâtre de la maintenance,[9] in which the maintenance staff initially explains and comments on the various techniques and devices of the theater is a famous (Rostand's *Cyrano de Bergerac*) play intermeshed at the outset with a completely different action. At its origin the intent of this play was purely pedagogical:

Ce texte me fut commandé par la Nouvelle Compagnie Théâtrale, en 1973, pour être présenté dans le cadre des "opérations-théâtre" de cette compagnie, cette création devait répondre à des exigences bien précises. Il s'agissait de présenter une oeuvre à la fois didactique et divertissante, pour un public de jeunes étudiants du secondaire I et II, non initiés au théâtre. . . . La gageure d'un texte comme celui-là, c'est d'essayer d'initier des jeunes à un médium, comme le théâtre, tout en tentant de les divertir.[10]

A wager won, it seems, since according to Laurent Mailhot:

les principales questions qu'on se pose sur le théâtre, depuis vingt ans, depuis cent ans, sont mentionnées, effleurées par le *Théâtre de la maintenance*. En tirant des ficelles, en déplaçant des meubles, ce sont des clichés, des concepts, des théories, des méthodes, des interprétations que remuent—sans ménagement mais sans bouleversement inutile—ces femmes et ces hommes de ménage. Ils s'interrogent sur leur situation, leurs sentiments, leurs actions, leur paraître, sur l'effet qu'ils font sur les autres ou que les autres font sur eux; sur le rideau de la scène, l'éclairage, les costumes, le rôle du chef d'équipe, l'envers du décor, et même (surtout) le texte.[11]

In order to promote a better acceptance of these theoretical considerations, Barbeau has included them in a plot that serves his demonstration. On a deserted stage, the clean-up crew is content at first to comment on the various elements of the world of theater: "La droite, placée du point de vue du spectateur, c'est le côté cour. La gauche, c'est le côté jardin."[12] Gradually caught up in their own game, they move from theory to practice, and attempt to stage an excerpt of *Cyrano de Bergerac*, a modernized version of the kissing scene. This is made clear by the crew chief functioning in this instance as the *porte parole* of Barbeau:

Ecoute! *Cyrano*, c'est une pièce, écrite à la fin du dix-neuvième siècle, et qui nous parle d'un personnage qui vivait au seizième siècle. Nous, on est au vingtième. . . . On ne monte pas la pièce. On ne monte pas la pièce, on s'en sert. On se sert d'une scène de la pièce, on en prend les mots et on l'adapte à notre situation, à notre principale préoccupation qui est la séduction.[13]

167

So it is that the characters of the cleaning crew, Roxanne ("jeune femme romantique"), Bergeron ("un original, un curieux, qui possède ce qu'on appelle, selon certains canons, un physique ingrat"), and Christian ("jeune homme timide et de belle apparence") will begin to act out a text of Rostand. But, by way of a mental slip reminiscent of Marivaux, Pirandello, or Anouilh,[14] they will soon be acting in their own names the text of Rostand and actually experiencing the declaration of love in the scene of Cyrano's death. Consequently, lines of the heroic French play are mingled with the more prosaic lines of *québécois* reality:

ROXANNE: Vous m'aimez. . . .
BERGERON: C'était l'autre. . . .
ROXANNE: Vous m'aimiez. . .*Elle baisse le livre.* Tu m'aimes, Bergeron. . .
BERGERON: Non. . .
ROXANNE: Non, c'est la réplique du livre. . . . La tienne, qu'est-ce que ce serait?
BERGERON: On. . .on joue plus, maintenant?
ROXANNE: Tu m'aimes, Bergeron?
BERGERON: *moins catégorique* - Non. . .
ROXANNE: *Ouvre le livre*—Déjà vous le dites plus bas. . .
BERGERON: Non, non, mon cher amour, je ne vous aimais pas. . .[15]

"Est-on au théâtre ou non? dans le livre ou dans la vie? Dans les deux, dans un entre deux," asks Mailhot, echoing the uncertainty of the characters themselves.

BERGERON: *impatient*—A qui tu parles, Roxanne? A Bergeron ou à Bergerac?
ROXANNE: On joue *Cyrano,* non?
BERGERON: J'le sais plus, moi. . .
ROXANNE: Comment ça, donc?
BERGERON: Pour une fois, j'aimerais ça. . .que ça soit pas du théâtre. . .
ROXANNE: C'est dommage, mais c'en est. . .
BERGERON: Bon, si c'en est. . .
ROXANNE: Par boutte, oui. . .Par boutte, non. . .[16]

Barbeau by way of his educational project would set in place a technique that would give to the rehearsal of a well-known play, inserted into contemporary *québécois* reality, a more reflexive form than that created by the other playwrights of the period. So doing, he anticipated the flurry of experimental productions that would follow.

The 1980s

In the 1980s five important plays explicitly presented the theatrical universe. Four works by young authors appeared during the decade: *Provincetown Playhouse,* by Normand Chaurette (1981), Michel-Marc Bouchard's *Les Feluettes ou la répétition d'un drame romantique* (1987), *La Répétition,* by Dominic Champagne (1990), and J.-F. Messier's *Le Dernier Délire permis* (1990); to which may be added *Le Vrai Monde?* (1987), by Michel Tremblay, the acknowledged standard-bearer of *québécois* theater.

In their different ways, all of these plays speak of theater at a more-or-less pronounced level of supertheatricality. Three deliberately situate themselves within the theatrical universe, explicitly and completely (*Provincetown Playhouse* and *La Répétition*), or partially and indirectly (*Les Feluettes*). The two others evoke the theatrical world, but rather by allusion, presenting just one author/character or one reference drama. However, all five plays, with individual variations, have recourse to *the play within the play* used so frequently by Shakespeare and the baroque theater and later taken up by Pirandello and the creators of contemporary metatheater. Three of these plays summon up already-existing and well-known theater texts, which they incorporate into their plot. In a way, they aim at re-presenting them, if we can give to this term the positive meaning of "reproduce" or "recreate" rather than "plagiarize."

While a first reading of *Le Dernier Délire permis* may not suggest any hypertextuality, Messier explicitly announces in the sub-title: (Vaguement d'après *Dom Juan*).[17] In the text itself, Molierè's work is cited in several places. The scene entitled "Prélude" is presented as a parade of classical characters: "Elvire prend l'exemplaire de *Dom Juan* de Molière qui était à côté de lui et va le placer dans l'espace vide de la ligne de livres qui traverse le plateau." Elvire herself declares: "Tous les personnages sont inspirés du *Dom Juan* de Molière." Upon hearing his name, each actor comes on stage, saying one or two lines from Molière.[18] Furthermore, in the very midst of the

169

action of scene IX, when Elvire reappears holding a book "dans ses mains crispées," Domme asks her: "C'est quoi le livre que tu lis?"

> ELVIRE: Ah! . . .C't une pièce de théâtre. *Dom Juan.* . .
> DOMME: *Dom Juan?* C'est vieux.
> ELVIRE: Oui, mais c'est bon. C't une pièce de théâtre sur l'amour, la
> passion. . .la séduction" (*Un temps. Malaise*).[19]

More precisely, in scene XI, subtitled *Ne soyez point surpris, Dom Juan,* "Elvire récite de mémoire des extraits du monologue d'Elvire, dans la scène 6 de l'acte IV du *Dom Juan* de Molière comme une sorte de condensé de cette très pathétique déclaration d'amour."[20] The classical text thus insinuates itself throughout, like a sort of guide or model, or guarantee—even if the plot, the psychology of the characters, and the general meaning of the play are, one must admit, only very "vaguement d'après *Dom Juan.*"

In the sub-title of his somewhat enigmatic *Feluettes,*[21] Bouchard evokes "la répétition d'un drame romantique." He does in fact make use of a text—rather more neo-romantic than romantic—written in French by the Italian poet Gabriele D'Annunzio: a *mystère* entitled *Le Martyre de Saint Sébastien.*[22] The play incorporates in no discernible order excerpts from this emphatically lyrical oratorio. The most significant passages—borrowed from the end of the fourth *mansion,* entitled "Le Laurier blessé"—portray the death of Sebastian via patently erotic dialogues between the Saint and his beloved archer, Sanaé. Episode four contains another long quotation from d'Annunzio, this time from the third *mansion,* "Le Concile des faux dieux." It is a declaration of love by the emperor to the handsome soldier who refuses the immortality offered him in the name of his new religion. These quotations from D'Annunzio, far from being centered in a particular episode, permeate Bouchard's play while providing a counterpoint to the adventures of heroes who, until the tragic ending, unceasingly identify themselves with the characters of this "drame romantique."

Dominic Champagne's play, *La Répétition,*[23] openly takes up Beckett's masterpiece, *En attendant Godot,* noting in the margins variations of his own *québécois* re-writing of the play. The characters, Victor and Etienne, go to an audition after reading an announcement: "Théâtre cherche désespérément deux vrais amis de toujours pour vivre drame existentiel profond, comédiens s'abstenir." Although several times bits of well-known plays are quoted,[24] Beckett's *En attendant Godot,* on which the entire action is based, is never quoted textually. It is, however, omnipresent, constantly named, and evoked in the decor and situations.[25] The atmosphere of Godot in sum permeates the universe of Champagne[26]:

> LUCE: Imaginez. . .imaginez deux hommes. Deux vieux amis de toujours. Qui attendent. Sur une route. A côté d'un arbre. Que Godot arrive. En l'attendant, qu'est-ce qu'i font?
>
> VICTOR: Ben moi je. . .
>
> LUCE: I se parlent de leur vie. I mangent. I dorment. I s'engueulent. I se réconcilient. I parlent, i parlent, i parlent. Pis à la tombée de la nuit, quant un enfant vient leur dire que Godot viendra pas aujourd'hui mais sûrement demain. . . c'est le rôle que va jouer Blanche, alors qu'est-ce qu'ils font?
>
> VICTOR: Ben moi je. . .
>
> LUCE: I s'en vont se coucher, quelque part, chacun de leur côté. C'est la fin de l'acte un. A l'acte deux, le lendemain, même histoire. I se passe la même chose.
>
> ETIENNE: I se passe quoi?
>
> LUCE: Rien.[27]

Another way of devising a *play within the play, theater within the theater,* is the "original reprise"; into the story of the play a fragment of another "play" that has no previous or independent existence, written especially for the purpose by the author of the primary play; this is the original procedure Normand Chaurette and Michel Tremblay used to give such a text, *mise en abîme,* the function of a mirror, of a more-or-less faithful, more-or-less deformed, reflection of their primary text.[28] Examples of this device include *Provincetown Playhouse* and *Le Vrai Monde?*

Normand Chaurette's play *Provincetown Playhouse* is the staging, on a July evening in 1919, of a play entitled: "Le Théâtre de l'Immolation de la beauté." This work is attributed to the principal character, Charles Charles, and is interpreted by three young professional actors, Alvan, Winslow, and the author himself who is responsible for the staging.[29] The play, a parody of symbolist style, is in fact reduced to twenty-odd lines. Interrupted several times during scene 6, repeated softly in a recorded background to scene 7, reduced to three lines in scene 8, it develops (but is it really the play by Charles Charles, or does it rather belong in its entirety to Normand Chaurette?) in scene 9 in an increasingly accelerated fashion,[30] ending in a verbal delirium similar to the final disorder in *La Cantatrice Chauve*. Apart from the murder of the child enclosed in the bag (this theatrical murder, which is transformed mysteriously into a real murder, represents the high point of this melodrama with poetic pretensions), the audience will learn nothing more of the "play." One of the actors even declares: "Cette pièce n'a qu'un début!"[31] Still, although reduced to no more than a few sentences, it nonetheless besieges Chaurette's play almost to the point of blending with it in a troubling symbiosis.

Le Vrai Monde?, a recent work by Michel Tremblay, shows the difficulties encountered by a young playwright, Claude, who attempts to have his mother read the first play that he has written—a play without a title. In the play, Claude depicts from his own perspective the situation in his family. He exposes, via the power of words, conflicts between father and mother and father and daughter, while suggesting explanations, revolts, and break-ups that the real protagonists have until now avoided, and which they still refuse to confront. A true staging cannot take place with production and actors because Claude's "play" remains at the textual stage, a manuscript only. At the same time, in the family living room, alongside the real protagonists from the "real world"—their theatrical doubles pass like spectres and quickly gain access to words and action. "Les personnages de la pièce de Claude—says an introductory note—sont habillés exactement comme ceux de la réalité avec, toutefois, quelque chose de transposé qui en fait *presque* des caricatures." This play within a play presents itself at first in distinct scenes: Madeleine II and Alex II, theater parents, reinterpret in their own extroverted and aggressive way the situations that the "real" parents, Madeleine I and Alex I, live out in their muffled, silent minor mode. As Tremblay's play develops, however, the clear-cut alternation between the two worlds—the world of reality and the inversely symmetrical and parallel world of theater—becomes more complex and muddled.

When Mariette, Claude's "real" sister appears, a third character, Mariette II, enters Claude's play to suggest that the abundant caresses given the little girl by her father, and later his exaggerated admiration of her performance as a gogo dancer, hint at an incestuous relationship never realized but always secretly desired. At this point in the play, Tremblay's technique interpolates into a tangled web the lines of the "real world" and those of Claude's characters, thus obscuring the boundaries between concrete, everyday reality and this other reality, this perhaps more-true-than objective truth that can be revealed only through dialogue and scene. Unless of course the truth is that only of the author, Claude—the truth of his fantasies, his urges, or his repressions.

By placing themselves directly in the world of the theater, two of these plays use actors, directors, managers, and public, and stage both rehearsals and plays, presenting theater about theater.

In the play with its transparent title, *Provincetown Playhouse,*[32] Normand Chaurette evokes the famous Cape Cod playhouse and the shades of several great names in the history of the theater. Charles Charles 19, tells us: "J'ai écrit à Monsieur Stanislavski et il fera le voyage exprès." Charles Charles 38, adds later:

> Il était effectivement des nôtres, le monsieur Stanislavski. Il était assis de biais, il attendait impatiemment que le spectacle commence. . . . Une minute avant le début de la représentation, j'ai pu voir qui était dans la salle. . . . Ah. . .Lee Strasberg, grand perruquier de New-York, assis dans la première rangée. . . . Et derrière. . . Monsieur Eugène O'Neill! Ah, Monsieur O'Neill, il ne faut pas vous attendre à du génie, mais vous allez voir qu'on a du talent!. . . Oh, monsieur Vaughn Moody, fallait pas vous déranger pour si peu. . .bonjour Monsieur. . .et vous, ah! je ne vous avais pas reconnu.[33]

All of this, of course, is seen through the somewhat delirious memories of the main character Charles Charles, divided, as his names implies, into his two selves, that of 1919 (when he was 19) and that of 1938 (when he was 38);[34] but this evocation is tangibly paralleled by the action of the play. Directorial techniques are discussed one by one: "Le sac n'est pas éclairé! Comment voulez-vous que les gens comprennent l'importance du sac s'il n'est pas éclairé! Je me mets dans la peau d'un spectateur moyen, eh bien je ne comprends rien" (scene 6, 55). Or, the somewhat droll liberties taken by a director who arrogates authorial rights to himself:

> Il y a des soirs où j'apporte certaines modifications à ma pièce. Des fois j'allonge des répliques, d'autres fois, je coupe ce qui est écrit pour

m'éloigner un peu de mon sujet. Un soir j'ai décidé de remplacer le sac par un petit lapin! A chaque fois qu'on disait 'projecteur sur un sac' le petit lapin se mettait à sauter, c'était assez baroque, les gens comprenaient difficilement pourquoi on faisait autant d'histoires autour d'un petit lapin, mais moi je me suis amusé follement! Alors ça m'a donné des idées, à chaque premier jeudi du mois, je remplace le sac par quelque chose d'autre. . .un soir je l'ai remplacé par un tracteur. . .alors là, c'était ambigu! (scene 17, 100)

The public is also present, with its empty remarks and its sterotyped critiques: "Des coulisses, j'entendais les commentaires venant de la salle, une voix de femme qui disait: 'Moi, j'adore, moi j'adore, . . .' une autre voix de femme qui disait: 'enfin, un jeune auteur qui va nous parler de la beauté'" (scene 7, 59). Or, anonymous judgments that are equally applicable to the play by Charles Charles or to Chaurette's play: "Le début de la pièce est pour le moins bizarre," or "C'est l'oeuvre d'un fou" (scene 5, 43). Then there is the episode of the late-arriving spectator who disturbs everyone, asking "à gauche et à droite qu'est-ce qui s'est passé," whose conversation interrupts the play, ruins the dramatic effect, and forces the replay of everything from the beginning. These elements of theatrical life take on so much importance in Chaurette's play that the public staging cannot develop normally; it turns into a rehearsal, repeated over and over, the interrupted rehearsal: "il a fallu tout recommencer à cause de lui, tout recommencer depuis le début" (scene 7, 65).

Dominic Champagne's *La Repétition* presents a contemporary theater: actors, manager, director, and dresser belong to the world of today, the world of the spectator who has come to see the play. In his preliminary remarks, the author suggests that "les éléments du décor, de la régie, des éclairages, des costumes et des accessoires soient à la vue du public. Que ça sente l'envers du décor. Et autant que possible, qu'on utilise tout le théâtre comme lieu de représentation—et jusqu'au balcon si possible, l'action se passant dans un théâtre, celui de Pipo."[35]

Rather than a true rehearsal, this is an audition and a working discussion for the staging of Beckett's play, the perfect setting for the elaboration of metatheater. The characters are exclusively professional: an actress, a wardrobe girl, a makeup girl, an ex-actor manager, and two somewhat improvised "actors." What is at stake in this droll "theatrical" drama—mocking like a text by Beckett—is a performance of *Godot* that will of course never take place. Luce, an inspired director, a talented and adored actress who is nonetheless tormented by doubt, fear, and alcohol, will not appear; she will let Victor/Vladimir and Etienne/Estragon wait, wait "que quelque chose arrive. . .attendre pour rien."[36]

If Michel-Marc Bouchard's *Les Feluettes*, unlike the two preceding texts, does not specifically speak of the theater in the professional sense of the term, the notion of staging and spectacle evoked in the sub-title "the rehearsal of a romantic drama," presents throughout the text a complex interplay of several levels of dramatic creation, a theater of passion. Not content with including a rehearsal of d'Annunzio's play in the plot, Bouchard has imagined three separate levels of fiction set in three different eras.

The "real" level, belonging to the Prologue and Epilogue, takes place in 1952, in a sort of garage where a bishop, Monsignor Bilodeau, appears at the invitation of his former high-school friend, Simon, just out of prison having served a long sentence. The main body of the play is performed in this framework. Ten episodes make up a drama acted out for the bishop by former prisoners, who are pressed into service as actors.[37]

> LE VIEUX SIMON: Y ont tous été comme moi, victimes d'erreur judiciaire. Tu sais, on apprend beaucoup de choses en prison. . .même à tuer. On a travaillé pendant trois ans not' spectacle, pis seulement pour vous, Monseigneur. . . . Ça serait dommage que tu nous quittes prématurément. . . (*Il lâche l'évêque*).
>
> MONSEIGNEUR BILODEAU: Vous rendez-vous compte que vous êtes en train de séquestrer un évêque?
>
> LE VIEUX SIMON: J'ai seulement invité mon vieux camarade de collège à une petite soirée théâtrale comme on en faisait dans le temps.[38]

They show him events of 1912, when Simon, a dazzlingly handsome young *Québécois,* and his friend Vallier, a ruined French aristocrat, have had a romantic homosexual affair at Roberval. Because of social repression and in particular because of the jealousy that Bilodeau—despite his prejudice—had harbored toward his two fellow students, everything ends tragically, like a true "drame romantique." The past is recreated before the bishop's eyes by Simon's prison companions—eight men who act out all the roles in the play, including the role of the

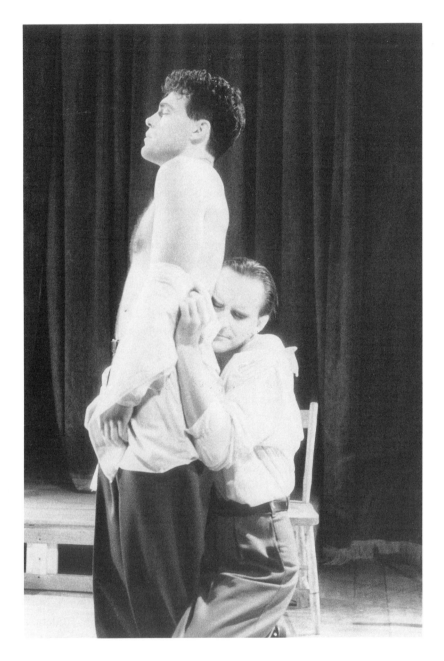

Les Feluettes, 1987. Photograph by Robert Laliberté.

three French women, the Baroness of Hue, Lydie-Anne des Roziers, and Vallier's mother, the Countess.

In this second level, however, there is embedded a third level. The evocation of Roberval, played by makeshift actors, begins with a play rehearsal set in the Roberval *collège*. The students are to perform the *Le Martyre de Saint Sébastien* by Gabriele d'Annunzio.[39] This amateur rehearsal takes up the entire first episode, which M.M. Bouchard uses to recall the role of the clergy in the development of theatrical activity in French at the beginning of this century in Quebec. He also takes the opportunity to denounce the narrow-mindedness of the average *Québécois* and the lack of interest in avant-garde theatrical experimentation. Father Saint-Michel, a director both ambitious and inexperienced, is the agreeably caricatural spokesman for these metatheatrical declarations. However, this "rehearsal" also plays a determining role in the ordering of events, through the mirroring effect it occasions in the roles later assumed by the two protagonists. Added to this is the unexpected arrival of the Countess of Tilly, Vallier's mother, who chances to catch sight of the first kiss—which bears little resemblance to a theater kiss—of the two lovers.

> LA COMTESSE: Allons-nous avoir enfin l'occasion de voir la suite? A chaque fois que je rentre, à ce moment précis vous arrêtez. Et ce baiser? (*Citant*) "Amour! Amour!". . .
> SIMON: Vous êtes sûre?
> LA COMTESSE: Nous n'attendons que ça!
>
> *Ils s'enlacent.*
>
> SIMON: Je vais revivre Sanaé. J'atteste mon souffle et le ciel que je vais revivre. . .Je vous montrerai mon visage tourné vers l'Orient. Alors vous serez prêts. Nous trouverons des voiles, des voiles gonflées. . .[40]

The two other plays maintain a less obvious or direct relationship with the world of the theater. Claude, the protagonist of *Le Vrai Monde?*, does indeed write for the stage, and he fully intends to have his play staged. "On va la monter, mes amis pis moi, dans un petit théâtre, à l'automne";[41] but Tremblay's play never engages the problematic of the theater, except to raise the essential question of whether an author has the right to borrow from his own world the subjects of his dramatic fictions:

> MADELEINE 1: . . .T'as pris la parole pour nous autres, Claude, qui c'est
> qui te donnait ce droit-là? Pis en plus c'est la seule qui va rester parce
> que c'est la seule qui est écrite! t'as pas le droit de faire ça! T'as pas le
> droit! Prends la parole pour toi tant que tu voudras, exprime-toi,
> conte-nous tes malheurs, mais laisse-nous tranquilles! . . .
> CLAUDE: Tous les écrivains font ça, maman, prendre des choses autour
> d'eux pis les restituer de la façon qu'y les voient, eux. . .
> MADELEINE 1: C'est pas une raison! Les autres écrivains, j'les connais
> pas pis y'écrivent pas des mensonges sur mon compte![42]

The insertion of theater is perhaps least apparent in *Le Dernier Délire permis*, if one excepts the constant references to Molière. Elvire is indeed a writer, but he is completing a novel, the novel of his unhappy love for Domme. The latter, a modern incarnation of the female Don Juan, enters show business, on Charlot's advice, to do a show in a New York club with Mathurine. Scenes 14 and 15 take place at the makeup tables in the dressing rooms—but the dialogue evokes the world of the theater only briefly and then only in the context of the personal concerns of the heroine who wonders if she sings poorly and how the audience reacts to her French accent.

An Esthetic of La Répétition

Several of these plays, by the doubling of the main characters, created a sort of concrete evocation of the "répétition." This is the case in *Les Feluettes* wherein the spectator sees Bishop Bilodeau and Simon Doucet on the same stage in 1952, as they watch their 1912 lives being reenacted for them. Concurrently, the spectator is permitted to discover the relationship between young Simon and his jealous and hypocritical classmate and to view, forty years later, the result of this episode, and the evolution of the characters.

Even more troubling is the doubling of the characters in Tremblay's *Le Vrai Monde?* The same author had already presented a more complex mutation of this theme in *Albertine en cinq temps* where a single character, Albertine, appears simultaneously as the incarnation of five separate moments in her life: thirty, forty, fifty, sixty, and seventy years of age, each caught up in a discussion with all the others. In *Le Vrai Monde?* the effects of the doubling are simpler:

Albertine en cinq temps, 1984. Photograph by Guy Dubois.

each character of the the "real world," with the exception of Claude, is doubled by a fictional character. There is no dialogue between characaters of the two different levels, but rather a juxtaposition of scenes and speeches that little by little criss-cross and finally intermingle, thereby leading the spectator to ask: Which is the real world?

Is the character of Normand Chaurette in *Provincetown Playhouse* really crazy? He talks to himself and the audience sees two actors who play Charles Charles at the ages of nineteen and thirty-eight. This doubling of characters is added to the doubling of levels of theater, to the echoing of texts brought from elsewhere, to fragments repeated in various ways and in different contexts. By choosing Beckett's play, whose structure reposes in an exemplary fashion on *répétition*, did not Dominic Champagne go to the heart of the questioning inherent in the use of this technique?

"The theater of the eighties asks questions but provides few answers," concludes Jonathan Weiss on the last page of his *French-Canadian Theater*.[43] For certain *québécois* authors, the 1980s have been a time of reflection that has succeeded a period of affirmation, proclamation, and conquest. This reflection has permitted them via their dramatic action to theorize on their situation as writers for the theater while they have been able to show a remarkable originality and creativity in the transformation of a still-effective trope, that of the theater within the theater.

Notes

1. Translated by Leonard Rahilly, Michigan State University.
2. "His successful 'prophetic political fiction' of 1968, *Hamlet, prince du Québec,* uses Shakespeare's plot to hypothesize what was to be the political situation ten years later as René Lévesque having become premier of Québec (Horatio in the play), duels with Pierre-Elliott Trudeau, prime Minister of Canada (Laertes in the play)." Jonathan M. Weiss, *French-Canadian Theater* (Boston: Twayne, 1986), 136.
3. R. Gurik, *Hamlet, prince du Québec* (Montréal: Leméac, 1977), Avant propos, 21.
4. L. Mailhot, "Hamlet, *spectre* du Québec: d'un spectre à l'autre," in *Hamlet, prince du Québec,* ed. R. Gurik, 12, 16.
5. The play was created in 1968. "The plot changes indicate that Ducharme's intentions go far beyond dressing *Le Cid* in modern clothing. By presenting a King who is powerless, by ending the play in disorder, by giving us a Rodrigue who is full of hot air and drink, Ducharme (as most of the critics remarked) holds the mirror to Quebec society. He sees a society that resembles the world of the western movies more than the well-ordered France of Louis XIV, Weiss, *French-Canadian Theater,* 85–87.
6. The play was created in Montreal in September of 1978 by the Théâtre du Rideau Vert.
7. Antonine Maillet, *Le Bourgeois gentleman,* act II, scene 3 (Montréal: Leméac, 1987), 133.
8. In his *Folle du Quartier Latin,* Roland Lepage has likewise revived *La Folle de Chaillot* by Jean Giraudoux.
9. Created in 1973, the play was revived again in 1975 by the Nouvelle Compagnie Théâtrale in its greatly revised but definitive version.
10. Jean Barbeau, "A propos du *Théâtre de la maintenance*," *Le Théâtre de la maintenance* (Montréal: Leméac, 1979).
11. Laurent Mailhot, "Le ménage de la scène ou la représentation machinée," *Le Théâtre de la maintenance* (Montréal: Leméac, 1979).
12. Barbeau, *Théâtre de la maintenance,* 46.
13. Ibid., 72.

14. The situation resembles that in Marivaux's *Acteurs de bonne foi*; Pirandello's *This Evening We Improvise*; and Anouilh's *La Répétition ou l'amour puni*.
15. Barbeau, *Théâtre de la maintenance*, 85.
16. Ibid., 86.
17. *Le Dernier Délire permis* was created in Montreal in January 1990.
18. Jean-Frédéric Messier, *Le Dernier Délire permis* (Montréal: Les Herbes Rouges, 1990), 15–16.
19. Ibid., 83–84.
20. Brigitte Jaques made use of the actor's work on Elvire's tirade (*Dom Juan*, IV, 6) as the subject of a play, *Elvire-Jouvet 40,* according to lessons that Jouvet gave at the Conservatoire in 1940. Created in France in 1986, this play was staged with great success in Europe and on a world tour.
21. Bouchard's *Les Feluettes* was given in September 1987 at the Salle Fred-Barry by the Théâtre Petit à Petit in collaboration with the French theater of the Centre National des Arts. This play, staged at the Francophonies de Limoges (autumn 1988), toured in France during the 1989–90 seasons.
22. Set to music by Claude Debussy, this mystery play was interpreted at the Châtelet by Ida Rubinstein in 1911.
23. Dominic Champagne, *La Répétition* (Montréal: VLB Editeur, 1990). Created in January 1990 at the Salle Fred-Barry, this play won the prize of the Association québécoise des critiques de théâtre for the best text of the 1980-90 seasons.
24. *The Seagull* of Chekov (scene 1, 15), Shakespeare's *Titus Andronicus* (scene 3, 51), or *Mademoiselle Julie* by Strindberg (scene 4, 71–72).
25. The famous hat scene is transposed to a Quebec mode in scene 6 of *La Répétition,* 108-9. Etienne concludes: "Eille! Te rends-tu compte qu'on est après pogner le fond de l'insignifiance, là, nous autres, ciboire de christ!" (109).
26. See his *Postface pour saluer Samuel Beckett*: "J'ai une passion pour l'oeuvre de Samuel Beckett. . . . Aujourd'hui, alors que j'apprends sa mort, je suis encore à m'y coller, avec cette *Répétition* bien personnelle écrite dans l'esprit de Godot, moi qui depuis des mois me suis gavé de cette inquiétude impitoyable et de la beauté de ce désoeuvrement" (147).
27. *La Répétition*, scene 3, 53–54.
28. This current procedure has been practiced from *Hamlet* to *The Seagull,* as well as in *L'Illusion comique* of Corneille and in the work of Pirandello.
29. "Autrefois l'acteur l'un des plus prometteurs de la Nouvelle-Angleterre," *Provincetown Playhouse,* scene 1, 26.

30. "Gestes et paroles des comédiens à peine compréhensibles. La pièce recommence, les répliques se chevauchent, les mots sont escamotés"; *Provincetown Playhouse*, scene 9, 67.

31. *Provincetown Playhouse*, scene 6, 57.

32. "C'était un théâtre au bord de la mer. Le Provincetown Playhouse Provincetown. Sur les quais, offert au vide étale. Un lieu où l'on a joué sur le sable, de 1915 à nos jours. Où les jeunes créateurs de l'époque, dont Eugène O'Neill, proposaient leur nouveau théâtre." "Dans la soirée du 25 mars 1977, à 21h25, le service des sapeurs pompiers de Provincetown était alerté au sujet d'un bâtiment qui brûlait sur la plage. Le Provincetown Playhouse-on-the-wharf était en feu." See the preface by Gilles Chagnon, "La Scène cautérisée," Normand Chaurette, *Provincetown Playhouse* (Montréal: Leméac, 1981), 9, 17.

33. *Provincetown Playhouse*, scene 5, 48–49.

34. This could explain why the playwright William Vaughan Moody is mentioned, although he had in fact died a good ten years before, in 1910.

35. *La Répétition*, 9.

36. Etienne: "Rouvre-toi les yeux, Victor, a viendra pas! A viendra pas!" *La Répétition*, scene 8, 143.

37. They form an association that is suggestive of Montriveau's band in *La Duchesse de Langeais* and Balzac's *L'histoire des Treize*. As F. Frangi says in his *Préface à la Duchesse de Langeais* (Paris: Livre de Poche classique, 1972): "tous les membres de cette société secrète sont un perpétuel défi des forces vives de l'homme à une société qui étouffe, "s'étant acceptés tous tels qu'ils étaient, sans tenir compte des préjugés sociaux: criminels sans doute, mais certainement remarquables par quelques-unes des qualités qui font les grands hommes, et ne se recrutant que parmi les hommes d'élite (Préface de *Ferragus*)."

38. Michel Marc Bouchard, "Prologue," *Les Feluettes* (Montréal: Leméac, 1988), 22-23.

39. The role of Saint Sebastian had been created at the Théâtre du Châtelet in 1911 by Ida Rubinstein, who had commissioned it of the authors.

40. *Les Feluettes*, episode 5 (Montréal: Leméac 1988), 106. The quotation from d'Annunzio is an abbreviated speech of Saint Sebastian (*Opere* 4, Einaudi, 574–75).

41. Michel Tremblay, *Le Vrai Monde?* (Montréal: Leméac, 1987), 53.

42. Ibid., 50.

43. Weiss, *French-Canadian Theater*, 156.

Responding to Quebec Theater[1]

Elaine Nardocchio

Text and Context

When *Les Belles-Sœurs* played in Montreal in 1968 it sparked a language debate at all levels of Quebec society,[1] influenced the choice and form of language used by numerous Quebec playwrights,[2] and preoccupied theater critics for several decades. When *Les Belles-Sœurs* premiered in English as *The Sisters-in-law* at Toronto's Saint Lawrence Centre for the Arts in 1973, or when it was produced in English as *Les Belles-Sœurs* in 1991 at the Stratford Festival, few critics in Ontario mentioned language, however, preferring to comment on the play's social themes or humor. On the other hand, when the *The Guid Sisters*[3] was presented in Scots at the Edinburgh Festival in 1987, and in Toronto, in 1990, once again reviewers talked about language.[4]

This is but one illustration of how many aspects of a play, in this case, its language, can become the focus of critical and popular attention. Although language is both extrinsic and intrinsic to the positive or negative reception of *Les Belles-Sœurs* and other works, there are other, purely extrinsic, factors that affect popularity. A new piece by Michel Tremblay or Gratien Gélinas, for instance, attracts immediate and generally sympathetic attention among theater-goers across Quebec and throughout Canada. There is also the question of the surroundings in which a play is produced, whether it is produced in Montreal, in Vancouver, or in New York, even the name of the theater troupe or that of the director, can all play a role.

Being at Home with Claude, 1985. Photograph by Robert Laliberté.

Many factors, such as choice of language, are both intrinsic and extrinsic to a play's success or failure. The theme or subject matter can, in itself, for instance, affect reception positively or negatively. In 1978, when Denise Boucher's *Les Fées ont soif* was presented at Montreal's Théâtre du Nouveau Monde, the fact that one of the main characters was a critically feminist version of the Virgin Mary was enough to cause one of Quebec theater's biggest controversies and political debates. The Montreal Arts Council withdrew its financial support of the production, even before it opened, and the Bishop of Montreal had the show temporarily closed down, by injunction, on the grounds it was "blasphemous libel." Critics and concerned citizens rose to protest these various attempts at censorship. This situation of course guaranteed sold-out performances and rave reviews![5]

Some themes are simply ignored. Homosexuality, for instance, is a subject that many critics tend to avoid. *Being at Home with Claude,* a play by René-Daniel Dubois about homosexual love and violence, is a case in point.[6] This work was presented in Montreal in 1985, in Quebec in 1986 and Toronto in 1987, premiered as a film in 1992, and has been widely reviewed, without, however, having stimulated much discussion of homosexuality or of the sensitive but violent image of homosexuals it projects. In the same way, reviewers of Michel Tremblay's *Hosanna* or Michel-Marc Bouchard's *Les Feluettes* scarcely mention homosexuality, preferring to focus on the writing, the acting, or the staging of these plays.

All of these examples serve to illustrate my central thesis: that our response to Quebec plays, what we think they mean and how significant we may find them, incorporate, explicitly or implicity, elements that go beyond the analysis of textual features. For this reason, the study of response to Quebec theater should integrate, or at least recognize, the many contextual and psychological elements that can affect reception. In fact, once we recognize that the interpretation of Quebec plays (and indeed all literary texts) is a complex, multi-layered, and multi-faceted process, then any attempt at understanding them requires a polydimensional approach to meaning and interpretation. Of course, one scholar or one study cannot aspire to be all encompassing. Nevertheless, keeping the multi-faceted nature of response in mind can help put our own responses, at least, into perspective.

As circumstances allow, we may want to focus on specific elements of reception and to conduct empirical studies that will help advance our understanding of response to Quebec theater. This is what I do when I design and carry out empirical studies, two of which I would like to discuss here. The first deals with readers of a play by Marie Laberge: *C'était avant la guerre à l'anse à Gilles*.[7] The second, with spectators of a work by Michel Garneau: *Les Guerriers*.[8] My objective in these and other studies is to map the effect different levels of critical and cultural knowledge may have on readers/viewers' response.

Reading Response and Expertise: The Example of *C'était avant la guerre à l'anse à Gilles*

Set in rural Quebec during the 1930s, this play revolves around a strong-willed but kind and pleasant widow, Marianna, the man who loves her, Honoré, her tight-lipped relative, Aunt Mina, and a young friend, Rosalie, an orphan and servant girl. The play was first performed in Montreal in 1981, was awarded the Governor General's award in 1982, and has been produced regularly in English and French in Toronto and Montreal. Critics have especially praised Laberge's rich use of language and her portrait of Quebec's simple rural life of the past. They have also noted the independent spirit and feminist traits of Marianna and the tenderness of her relationship with her entourage.[9]

In the late 1980s I had graduate students studying Quebec literature, in the French program at McMaster University, read the text and analyze it in detail. They used a computerized, analytical grid to indicate their choice of various actantial Subjects, Objects, and Opponents, along with what they thought were the overall meaning (convergence) of the different stage elements (as indicated in the text) and their connotations. I later had the opportunity to have students in France perform a similar task, although only for the first scene of the play. These were Moroccan teachers of French literature attending graduate-level courses in the linguistics department of the Université de Toulouse-le-Mirail, and graduate students of theater, studying at the Université de Paris VIII. I tested the results for the three groups against levels of expertise, both critical and cultural, and reported my findings in "The Critic as Expert: Part II."[10] The overall conclusion was that although expert readers tended to pick up the same text markers that other, non-expert, readers did, high-knowledge readers

C'étaient avant la guerre à l'anse à Gilles, 1981. Photograph by André Panneton.

generally performed differently. For instance, responding consistently as a group, they produced more numerous and more complex explanations than did the low-knowledge subjects.

In the context of the present article on Quebec theater, I thought it would be interesting to look closely at what those "more numerous and more complex" responses actually entailed. My examples come from responses to the first scene, a scene in which Honoré arrives to deliver some washing, is invited to test freshly baked pie, and chats with Marianna, who irons most of the time. They talk about Marianna's fine domestic qualities, Honoré offers snippets about gardening and the family he works for, and the two of them discuss whether or not women inherit their ability to cook and iron, and if Marianna is working too hard.

The most informed group[11] designated Honoré as the main Subject of this scene, and his, and Marianna's desire to please and to be sociable as the main Object. Less-informed readers also designated these same subjects and objects although only 30-40 percent did so as opposed to 100 percent of the expert group. The socially oriented nature of the main object was designated by a variety of terms (*faire plaisir, accueillir, flatter, complimenter* . . .). Other choices of objects included exchange of information, a desire to persuade or convince the other, and Marianna's determination to work (*persuader, convaincre, faire faire, obliger, travailler, faire quelque chose, ménager* . . .). Expert readers classified the various stage directions and non-textual, theatrical elements under many more sub-headings than did the non-experts: *amitié, curiosité, extérieur, gêne, rapports humains chaleureux, pauvreté, plaisir, temps, travail, tradition* are just some of the convergences indicated by this group. While both groups noted the warm interpersonal atmosphere of the scene, only the expert group regularly designated work and tradition as part of the overall, audio-visual impression the scene creates.

When subjects were grouped by type as well as level of expertise, those who knew the most about Quebec theater consistently ranked work and tradition at the top of their list of convergences, and balanced Honoré's desire to please and court against Marianna's need to work and to exchange information. As I pointed out in "The Critic as Expert: Part II," this group actually designated *fewer* objects and convergences than did those with high levels of knowledge about Canada or Quebec, or about dramatic criticism. In other words, readers with high-knowledge both in a genre and in a culture, i.e., Quebec theater, saw beyond the surface niceties of the scene and extrapolated the determinant socio-economic exigencies (lack of money and tradition) that constrain Marianna's ambitions.

That study was conducted in the late 1980s. Since then, I have had other students of French and Quebec literature, and of Quebec theater, analyze this play with particular emphasis on scene one. Expert readers of the 1990s tend to downplay, even more than the 1980s parallel group, the apparently warm, friendly atmosphere of the first scene in favor of a struggle for control between Honoré and Marianna, and what they see as two different world views. Some even classify Honoré as an intruder, an opponent who, despite his friendly behavior, is actually keeping Marianna from working and improving her life! The struggle then becomes one between a desire on Honoré's part to control and constrain and Marianna's need to work, to think for herself, and to change her life.

Over time, as we all know, and as this result indicates, views of a text change. An important lesson to be learned from this study is that levels and types of knowledge affect our response to Quebec theater. What really constitutes "domain knowledge" and, by extension, "expertise" remains one of many open questions. How should expertise be measured? How can we assure the validity of the designation "expert"? Should all respondants be interviewed and given written recognition tests? What about different levels of expertise displayed by graduate students as opposed to theater critics or university professors? Measurement and evaluation is a discipline unto itself and I have no immediate answers to these questions. Nevertheless, it is clear that it is important to test for different types of expertise when studying reader and viewer response.

In the study cited above, for instance, when subjects were ranked by their knowledge of Canadian and Quebec culture, results were consistent with other studies of high versus low levels of expertise, i.e., high-knowledge individuals behaved differently from low-knowledge subjects, essentially by producing more and different levels of meaning. Knowledge of Quebec theater, however, not only served to differentiate high- and low-knowledge readers, it also turned out to be a determining factor in distinguishing experts from one another— those with cultural or linguistic or theatrical expertise responded differently than did those with a very specific, and text-related, type of expertise, that is, knowledge of Quebec theater. This implies that studies of reader response should be sensitive not only to different *levels* but also to different *types* of expertise. Knowledge of culture and knowledge of literature and criticism related to a specific text or genre, for instance, could very well introduce forces that change the response patterns that usually differentiate experts from non-experts.

Culture and Response: *Les Guerriers* and Other Plays at Toronto's French Theatre

Cultural background and knowledge, along with one's sense of identity and even relevant cultural status, have become the focal point of my research into response to Quebec theater. My underlying premise is that although there may be common threads that link readers and viewers, cultural knowledge and alliances create specific views of the world and these unique world views are reflected in the "texts" that are perceived and received. The study of the perception and reception of

189

cultural differences and plurality of cultures is a complex process and even more so when undertaken within the context of the theories and practices of reader response and audience reaction to stage and print. To understand the way we receive, read, and react to images of others and otherness, we must take into account a variety of factors from the cognitive to the social, from the cultural to the political.

I would like to report here, however, on one small study related to this ambitious research program and that is a "micro" level study that concentrates on the reception, in Toronto, of French-language theater, by theater goers attending productions at the Théâtre français de Toronto. Francophone patrons of this theater are Franco-Ontarians, *Québécois*, French from France, and other Francophones. Many are Anglophones or allophones who have learned French either at school or through life experiences. They, too, come from Ontario and Quebec and all over the world and are part of the rich pool of viewers with whom I dealt.

In the 1993–94 season, the TfT presented two musicals (*Good* by C.P. Taylor, translation by S. Karmann, and *Le Pays dans la gorge* by Simon Fortin) one Franco-Ontarian play (*Le Chien* by Jean-Marc Dalpé), one *québécois* play (*Les Guerriers* by Michel Garneau), and an evening of French farces by Georges Feydeau (*Feu la mère de madame* and *Mais n'te promène donc pas toute nue!*). Short questionnaires were distributed at the performances of the Dalpé, the Garneau and the Feydeau pieces. Some interviews were conducted, and, at the end of the season, a long questionnaire was mailed to all subscribers. I will comment here on the response to *Les Guerriers* and compare results with those of the Dalpé play.[12] Two hundred and sixty-one questionnaires were completed for the *Les Guerriers* (or 34 percent) and ninety-five questionnaires (or 23 percent) for *Le Chien*.[13]

Les Guerriers is about Gilles and Paul, two Montreal image makers or ad men, working for ten days straight on a campaign slogan for the Canadian Armed Forces. In the process, they reveal their own lower instincts and become increasingly aggresive toward each other. All of this takes place in stark, somewhat surrealistic (or ultra modern) surroundings. Co-produced by the Atelier of the Centre National des Arts, in Ottawa, and the Théâtre d'Aujourd'hui, in Montreal, the play was first presented in French, in April 1989, at the Centre National des Arts. It has also been produced, both in English and French in Toronto, Montreal, and Calgary. Reviews have been mixed, with some critics stressing Garneau's clever writing styles while others called the play dramatically weak and criticized its lack of character development.[14] Some reviewers of the 1994 production at the Théâtre français de Toronto focused on the play itself, particularly the subject of war and the military mentality, and the corresponding cold and calculating world of ad agencies and image makers.[15] Others praised Garneau's "smart and tightly crafted dialogue" and "first-rate" acting but criticized the staging.[16]

Of the spectators surveyed, most of whom were over 35 years of age,[17] 8 percent were allophones, 23 percent were Anglophones, 66 percent were Francophones, and 3 percent were what I will call "biculturals," that is, Francophone subjects who claim both Ontario *and* Quebec as their place of origin. With few exceptions, the Anglophones did not indicate where they were from or where they had learned their French. The others did, however. The allophones came from several countries (e.g., Germany, Hungary, Italy, Rumania, Russia), the Francophones were from France (24 percent), and Canada (74 percent). Two percent were from the diaspora (e.g., Haiti, Africa). Francophone Canadians came from Ontario (19 percent), and Quebec (76 percent). Five percent were from other parts of Canada (e.g., Alberta, Manitoba, New Brunswick, Nova Scotia, Saskatchewan). All in all, an impressive collection of cultural communities, perhaps not surprising in a city as multicultural as Toronto. As the demographics for the other plays surveyed are similar,[18] one can conclude that there is broad-based support in Toronto for French-language theater, including plays from Quebec.

Scores were calculated for each segment of this culturally rich audience so as to better reveal any difference in response by cultural community. Of course, as could be expected from the results of other studies previously discussed, there were many areas of agreement. For example, both the play and the production of the play were generally not well received: only 43 percent of the public noted the text as either *très bien* or *remarquable*; only 42 percent appreciated the stage production. The acting was praised by all groups as the best part of the production.

However, there were also real differences between groups. The bicultural group, for instance, was the most supportive of the play (56 percent), and the Francophones from the diaspora liked it the least (25 percent); biculturals favored the stage production the most (67 percent), and the diaspora group the least (25 percent). When asked about their programming preferences for the next season, 33 percent of the diaspora Francophones called for more plays from the classical repertoire, while 50 percent of the Franco-Ontarians chose comedies. The other groups spread their choices fairly evenly, except for the biculturals, of whom 83 percent expressed no preference.

Finally, there were some interesting inter-group affinities: the Franco-*Québécois*, and the Anglophones had similar scores for their support of the text (46 percent and 41 percent, respectively). The Franco-*Québécois*, the Anglophones, and the allophones each approved the production to a similar degree (47 percent, 42 percent, and 48 percent, respectively). The biculturals and the Franco-Ontarians were particularly supportive of the acting: 78 percent and 75 percent as compared to an average among the other groups of 67 percent. The biculturals, the youngest group, identified the most with the characters or the subject of the play (44 percent), followed by the Anglophones (33 percent). Only 16 percent of the French from France and 10 percent of the diaspora Francophones were able to identify with the play, its themes, or its characters. The Franco-*Québécois*, the Franco-Ontarians, and the allophones related somewhat better to the play. Their "identity scores" were 27 percent, 21 percent, and 20 percent, respectively.

Overall results were similar for the Franco-Ontarian play, *Le Chien*, by Jean-Marc Dalpé,[19] in that between groups there were similarities, differences, and affinities. The Franco-Ontarians (89 percent) and the Franco-*Québécois* (76 percent), for instance, liked the play the most; the French from France, the Francophones from the diaspora, and the allophones liked it the least (50 percent for each group). The two allophones, the Franco-Ontarians (89 percent) and the Franco-*Québécois* (77 percent), liked the stage production the most. The French from France and the diaspora Francophones liked it least (50 percent and 43 percent, respectively).

One difference in the reception for the two plays was the fact that the majority of the spectators for *Le Chien* lauded both the play (71 percent) and the production (72 percent). Another was the relative level of cultural knowledge of the audience. Although 89 percent of the Franco-Ontarians were regular theater goers, and claimed to have seen other Franco-Ontarian plays, the overall score for attendance of other Franco-Ontarian plays was only 54 percent.[20]

This could mean that the Franco-Ontarian play was less attractive to non-Franco-Ontarians while the Franco-Ontarians came out especially to see a "local" play and playwright. Indeed, when asked whether they could identify with different elements in the play, 78 percent of the Franco-Ontarians said they could identify with elements of *Le Chien*: the family drama, the daily hardships, terrible relationships, and poverty. The scores for all other groups ranged from 20 percent to 25 percent. On the other hand, when asked to identify other Franco-Ontarian plays previously seen, very few members of the audience could name other Franco-Ontarian plays. They did, however, cite works by québécois authors Michel Tremblay, Jean Barbeau, Marie Laberge, and Gratien Gélinas in their list of "Franco-Ontarian" plays. This indicates that the Franco-Ontarian repertoire is really not well known. It also indicates that there is confusion or merging of the *québécois* and the Franco-Ontarian identities, at least on the artistic level. In any event, although the audience knew little about Franco-Ontarian plays or playwrights, this Franco-Ontarian play did draw a large Franco-Ontarian audience and touched this group more than any other.

Conclusion

If it is clear from these various studies that competence, culture, distance, and proximity variously affect response, it is equally true that there is still much to be explored in the field of cultural knowledge and appartenance when studying response to French-language theater productions in Toronto. One element I have merely touched on here but which needs further research is the relevant status of the cultural community being represented on stage and viewing the production.[21]

As the sociolinguist Richard Bourhis has demonstrated, status and power relations, as well as marginal and dominant cultures, are all elements affecting reception in every act of communication.[22] Bourhis has simulated real-life situations in which a client and a clerk in a Montreal retail store engaged in a dialogue, first in his or her native language (English or French), then in different combinations of French and English. When Bourhis asked University undergraudates in Montreal to react to these situations and to assess the personality of the speakers, he found that ingroup favoritism, situation norms, inter-personal accommodation, *and* language status were all factors that oriented listeners' evaluations of dialogues. Bourhis concluded that status affects listeners' feelings toward speakers and that it was because the English language still enjoyed a great deal of prestige in Montreal that all listeners, including Quebec Francophones accorded preferential evaluation to English usage by Quebec Anglophone *and* Francophone speakers.

It is not surprising to learn that, if you are part of the dominant culture or use some of the tools and codes of that culture, people tend to react more favorably toward you. What is important to note is that status and language usage can adversely or positively affect communi-cation and personality evaluations. I propose that this is also true in the response to theater of and by different cultural communities. As status and power increase so do the value and interest accorded plays and playwrights from different cultural communities. Our reaction to Quebec theater and to Franco-Ontarian theater does not take place in an aesthetic vacuum.

This is not to say that groups never overcome obstacles or cannot profitably interact with each other. On the contrary, within the con-text of our Toronto studies, it has been shown that French-language theater has the power to attract and retain a large and culturally diverse audience. Indeed, as we have seen, there are many surprising affinities in response to *québécois* and Franco-Ontarian plays: Franco-*Québécois* and Franco-Ontarians, Franco-*Québécois* and Anglophones, and allophones and Anglophones can all be paired at some point and on some levels. Nevertheless, there are differences and it is these differences that we must respect and incorporate into stud-ies of response to theater and, indeed, of inter-cultural communication and interaction.

Notes

1. The use and implications of *joual* (working-class, Montreal French) became a very hot topic of public discussion in the early 1960s, espe-cially as it related to the education system and the level of language spoken and used by teachers and students. Tremblay's play moved the debate from the educational sphere to the political realm where questions of national pride and identity were inextricably linked to

questions of language form and usage. See Françoise Tétu de Labsade, "Langue et politique" in *Un Pays, une culture* (Montréal: Editions Boréal, 1990), 99–111.

2. Including Jean Barbeau (e.g., *Joualez-moi d'amour* [Montréal: Leméac, 1972]) and Jean-Claude Germain (e.g., *Les Hauts et les bas dans la vie d'une diva, Sarah Ménard par eux-mêmes* [Montréal: VLB Editeur, 1976]).

3. *The Guid Sisters*, a translation of *Les Belles-Sœurs* by Martin Bowman and Bill Findlay. Toronto: Exile Editions, 1988.

4. For example, Pat Donnelly, "*Les Belles-Sœurs* in Scottish? It Works: Tremblay Play Loses Nothing by Translation into Dialect," *The Montreal Gazette* (June 1990): B8; Robert Levesque, "Les grandes langues des *Belles-Sœurs*," *Le Devoir* (29 September 1992): B3.

5. See Martial Dassylva, "Le Conseil des Arts accorde $82,000 au TNM mais *Les Fées ont soif* restera à l'index," *La Presse* (16 June 1978): B6.

6. René-Daniel Dubois, *Being at Home with Claude* (Montréal: Leméac, 1986).

7. Marie Laberge, *C'était avant la guerre à l'anse à Gilles* (Montréal: VLB Editeur, 1981).

8. Michel Garneau, *Les Guerriers: Théâtre* (Montréal: VLB Editeur, 1989).

9. See Murray Maltais, "L'Eveil d'une femme et d'une Québécoise," *Le Droit* (30 December 1981): 24. Martial Dassylva, "La Veuve, l'orpheline et le jardinier," *La Presse* (21 January 1981): A11.

10. Elaine Nardocchio, "The Critic as Expert: Part II," in *Reader Response to Literature: The Empirical Dimension,* ed. Elaine Nardocchio (Berlin: Mouton de Gruyter, 1992), 265–77.

11. Expertise was not limited to any one group. For example, there were experts on Quebec theater in the Paris group, semiotic experts in the Moroccan group, and non-Canadian experts of theater and Quebec culture in the McMaster group!

12. Results for the Feydeau plays and the overview for the entire season were not available at the time of publication. They were presented however, in August 1994, in Budapest, at the Fourth meeting of the International Association for the Empirical Studies in Literature.

13. The higher response rate for *Les Guerriers* can be attributed in part to two external factors: there was more personal contact between the spectators and the members of the research team who spoke with the public and distributed pencils and the order of the questions was changed so that purely factual information was requested first (e.g., mother tongue, age . . .) and questions were grouped into BEFORE and AFTER the show clusters (two small but apparently effective changes). Of course, one could also argue that since *Les Guerriers* was far more disliked than *Le Chien*, spectators were incensed enough to

want to vent their feelings. On the other hand, it is quite possible that a lively comedy evening, such as the Feydeau *soirée,* scheduled for later in the season, will also stimulate a lot of favorable responses.

14. Pat Donnelly, "New Play about Anguish of Ad Men Reflects Quebec Yuppie Sensibility," *Montreal Gazette* (10 May 1989): B5; Stéphane Lépine, "Le Théâtre qu'on joue," *Lettres québécoises* 55 (Fall 1989): 38–40.

15. Pierre Karch, "Au Canadian Stage, *Les guerriers*: Le salut de l'armée par la pub," *L'Express* (1–7 March 1994): 7; Mariel Karch, "Les Guerriers de Michel Garneau," *Sameplaît*, Radio CJBC (26 February 1994).

16. Annoying to some and simply distracting to others was the lighting, which was was directed toward the audience either through miscalculation or, as one spectator thought, in order to make the spectators feel suitably unconfortable. Kate Taylor, "*Les Guerriers*' Staging Is at War with the Script," *The Globe and Mail* (28 February 1994): C3; Jon Kaplan, "Warriors Misfires," *Now* (3–9 March 1994): 51; Charles-Antoine Rouyer, "Qu'est-ce que vous en pensez . . . ," *L'Express* (1–7 March 1994): 7.

17. Practically all to the same degree: Franco-*Québécois*: 56 percent; French from France: 68 percent; other Francophones: 57 percent; Anglophones: 53 percent; allophones: 62 percent. Two exceptions: the Franco-Ontarians, of whom 83 percent were over 35, and the "biculturals" (those who ranked themselves as Francophones from Ontario *and* Quebec), of whom 44 percent were 18 years old or less. But as these were only a small proportion of the total (3 percent), it is fair to conclude that the TfT public is a mature one. It is also fairly sophisticated as from 70–91 percent of those attending *Les Guerriers* stated that they had attended performances of other Quebec plays; many provided titles. Here again the "biculturals" stand out, since only 56 percent of this group claims to have seen other Quebec plays.

18. The demographics for the subjects questionned on *Le Chien* were similar: 2 percent allophones (from Poland and Portugal), 16 percent Anglophones (from Ontario, Quebec, and elsewhere, although many did not indicate their place of origin) 82 percent Francophones (from Canada, France, Africa, and Guadeloupe). There were no biculturals surveyed in the *Le Chien* study. The youngest members of the audience of the Dalpé play were Anglophones (50 percent). For the Garneau play the biculturals were the youngest (44 percent). Of those counted in the Garneau play 61 percent were 35 years of age or over. Sixty-eight percent of those attending the Franco-Ontarian play, and answering the questionnaire, were in the same age group. Subjects tested for *Les Guerriers* had not previously been surveyed. In fact, 75 percent to 89 percent had not completed a questionnaire for any other play at the Théâtre français de Toronto.

19. Jean-Marc Dalpé, *Le Chien* (Sudbury: Prise de Parole, 1987). Set in a remote area of northern Ontario, the play revolves around a disfunctional, working-class, family and its mad dog, which the father *(père)* keeps locked up. The son Jay comes home from doing odd jobs in the U.S. too late to attend his beloved grandfather's funeral. He spends time though with his sister, Céline, still naïve and sadly cheerful, even after being impregnated by this father; his alcoholic but tender mother *(mère)*, and his cold, rough, cruel, and un-named father *(père)*. *Le Chien* was awarded the 1988 Governor General's medal for drama. The play was first produced in Sudbury by the Théâtre du Nouvel-Ontario, in 1988, in collaboration with the Théâtre français of the Centre National des Arts (Ottawa). It toured Toronto, Ottawa and Montreal that year in both English and French. In 1989 it was presented at several Theatre Festivals (the Festival des Amériques, in Montreal, and at the Festival international des Francophones in Limoges, France) and was produced in Sudbury that same year. It has since been performed in French in Saint-Boniface (1990 and 1993), and, of course, in Toronto at the Théâtre français de Toronto (October 1993). The play has been very well received. Critics have pointed out the intensity of the drama that is played between father and son, the exceptional acting that is required to carry the play and have linked Jay's return to his roots with the search for identity of the Franco-Ontarians. See Ray Conologue, "Sharp Writing, Strong Acting Make Powerful Family Drama," *The Globe and Mail* (19 November 1988): C10; Vit Wagner, "Northern Play Accents the French," *The Toronto Star* (19 November 1988): B18; Vit Wagner, "Bridging our Bunkered Solitudes," *The Toronto Star* (12 October 1993): B3; and the excellent article by Pierre Pelletier, "Pourquoi *Le Chien* de J.M. Dalpé, ne cessera jamais de nous émouvoir, Liaison* (15 March 1994): 19–30.

20. The score for attendance of Franco-Ontarian plays of the other groups was from 46 percent to 60 percent.

21. This is a point that Robert Wallace demonstrates on several levels, in his collection of essays on theater and criticism in Canada (Robert Wallace, *Producing Marginality: Theatre and Criticism in Canada* [Saskatoon: Fifth House Publishers, 1990]). See also François Paré's discussion of "vulnerable" literatures (*Les Littératures de l'exiguïté* [Hearst: Les Editions de Nordic, 1992]).

22. See Richard Bourhis, "Ethnic and Language Attitudes in Quebec," in J. Berry and J. Lafonce, eds. (Toronto: University of Toronto Press, 1993); Richard Bourhis, ed., *Conflict and Language Planning in Quebec* (Avon, England: Multilingual Matters, 1984), particularly "The Charter of the French Language and Cross-Cultural Communication in Montreal," 174–204.

The Problematic of Love and Identity in *Zone*

Joseph I. Donohoe, Jr.

Seigneurs, vous plaît-il d'entendre un beau conte d'amour et de mort?[1]

So begins Bédier's remarkable literary reconstruction of the myth of Tristan and Iseut and, according to Denis de Rougemont in his classic *L'Amour et l'occident,* the Western World of readers and writers has for centuries accepted the invitation of the putative bard. As it turns out, the insidious attraction of the tale of fatal love, which exalts passion while concealing its inevitable link to death, is not without effect on modern critics of the theater as well. Consider the instance of some recent critics who do not hesitate to invoke Tristan and Iseut and their impossible love in their analysis of Dubé's *Zone,* in *Théâtre québécois,* most recently edited in 1988. "Ce thème de l'amour impossible entre Tarzan et Ciboulette," They tell us, has, by the end of Act I, become "le ressort secret de la pièce."[2] In the following pages he will compare the two of them to the prototypical star-crossed lovers, Tristan and Iseut. The present study, while acknowledging the crucial importance to the play of the relationship between Tarzan and Ciboulette will attempt to show that it is not fatal love, but rather a kind of pre-political consciousness that shapes the landscape of post World War II Quebec as depicted in *Zone.* Along the way, it should become clear that whatever tragic resonance there is to the relationship between Tarzan and Ciboulette arises, not from the surrender of star-crossed lovers to passion, but rather from the contretemps which results when each of the lovers turns from love to duty or from duty to love at an inappropriate moment. Were one

199

to look then for a classical antecedent to the action of the play, one might more reasonably consider Corneille's *Le Cid,* except that things will turn out badly for the lovers of *Zone,* who no longer inhabit a Cartesien universe susceptible of harmonizing the otherwise uncompromising imperatives of love and duty.

For a brief time in Dubé's play, then, the tale of young lovers does appear somewhat to fit the paradigm of the myth of passionate love as elaborated by Rougemont. Tarzan and Ciboulette, we learn in the first act, have shared for some time an unspoken love, each believing more or less that to indulge his or her feelings could destroy the contraband operation to which both are deeply committed. The elements of the mythic tale: passion, opprobrium, and obstacles to overcome are all present, but unlike their mythic counterparts the lovers of *Zone* appear less than inflamed by the resulting confluence of difficulties. Ciboulette in fact appears more disposed to think of Tarzan in his role of messianic leader, or superhero, than as a lover or even as a man:

> . . .je fais partie d'une bande et j'ai un chef, un chef qui est plus fort que tout, un chef qui a peur de rien et qui rendra tout le monde de la bande heureux.[3]

Exception made for Passepartout, she is joined in her respect and admiration for their leader by the other members of the band who, like her, have been rescued from poverty and despair and given a purpose in life by Tarzan. "C'est pour ça," she tells 'Tit Noir, when the latter presses her to admit her feelings for Tarzan, "que j'ai pas le droit de lui parler d'amour, je le dérangerais dans ses idées et il pourrait plus me regarder comme il me regarde dans le moment, comme il nous regarde tous."[4]

According to 'Tit Noir, Tarzan also harbors feelings of love for Ciboulette which he chooses to conceal: "Je l'ai regardé et je suis convaincu," he tells her, "Il fait semblant de te parler durement comme à nous autres mais dans le fond de sa gorge il cache des mots d'amour, il se retient pour pas crier que tu lui plais.[5] 'Tit noir's perception is confirmed when the anxiously awaited leader appears dramatically toward the end of Act I and by accident finds himself alone with Ciboulette. Stimulated by the opinions of 'Tit Noir and a guarded comment of Tarzan about her falling in love one day, she begins uncharacteristically to question him. Has he ever been in love? Will he ever marry? What sort of woman would he choose? When Tarzan responds that at the proper time he will look for "une fille raisonnable," Ciboulette wishes immediately to know whether he considers her "raisonnable."[6] Ducking that leading question, Tarzan points out with nonetheless revealing harshness that there is work to be done. "Tu m'énerves avec tes questions," he snaps, "Laisse-moi tranquille, il y du travail qui presse."[7] Whereupon Ciboulette asks for and receives pardon for her indiscretion, and love is placed on indefinite hold in the interest of duty.

This situation can hardly be confused with that of Tristan and Iseut, where, as Rougemont has shown, obstacles separating the lovers serve merely to whet their appetites for the next reconciliation, thereby allowing the tale to rebound. Tarzan and Ciboulette, on the other hand, have not yet so much as avowed their passion. If, in point of fact, they choose to defer a declaration and thereby consummation, it is not to heighten the intensity of their feelings, but rather in the interest of a cause which appears at times for both to take precedence over passionate love.

Throughout Act II, the representations of Godin notwithstanding, the lovers maintain their non-relationship, that is to say that under interrogation, after their capture by the police, each tends to think of the other not as person and lover but rather in function of the role he or she plays within their extra-legal organization. When Ciboulette is grilled by the police, she calls out for her leader, Tarzan, to save her. When, on the other hand, the chief of police admonishes *him* for having led a young girl astray, Tarzan disculpates himself, evoking Ciboulette's position as a contributing member of the band: "Je l'ai pas pervertie. Ciboulette nous vaut tous, c'est même la plus dure, la plus vraie, la plus sincère des cinq."[8] Subsequent events will bear out fully the accuracy of Tarzan's estimate of the girl.

Like Rodrigue and Chimène, our two lovers are willing to sacrifice, or at least to defer, their love in the interest of a higher cause: that of becoming "someone," of lifting themselves and their friends out of "une certaine zone de la société où," the police chief himself admits, "le bonheur humain est presque impossible."[9] Given the chance under interrogation to explain why they are involved in smuggling, the usually vocal Tarzan becomes defensive: "Je me fiche des lois,"[10] he tells the police, and is unwilling or unable to respond when asked why the law should not apply to him. "Mais vous ne pourriez pas comprendre," he tells them, "Vous êtes pas là pour ça, vous, vous êtes là pour faire parler."[11] By the end of the act, the reason for his reluctance will become clear, Tarzan, prior to the action of the play, has killed a U.S. border guard. His familiar spiel: "on ne vole pas, on les trompe," or "on n'est pas des assassins," which he was still able to mouth in Act I, has in the intimidating presence of the authorities suddenly dried up, and he is left in the grips of an all-but-paralyzing guilt.

Later in prison, Tarzan reflects that the killing has brought everything to an end: the collective quest for identity, the future they hoped to shape, his leadership, everything. For months or years he had carried the pistol during his illegal crossings, apparently for the purpose of protecting himself and, thus, his band, from the police. When danger finally materialized in the form of a border guard, Tarzan's passionate belief in their cause, his unwillingness to see the group suppressed, dictated that he shoot. As Passepartout put it later: "a fallu qu'il se prenne au sérieux. . . ."[12] The latter's irony appears justified when Tarzan, unwilling to accept the consequences of his action, finds himself immobilized by the horror of his guilt. Finding his cause and his vocation of leader annihilated, Tarzan begins to think of the sole remaining element of meaning in his life, Ciboulette.

In Act III, having fled prison, Tarzan appears before Ciboulette. He has thought of no one and nothing but her in prison. He knows now that he loves her and has thought incessantly of the life they might have had together. "Depuis le premier jour," she responds to his confession ot love, "j'ai ton image dans mon coeur."[13] Does she consider him a coward, he wants to know. Why? she asks. Because I killed a man, he replies. Calmly, Ciboulette asks, would he have shot you if you hadn't shot him? Tarzan does not know. When he is reluctant to touch her—his hands, he says, are stained with blood, he says—Ciboulette tells him: "C'est des mains de chef, c'est des mains sans péché."

As the Act unfolds, it becomes increasingly evident that recent events have not devastated Ciboulette in the way they have the leader of the gang. Although she loves Tarzan and wishes to be loved in return, it is also clear that Ciboulette has not forgotten their common struggle to become "someone." Moreover, true to the assessment he made of her to the police: tough, loyal, and sincere, she is alone able, without blanching, to assimilate the notion of violence to the ongoing battle for identity and respectability. When she believes she is not sufficiently attractive for him, Tarzan pays her a compliment: she may not be beautiful in the way that other women are beautiful, he tells her, but your name is Ciboulette "et tes yeux sont remplis de lumière."[14] The light shining in her eyes is, of course, indicative of her love, but very specifically, as we shall see, her love for a leader whose stature and desirability is reckoned after the immensity of the task which remains to be accomplished. Tarzan, soon to shed his glorious *nom de guerre* for the comparatively pathetic "François Boudreau," wants nothing more than a few peaceful minutes with Ciboulette, after which he will give himself up if possible or, if not, be killed returning police fire. He has no need of his share of the money which he turns over to Ciboulette. At this, the normally reserved young woman explodes in indignation calling Tarzan a coward. "Tu ne veux plus courir ta chance," she accuses, "tu ne veux plus te battre et t'es devenu petit. C'est pour ça que tu m'as donné l'argent. Reprends-le ton argent et sauve-toi avec."[15] When Tarzan refuses to do either, she throws the money in his face, telling him:

> Oui. C'est à toi. Ce n'est pas à moi. Je travaillais pas pour l'argent, moi. Je travaillais pour toi. Je travaillais pour un chef. T'es plus un chef.[16]

Confused and feeling abandoned, Tarzan-François circles the courtyard, like a character in a *film noir* of the 1930s, calling on the police to shoot. Like Passepartout, he says, Ciboulette has now betrayed him. Beside herself, Ciboulette now encounters the terrible choice faced earlier by François himself: she can play it safe, i.e., encourage François to remain and give himself up, or she can encourage Tarzan to flee in spite of the odds in the hope that he will make it and return one day to lead once again. Like Tarzan earlier, in the presence of the border guard, Ciboulette refuses to acknowledge defeat; she pleads with him to make his escape and he reluctantly disappears into the night. Her faith, or rather her great need to believe, takes over as she celebrates prematurely his escape. "C'est lui qui va gagner, c'est lui qui va triompher. . . (-) Tarzan est le plus fort, il ne mourra jamais."[17] Within seconds, however, the body of the young man will slide derisively from the roof of an adjoining building back into the courtyard.

Earlier, François conceded that if he had really loved Ciboulette, he never would have fired the shot that made a normal relationship between them impossible. Now Ciboulette is forced to contemplate the consequences of her own fateful enthusiasm. Another woman might have restrained her lover, preferring that he live, go to prison and eventually, one day, return to her. Not Ciboulette. Unable to love a François diminished by his guilt, she has gambled in an effort to resuscitate Tarzan, a leader whose mythic stature alone responds to the need of a dispossessed *québécois* people to recover identity and hope. Before the inert form of François, she at first denies responsibility: "Ce n'est pas de ma faute, Tarzan. . .c'est parce que j'avais tellement confiance. . . ." A moment later, she will reverse herself, in a mixture of guilt and tenderness which is the lyrical highpoint of the play: "Dors avec mon image dans ta tête," she croons. "Dors, c'est moi Ciboulette, c'est un peu moi ta mort. . . . Je pouvais seulement te tuer et ce que je pouvais, je l'ai fait. . . . Dors. . . ."

It is difficult to conclude on *Zone* without referring to Dubé's earlier play, *De l'autre côté du mur*, staged the year before, in 1952. *Le Mur*, as we shall call it for the sake of convenience, seems in some ways to be the *schéma*—or better yet perhaps, the premonition—of the later play. (Parenthetically, although it is relatively unknown today, *Le Mur* was the first play ever to appear on Canadian television, a fact that seems to testify to the great interest it excited in the contemporary audience.) *Le Mur* concerns a small band of adolescents led by Fred, who live their days in the shadow of a mysterious wall that seems to have as its function to separate the child's world from that of adults. One day, Fred, after failing to convince his second-in-command, Robert, to follow him, will climb over the wall leaving Robert behind, in charge. When some time later, Fred unaccountably attempts to return, he will be killed by Robert, who refuses to relinquish his leadership. The parallels between the two plays are both immediately evident and striking: the leader of a group of disadvantaged youths crosses a wall—in the case of *Zone*, a political border—experiences reality in some extreme form and returns home, his ability to lead impaired, to find his death, directly or indirectly, at the hands of his lieutenant. The differences between the plays are however more instructive: whereas *Le Mur* seems to tell a timeless tale of coming of age, the action of *Zone* appears more rooted in the reality of the Quebec of the 1950s. Coming of age in *Zone* implies not the scaling of some subjectively conceived wall, but rather the illicit crossing of a political boundary that brings the perpetrator into confrontation with the police and the society they serve. Still, one play seems to beckon to the other, as if by moving from *Le Mur* to *Zone,* the playwright brings more clearly into focus the still shadowy stirrings of the collective psyche in Quebec. Irrespective of the metaphor chosen to express the reality, crossing the line or scaling the wall, the challenge of maturity and self-determination confronts the people of Quebec in these plays as never before in Quebec theater.

In *Zone,* Dubé created an impassioned leader and an equally impassioned follower. Although they love each other, it is clear that at critical moments their passion for a different life, for themselves and people that resemble them, transcends their feelings for each other and in the process brings misfortune upon them personally. What is most striking about the play, however, is precisely the manner in which passion invades the political consciousness of the lovers. François is a proto-political leader who in 1953 lacks the ideological vocabulary to admit violence in the context of what is essentially a liberation movement. In the impassioned resolve of Ciboulette not to abandon their dream, whatever it may cost her—or him—personally, we see the most vivid spark to date of the aggressive willfulness which, in a bare ten year's time, will spill the first blood, in association with Quebec's effort at last to control its destiny as a people. In the final analysis, the proper literary referent for *Zone* may be neither *Tristan* nor *Le Cid,* but rather *Les Mains sales* de Jean-Paul Sartre.

Notes

1. Joseph Bédier, ed., *Le Roman de Tristan et Iseut* (Paris: L'Edition d'Art H. Piazza, 1946), 1.
2. Jean-Cléo Godin and Laurent Mailhot, *Théâtre québécois I* (Montréal: Edition Hurtubise HMF, 1988), 126.
3. Marcel Dubé, *Zone* (Montréal: Leméac, 1969), 49.
4. Ibid.
5. Ibid., 48.
6. Ibid., 62.
7. Ibid., 62.
8. Ibid., 109.
9. Ibid., 138.
10. Ibid., 107.
11. Ibid.
12. Ibid., 151.

13. Ibid., 165.
14. Ibid., 166.
15. Ibid., 175.
16. Ibid., 176.
17. Ibid., 177.
18. Ibid., 178.

The Hermaphrodite as Cultural Hero in Michel Tremblay's Theater

Ruth B. Antosh

The subject of this essay is a mysterious and perverse figure who
flits in and out of Tremblay's work, teasing readers and spectators with its duality. I refer to this figure as "the hermaphrodite," after the mythical son of Aphrodite and Hermes, whose body
was forever entwined with that of the love-struck nymph Salmacis.

Although many dictionaries and studies on gender use the terms
hermaphrodite and *androgyne* synonymously, I accept the distinction
suggested by Kari Weil in her *Androgyny and the Denial of
Difference.* Weil contrasts the myth of the androgyne in Plato's
Symposium with the story of Hermaphroditus as presented in Ovid's
Metamorphoses, suggesting that although Plato's ideal beings
emblematize a "spiritual or psychological state of wholeness and bal-
ance,"[1] Ovid's description of Hermaphroditus's union with Salmacis
is far less positive, for the boy is virtually raped by the amorous
nymph, and struggles to escape her unwelcome advances. It is only
when the gods intervene that the two become one grotesque entity,
"no longer / Two beings, and no longer man and woman, / But neither, and yet both."[2] Thus, if the androgyne is a harmonious union of
male and female, the hermaphrodite is a wavering, imperfect mingling
of the two sexes. While the androgyne depends upon "a stable opposition between male and female," the hermaphrodite is a being in flux,
characterized by "constantly shifting lines of difference."[3]

Tremblay's troubled transvestites seem to me to fit Weil's definition of the hermaphrodite rather well, particularly in his plays *La
Duchesse de Langeais, Hosanna,* and *Damnée Manon, Sacrée Sandra,*

207

where sexual identity is in a constant state of flux. Although the protagonists of all three works have male genitalia, they insist on referring to themselves in the feminine, wear feminine clothing and makeup, and adopt feminine names. Their fragmented sense of self is manifested in a passion for multiple role-playing.

Although Tremblay has not specifically discussed the myths of the androgyne or Hermaphroditus in interviews or in his works,[4] it is likely that he is aware of the mythic dimensions of his transvestites. He has often mentioned his interest in Greek drama and myth, as well as his goal of creating a new, uniquely *québécois* mythology.[5] He has borrowed other figures from Greek myth and turned them into *québécois* characters, as in *Sainte Carmen de la Main,* in which the protagonist is loosely based on Antigone, and in the Plateau Mont-Royal novels, where four invisible women based on the Moirai knit the fates of the other characters. Since Tremblay is also an enthusiast of nineteenth-century French literature, Balzac in particular, he is doubtless familiar with the figure of the hermaphrodite in such works as Balzac's *Seraphita* and *La fille aux yeux d'or,* and has probably read Gautier's *Mademoiselle de Maupin.*[6] In nineteenth-century French literature, the hermaphrodite, "l'être . . .[qui] se féconde et s'engendre lui-même,"[7] is often linked to the figure of the artist.[8] I submit that Tremblay's own fondness for this mythical being is closely linked to his triple obsession with the creative process, sexual ambiguity and Quebec's cultural identity.

Gay Theater or Political Allegory? The Critical Debate

I have chosen to limit my discussion of the hermaphrodite to *La Duchesse de Langeais, Hosanna,* and *Damnée Manon, Sacrée Sandra,* although there is ample material for study in Tremblay's novels. In order to better understand this topic, it is helpful to review the critical debate these plays have sparked and Tremblay's own comments about them. From the beginning, he has steadfastly maintained that although they are about gay transvestites, the plays must not be viewed purely as "gay theater." As early as 1971, in a now-classic remark, Tremblay argued for a broad cultural and political reading of transvestism, "On est un peuple qui s'est déguisé pendant des années pour ressembler à un autre peuple. . . . On a été travestis pendant 300 ans."[9] For

Tremblay, the notion of dressing up as someone else, of assuming an identity other than one's own, is at the center of these plays. In a 1988 interview, he declared, "*La Duchesse. . .* , *Hosanna* ne sont pas des pièces sur l'homosexualité. Non que je ne veuille pas en parler, mais je me servais d'eux pour d'autres raisons, pour leur volonté d'être quelqu'un d'autre, à l'image de notre société."[10] Without the added dimension of political and cultural allegory, Tremblay insisted, the plays would fall flat and lose their complexity.

Clive Barnes, reviewing the New York production of *Hosanna* in 1974, seemed to prove that Tremblay's concerns were justified; admitting that the play's political level escaped him, Barnes declared, "The play is too simplistic. Once the story is out of the bag, the drama becomes over-obvious, and the ending, a nude clasp of lovers who at last have found understanding, seems as unlikely as it is sentimental."[11]

More recently, several critics have questioned the sincerity of Tremblay's declaration that his transvestite plays are not really about homosexuals. In an article on gay theater in Canada, Robert Wallace suggests that in these works Tremblay is really writing about his "propre homosexualité," and only tangentially about Quebec.[12] Yet once having asserted that these plays are about the homosexual experience and not Quebec, Wallace dismisses Trembley's transvestites in *La Duchesse de Langeais* and *Hosanna* as "conventionnels," and moves on to other, younger playwrights.[13] Once again, a critic who views these plays solely as a portrayal of the gay experience concludes that they lack complexity. I believe it is time for a reassessment of these works as studies in both sexual and cultural ambiguity. Current theories on sexual identity and gender blurring and their political and cultural ramifications may offer new perspectives. In this essay I am particularly indebted to Weil's aforementioned study of androgyny and to Marjorie Garber's *Vested Interests*.

The Hermaphrodite: Emblem of Change and Flexibility

The earliest full-scale appearance of this dual-sexed being is in *La Duchesse de Langeais* (1969). According to Tremblay, he originally set out in this work to portray "l'homme québécois. . .je voulais mettre à nu les deux faces de sa personnalité: son côté féminin. . .et son

209

côté masculin, mais je me suis laissé emporter par mon personnage et. . .j'ai raté l'effet que je voulais produire."[14] In true Balzacian fashion, the Duchesse took on a life of his/her own, evolving in ways the author had never intended, and bearing out Camille Paglia's remark that hermaphrodites have a way of disrupting the texts in which they appear.[15] Rather than portraying the Quebec male, *La Duchesse de Langeais* became the study of a man playing a woman—in fact, a series of women—so well that he is "plus femme que toutes les femmes."[16]

La Duchesse de Langeais is, on the one hand, a play about a pathetic drunk, an aging transvestite who has devoted a lifetime to pleasing lovers by assuming various personae modeled on famous women. On the other hand, it is a play about a consummate artist who is forever perfecting new roles, and who takes pride in his/her artistry. (From now on I shall refer to Tremblay's characters in the feminine, since that is how they refer to themselves.) The multiplicity of the Duchesse's roles and the fact that she is constantly striving to create new ones make her a figure of change and fluidity. She delights in crossing the borderline between the sexes, sometimes more than once; not only does she play at being a man playing a woman, but in perhaps her greatest role, Sarah Bernhardt in *L'Aiglon,* she plays a man playing a woman playing a man, exclaiming delightedly: "J'avais quasiment l'air d'un homme!"[17] (It is a mark of her artistry that she is careful to allow just a trace of Bernhardt's underlying femininity to show through her masculine disguise.)

Sexual categories are not the only kind of borderlines the Duchesse crosses; calling herself a "putain internationale. . .pis, après, duchesse,"[18] she crosses the borders of class and language, sprinkling her French and joual monologue with phrases in English such as ("Come up and see me some times [sic]."[19] She traverses geographical boundaries as well in her ceaseless quest for change: "J'ai fourré sur quatre continents, moi, vous savez! Amérique, Europe, Asie, Afrique!"[20] She assumes such culturally disparate roles as Claudette Colbert in *Cleopatra,* Galina Ulanova in *Swan Lake,*[21] and (to prove that racial differences are no barrier) Josephine Baker.

The audience is allowed only a glimpse of this character's former self; as a child of six, the Duchesse was sexually abused by an older cousin and became a gay prostitute at the age of twelve. It is, one assumes, both to deny and transcend this unhappy childhood that she has assumed a series of new identities. But it is also out of sheer artistic exuberance that she develops her roles, in an effort to create ever more complex illusions. The words of the French entertainer Coccinelle, alias Jacques Dufresnoy, famous for his female impersonations, are strongly reminiscent of the Duchesse: "I extended my repertoire and changed my appearance each year, trying to base myself on a different type of woman. . . I thoroughly enjoyed admiring myself. . . . There was no doubt at all that, as a *travesti,* I was freed from all my complexes."[22]

Both the Duchesse and Coccinelle share a pride and pleasure in the exercise of their art; in *travestissement* lies freedom. Both are quite aware that they are creating an illusion; although they develop their many roles with skill and dedication, there is a certain playfulness in their approach, a self-conscious irony, as in the Duchesse's quip "Quand tu peux arriver à faire croire à un homme qu'il couche avec une grande vedette internationale pis que c'te grande vedette féminine—là c'est quand même un homme, parce que c'est avec un homme qu'il veut coucher, ben chapeau!"[23] The Duchesse exemplifies Marjorie Garber's observation that the "subversive secret of transvestism" is that "gender exists only in representation."[24] In a dazzling display of theatrical expertise, she is able to play both genders simultaneously.

Unlike many of Tremblay's characters, the Duchesse regrets nothing; her art is her *raison d'être,* through which she finds her identity and power. Her true self is her series of masks. Far from being a false, contrived personality, she attains a unique authenticity through her role playing; she is an original in her own right, and as such she is the object of imitation by other gay transvestites.[25]

While it might be argued that the Duchesse's repertoire is too dependent on foreign models (she does not assume a single *québécois* role), the Balzacian title of Tremblay's play may be seen as a suggestion that *québécois* culture can draw inspiration from foreign models and still be original. Thus, if the play is read as a fable about Quebec literature, the Duchesse becomes an emblem of intertextuality.[26] Besides figuring the notion of literary hybridity, the Duchesse also can be read on a cultural and political level as a trope of change and flexibility. She is a "third term," a subversive force, exemplifying Garber's comment that "the cultural effect of transvestism is to destabilize all. . .binaries: not only 'male' and 'female,' but also 'gay' and 'straight,' and 'sex' and 'gender.' This is the sense—the only radical sense—in which transvestism is a 'third.'"[27]

The Naked Hermaphrodite: Strip-Tease as Self-Revelation?

The joyous energy of the Duchesse all but vanishes in *Hosanna* (1972), where the hermaphrodite confronts failure. Hosanna has spent a lifetime preparing for one great role: Liz Taylor in *Cleopatra*. As in *La Duchesse de Langeais,* this role involves blurring of traditional boundaries and categories. Tremblay himself has pointed out the multiplicity of this role: Hosanna is a *québécois* man playing an American actress playing an Egyptian queen. Camille Paglia offers another insight into Hosanna's choice of this role, calling Liz Taylor a manifestation of the Venus Barbata or Bearded Venus type, "a highly aggressive, corrosively verbal and hence masculine woman."[28] This deity, according to Marie Delcourt's study of the hermaphrodite in classical antiquity, "avait le corps et le vêtement d'une femme, la barbe et les organes sexuels d'un homme; elle portait le sceptre. Pour lui sacrifier, les hommes s'habillaient en femmes et réciproquement."[29]

As a modern version of this figure, Liz Taylor is a fitting idol for the hermaphrodite Hosanna, who worships her with near-religious fervor. Only after many years has Hosanna finally begun to feel ready for this ambitious undertaking: "J'm'étais toujours contentée de regarder Elizabeth Taylor, jusqu'icitte; j'm'étais jamais permis d'essayer d'y ressembler. . .du moins, pas devant le monde. . . . J'étais pas encore prête! J'attendais d'être. . .digne!"[30] In imitating her, Hosanna hopes to become powerful and to attain near divine status by triumphing at a gay costume ball.

Although it is apparent from the moment the play opens that something has gone awry, for Hosanna's disguise is dissolving (her makeup is running and her wig is disheveled), it is not until almost the end of the play that we learn the cause of her dismay—as a cruel joke, all her gay friends dressed up as Liz Taylor in Cleopatra, robbing her of the apotheosis she had hoped for. By replicating this role a multitude of times, Hosanna's friends call into question the authenticity of the original model, destroying her ideal. At the end of the play, realizing that she is ridiculous in her disguise, she strips off her feminine clothes, faces her lover and proclaims "Chus-t-un homme!"[31]

Hosanna, 1975. Photograph by Daniel Kieffer.

Most critics feel that Hosanna, stripped nude, has decided to be a man, to accept the biological reality. Jean-Cléo Godin, for instance, states that "A la scène finale, très belle et douce, ils sont deux hommes qui acceptent de s'aimer tels qu'en eux-mêmes, enfin, . . .ils se retrouvent, dépouillés (moralement et physiquement) de leurs oripeaux."[32] However, I find the ending ambiguous. First of all, Hosanna's "true" name, Claude, can belong either to a man or a woman. Furthermore, despite the nude male body on full view to the spectators, Claude/Hosanna is still wearing a woman's makeup and wig at play's end. Tremblay's use of the half-disguise leaves us perplexed; we see the artificiality of the feminine mask and the undeniable masculinity of the body, but still we hesitate—is the nude body not itself a mask? Where will Claude/Hosanna go from here? Since her public humiliation, she is aware of the absurdity of her predicament, and of the impossibility of resolution: "Chus ridicule quand chus deguisée en femme. . . . Pis chus t'encore plus ridicule quand chus poignée comme ça, entre les deux, avec ma tête de femme, mes sous-vêtements de femme, pis mon corps. . . ."[33] It is hard to believe that Hosanna will not continue to vacillate between the sexes, much like the blinking red and yellow neon sign that is so prominent in the play.[34]

213

Hosanna, 1973. Photograph by André Cornellier.

Perhaps what saves the Duchesse from the fall suffered by Hosanna is that the Duchesse retains an ironic distance as she plays her roles. She seems never to forget that she is an artist creating an illusion, while Hosanna loses that self-conscious control. There are mythic overtones to Hosanna's disgrace. In attempting not to play a woman, but to become one,[35] she is guilty of *hybris,* of overstepping the bounds of cosmic and social order. For this, she is punished by being reduced to a role that is forever in flux, and her painful search for what Garber calls a "core gender identity" is doomed to failure.[36]

If, as Tremblay insists, *Hosanna,* like *La Duchesse de Langeais,* is a fable about Quebec as well as a play about gender blurring, then that fable may be far more ambiguous than has previously been suggested. In the past, the play has often been interpreted as a call for Quebec to strip off foreign culture; Cuirette's declaration near the end of the play, "L'important c'est que tu soyes toé, Hosanna!"[37] is frequently seen as Tremblay's plea to Quebec to be true to itself. Tremblay has suggested a seemingly straightforward political interpretation: "Hosanna deals in a symbolic way with the problems of Quebec. . .it is an allegory about Quebec. In the end they drop their poses and embrace their real identity. . . . He kills all the ghosts around him as Quebec did."[38] But perhaps the essential nature of Quebec is constantly changing. In the opinion of this writer, the play is a fable about Quebec's cultural complexity and the impossibility of defining that complexity. On a national level, Quebec's dilemma is the same as Hosanna's; it is a hybrid entity that has no "core identity" in conventional terms. As Quebec's demographics, economy, and politics change, its identity is increasingly subject to what Garber terms "slippage."[39]

The Hermaphrodite as Author

If *Hosanna* portrays the failure of the double-sexed being to achieve transcendence, *Damnée Manon, Sacrée Sandra* (1977), depicts a new and more playful treatment of the hermaphrodite, as the author himself dons the mask of the hermaphrodite and joins his characters in a game of hide and seek. In this play, two diametrically opposed characters, Manon, a religious fanatic dressed in black, and Sandra, a drag queen dressed in white, confess their innermost thoughts and desires in parallel monologues. Sandra, the transvestite, is a decadent objet-d'art come to life. Entranced with her own reflection, she preens and primps, admiring her body ("mon beau corps d'albâtre") as if it were a statue.[40] Of the three hermaphrodites discussed in this essay, Sandra seems the least vulnerable, as she sits in narcissistic detachment, contemplating "mes cuisses trop musclées pour une femme mais qui savent se ramollir le temps venu; mes bras, ah! mes bras: des ailes. . .que dis-je, des ailes, des plumes! Pas d'autruche, de cygne!"[41] She, alone among the three transvesitites, is a writer as well as an impersonator, though her "book" consists of green graffiti written on her lover's body. She seems a mix of clown and shaman as she fantasizes about inscribing "des brouillons hermétiques,"[42] "ma Bible à moé, la Genèse selon Sandra la Martienne!"[43]

Sandra's antithesis, Manon, is really her double, though their relationship is uneasy. Manon the mystic is highly erotic, while Sandra the sensualist is deeply spiritual. Just as Sandra delights in writing in secret signs and symbols, Manon delights in reading and decoding. She is constantly searching for "signs" that relay God's messages. If Sandra is an emblem of the writer, Manon is a persona of the reader; their natural affinity for each other may be explained in these terms, as well as in the more obvious pairings of body/soul, good/bad, black/white, etc. Although they are drawn to each other, they do not really communicate until the end of the play, and even that communication is cryptic at best.

Sandra writes only for herself, on her lover's back, as part of sexual foreplay; when the lovemaking is over, she will destroy her text: "j'vas toute éffacer. J'vas toute barbouiller c'que j'vas avoir écrit pour garder ça pour moé tu-seule!"[44] Manon has a similarly egotistical and self-absorbed concept of reading: "Si tout le monde comprenait ce qui se passe dans le monde comme moé j'le comprends. . . . Mais y'en n'a pas gros qui savent comment déchiffrer les messages."[45] She interprets signs according to her own rigid personal logic; a missal in the trash can becomes a commandment from God to throw away her new rosary. Writing and reading appear as comically narcissistic activities.

It is only when Sandra reveals that her "true" name is Michel, and that she was born and grew up on rue Fabre in Montreal, had a rebellious cousin named Hélène, and "[une] énorme moman. . .étouffante comme une journée de canicule,"[46] that the reader/spectator begins to suspect an enormous hoax is taking place, for Sandra shares these characteristics with the author. Just as Sandra has amused herself writing a text that no one will read or understand, Tremblay has been deliberately mystifying his audience. While the reader/spectator has willingly suspended disbelief, assuming that the characters of Manon and Sandra are to be viewed within the universe of the play as representing "real" people, with distinct personalities, they are now exposed not only as illusions, but as self-conscious, counterfeit characters who themselves recognize that they have no independent existence.[47] Once the audience's basic assumption that Sandra and Manon are "real" is undermined, nothing seems stable. Chaos overruns the text: identities appear fragmented, details contradictory, and symbols unreliable. Sandra declares that she has created Manon, or perhaps that she would have created her if she had not already existed.[48] Manon dreams that a statue of the Virgin Mary comes to life, first as Michel's cousin Hélène, then Sandra/Michel and tries to seduce her.[49] (When the Virgin Mary becomes a hermaphrodite who wears the mask of the author, even the most placid reader is apt to become unsettled.) Tremblay appears to be demonstrating that not only can he draw spectators into his illusion, but he can also play games with them, teasing them with clues that lead only to more questions.

The play ends with Manon in a sort of religious ecstasy, imagining that she is rising into the sky while Sandra shouts words of encouragement and asks to accompany her in flight. Although they do not merge into one character, and remain distinct in their roles on stage, many critics interpret this ending as a perfect union of opposites.[50] In fact, it is unclear what happens, for the play culminates in a blaze of light, blinding the spectators. The ending, as always with Tremblay, lacks closure.[51]

As I read the play, Tremblay is teasing the audience, daring them to try to decode the myriad signs and symbols he has presented, when in fact he has made definitive interpretation impossible. (What, for example, are we to make of the broken hand on the statue of the Virgin Mary and her various metamorphoses? Why does Sandra love green lipstick and nail polish? What exactly is the relationship between the author and his characters?) Like Manon, the would-be reader-decoder, one is tempted to protest, "Si vous commencez a m'envoyer des signes que je comprends pas. . .j'vous avertis, vous m'aurez pas!"[52]

Perhaps the real solution to the puzzle of this play is that in reading and writing there are no definitive truths; perhaps Sandra's words to Manon at the end of the play: "Monte plus haut. . .monte!"[53] are Tremblay's invitation to the reader/spectator to participate in the creation of the play, and to interpret it as he/she sees fit. In this realm of sexual mobility, shifting signs and shattered symbols, nothing is certain, not even in the author's mind.

When Manon and Sandra disappear in a blinding light, it may be said that the hermaphrodite has reached the vanishing point, returning to the mind of the writer from whence he/she came. At this juncture, (1977) Michel Tremblay stopped writing for a year and a half and the hermaphrodite disappeared from his theater, only to be reborn in his fiction as two distinct characters: "le fils-fille de la grosse femme," and Edouard (otherwise known as the Duchesse de Langeais).[54]

In conclusion, Tremblay's hermaphrodite plays offer a rich variety of readings. As studies in gender ambiguity, they are already of great interest. As cultural fables, they are more complex than has generally been recognized; the hermaphrodite as cultural icon embodies change, creativity, disorder, and flexibility. By crossing conventional barriers delineating gender, race, class, geography, and culture, the hermaphrodite becomes a sort of intermediary, a hybrid, certainly not "pure laine." Garber's comment that "crises of nationalism and sexuality [are] troped on the transvestite figure"[55] applies to the plays discussed here. I submit that this figure is a fitting trope for the new Quebec as it faces an uncertain future and continuing debate over its identity.

Notes

1. Kari Weil, *Androgyny and the Denial of Difference* (Charlottesville: University Press of Virginia, 1992), 63.
2. Ovid, *Metamorphoses,* trans. by Rolfe Humphries (Bloomington: Indiana University Press, 1955), 93.
3. Weil, *Androgyny,* 47.
4. Tremblay does use the term "hermaphrodite" in his novel *Des Nouvelles d'Edouard* but in a different sense, to denote a man who has undergone a surgical change of sex (something of which Tremblay strongly disapproves because it negates the importance of the imagination in transvestism).

5. See, for example, the interview with Tremblay in *La Presse* (2 September 1989): 3.

6. Tremblay's interest in the notion of the hermaphrodite manifested itself in an early unpublished short story, "Anne," which resembles a nineteenth-century *conte fantastique*. The story describes a man's encounter with his feminine double, who appears as his reflection in the mirror, then steps out, gets into his bed, and falls asleep. The story ends inconclusively, with the man watching the sleeping woman. (Michel Tremblay, "Anne," National Library of Canada, Fonds Michel Tremblay [14 ch. 81]).

7. Marie Delcourt, *Hermaphrodite, mythes et rites de la bisexualité dans l'antiquité classique* (Paris: P.U.F., 1958), 110.

8. Weil, *Androgyny*, 84.

9. Rachel Cloutier, Rodrigue Gignac, and Marie Laberge, "Entrevue avec Michel Tremblay," *Nord* 1 (1971): 64.

10. Pierre Lavoie, "Il y a 20 ans, *Les Belles-sœurs* par la porte d'en avant," *Cahiers de Théâtre Jeu* 47 (1988): 73.

11. Clive Barnes, *New York Times*, 15 October 1974: 46.

12. Robert Wallace, "Homo création: pour une poétique du théâtre gai," *Cahiers de Théâtre Jeu* 54 (1990): 25. For another approach to this question, see also Jane Moss's interesting article.

13. Wallace, "Homo création," 36.

14. André Vanasse, "Michel Tremblay: Les Bibittes des autres.'" *Le Maclean* (September 1972): 39.

15. Paglia's exact words are "Hermaphrodite visions have a life of their own. They are vampires upon their own texts" (Camille Paglia, *Sexual Personae: Art and Decadence from Nefertiti to Emily Dickinson* [New York: Vintage, 1991], 44). (It is, of course, possible that in claiming his own character ran off with the text, Tremblay is doing a bit of mythologizing about himself and one of his most memorable creations. Gobin feels that, of all Tremblay's characters, la Duchesse is the one who "peut se réaliser pleinement sur le plan du mythe" [222].)

16. Michel Tremblay, *Hosanna suivi de La Duchesse de Langeais* (Montréal: Leméac, 1973), 101.

17. Ibid., 90.

18. Ibid., 94.

19. Ibid., 91.

20. Ibid., 20.

21. One is reminded by this role of Les Ballets Trocadéro de Monte Carlo, a male troupe which is both serious about impersonating female dancers, yet aware of the comic aspects of this undertaking.

22. Cited in Peter Ackroyd, *Dressing Up: Transvestism and Drag: The History of an Obsession* (London: Thames and Hudson, 1979), 107.

23. Tremblay, *Hosanna*, 89.

24. Marjorie Garber, *Vested Interests: Cross-Dressing and Cultural Anxiety* (New York: Routledge, 1992), 374.

25. Tremblay, *Hosanna*, 87.

26. The Duchesse's final lines, in which she expresses a wish to "mourir sœur, Carmelite. . . . En buvant du thé!" (106) are difficult to interpret. Is Tremblay tipping his hat to Balzac, his master, while at the same time underlining the parodic nature of this tribute? It seems clear that the Duchesse is demonstrating a self-conscious awareness of her own origins.

27. Garber, *Vested Interests*, 33. As a "third sex," the Duchesse would be a fitting resident of the Maison Vauquer, "Pension bourgeoise des deux sexes et autres."

28. Paglia, *Sexual Personae*, 87.

29. Delcourt, *Hermaphrodite*, 44.

30. Tremblay, *Hosanna*, 59.

31. Ibid., 75.

32. Jean-Cléo Godin, "Héros ambigus, rois sans royaumes," *Small is Beautiful*, under the direction of Claude Schumacher and Derek Fogg (Glasgow University: Theatre Studies Publications, 1990), 178.

33. Tremblay, *Hosanna*, 59.

34. The link between Hosanna and the neon sign is stressed at several points in the play, as when Cuirette remarks "tu clignotes comme l'annonce de la pharmacie" (23).

35. Hosanna remarks that in her youth, she realized one day that "être tapette ça voulait pas juste dire que t'as l'air d'une fille, mais que tu peux aussi avoir vraiment envie d'être une fille, une vraie fille, pis que tu peux t'arranger pour y arriver" (41). To this end, before donning her Cleopatra costume, she takes a ritualistic bath, emerging "Une matière vierge. . .comme une statue de la sainte du même nom!" (63).

36. Garber, *Vested Interests*, 134.

37. Tremblay, *Hosanna*, 37.

38. Cited in Anthony, 284.

39. Garber, *Vested Interests*, 134.

40. Michel Tremblay, *Damnée Manon, Sacrée Sandra* (Montréal: Leméac, 1977), 36.

41. Ibid., 37.

42. Ibid., 45.

43. Ibid., 46.

44. Ibid.

45. Ibid., 44.

46. Ibid., 62.

47. Ibid., 65, 66.

48. Ibid., 63.

49. Ibid., 51–52.

50. See, for instance, Usmiani: "the play ends with all opposites coming together, all contradictions resolved" (145).

51. Jonathan Weiss comments that the ending of this play is "artificial and unconvincing" (46). I agree with this statement; however, as I have indicated, I suspect that the effect is deliberate on Tremblay's part.

52. Tremblay, *Damnée Manon*, 52.

53. Ibid., 66.

54. Tremblay's continuing fondness for the Duchesse de Langeais and his identification with her are clear in his comment "Quand je mourrai, peut-être que la Duchesse de Langeais sera un personnage complet" (Lévesque interview: n.p.). In *Des nouvelles d'Edouard,* la Duchesse, like Sandra in *Damnée Manon. . . ,* assumes the role of writer-story-teller.

55. Garber, *Vested Interests*, 240.

Biographical Notes on Contributors

Ruth B. Antosh received her Ph.D. from Indiana University and is currently Professor of French at SUNY, Fredonia. She is the author of *Reality and Illusion in the Novels of J.-K. Huysman* (Amsterdam: Rodopi, 1986) as well as articles on *fin-de-siecle* art and literature. She is presently preparing a book on myth and fairy tale in the work of Michel Tremblay.

Annie Brisset is a Professor in the School of Translation and Interpretation of the University of Ottawa. Her book, *Sociocritique de la traduction: théâtre et altérité au Québec, 1968–1988* (Montréal: Editions Balzac-Le Préambule, 1990) was awarded the Ann-Saddlemyer Prize for research in the theater. She has published articles on the translation of poetry and is a member of the staff of the review *Spirale*.

Gilbert David is the founder of *Cahiers de théâtre JEU* (1976), which he directed until 1983. Since 1980 he has taught playwriting and the history and theory of theater at various Quebec universities. Mr. David has written numerous articles for reviews and has contributed to several reference works on theater, including *Le Monde de Michel Tremblay* (Montréal: Cahiers de théâtre JEU, 1993), which he edited with Pierre Lavoie. He is presently at work on the aesthetic and ideological orientation of contemporary Quebec theater.

Joseph I. Donohoe, Jr. has a B.A. from La Salle College, a Ph.D. from Princeton University, and is currently Professor of Romance Languages at Michigan State University. He has published articles on French and Quebec literature and film; a book, *Essays on Quebec Cinema* (1991); and he has co-authored *A Fulfulde (Maasina)-English-French Lexicon* (1993), the latter books published by Michigan State University Press.

Gilles Girard earned his doctorate in France and is Professor of Theater and Literature at Laval University. He has published a number of articles on the history and theory of theater; he is the co-author of the *Univers du théâtre* (Paris: Presses Universitaires de France, 1994) and the *Dictionnaire des oeuvres littéraires du Québec VI* (Montréal: Fides, 1994).

Chantal Hébert is Professor of Theater Studies at Laval University. She has published a number of articles on Quebec theater and has edited a special number of *L'Annuaire théâtral* (Fall, 1990, no. 8) on "Le Théâtre repère." She is the author of two books, *Le Burlesque au Québec, un divertissement populaire* (Montréal: HMH, 1981) and *Le Burlesque québécois et américain* (Québec: Presses de l'Université Laval, 1989), which brought her the 1990 Ann-Saddlemyer Award for research in the area of theater.

Jane Koustas is Associate Professor of French at Brock University (Ontario). She holds a master's degree from the University of Montreal and a Ph.D. from Queen's University, Canada. Her current research interests include translation theory and practice and Quebec theater. She has published articles pertaining to translation in *Traduction, Terminologie et Rédaction* and regularly publishes in the *University of Toronto Quarterly*. She is currently working on a book that considers the theory and practice of theater translation.

Alonzo Le Blanc has a *licence* from Laval University and a doctorate from the University of Haute-Bretagne (Rennes). He is currently Professor in the Department of Literatures at Laval University. Professor Le Blanc is the co-author of the *Dictionnaire des oeuvres littéraires du Québec*, volumes II, III, IV and V (Montréal: Fides, 1980). He has also published a critical edition of *Aurore l'enfant martyr*

(Montréal: VLB, 1982), as well as more than twenty articles on Quebec theater in major literary reviews. His most recent work consists of nine articles to appear in volume VI of the *Dictionnaire des oeuvres littéraires du Québec* forthcoming from Fides.

Jane Moss is Robert E. Diamond Professor of Women's Studies and of French at Colby College, where she is also Director of Women's Studies. She has published numerous articles on Quebec and French literature in American, Canadian, and European journals. Professor Moss is at present the President of the American Council for Quebec Studies.

Elaine Nardocchio received her Ph.D. from Laval University and is currently Professor of French at McMaster University. She has published a number of articles on Quebec theater and civilization, reader response criticism, and the use of computers in the humanities. Professor Nardocchio is the author of *Theatre and Politics in Modern Quebec* (Edmonton: University of Alberta Press, 1986) and *Reader Response to Literature: The Empirical Dimension* (Berlin: Mouton de Gruyter, 1992). In 1994 she was elected President of the Canadian Federation of the Humanities.

Lucie Robert is Professor of literature and theater at the University of Quebec in Montreal. Her book *L'Institution du littéraire au Quebec* (Québec: Presses de l'Université Laval, 1989) received the Raymond-Klibanski Prize. Professor Robert has co-edited an anthology entitled *Littérature et société* (Montréal: VLB, 1994) and she is currently collaborating on a new volume of the literary history *La Vie litteraire au Quebec*.

Guy Teissier holds a *doctorat d'état*, with a thesis on Giraudoux. A graduate as well of the *Institut d'études politiques à Paris,* he has often taught in universities abroad (in Baghdad, Leningrad, and Prague), as well as in the United States. He is presently Professor of the Comparative Literature Institute of François Rabelais University, Tours. Professor Teissier has published a critical edition of the theater of Giraudoux and collaborated on the first two volumes of the Pléiade edition of the same author. Co-director of the *Cahiers Jean Giraudoux,* he also teaches classes on European, *Québécois,* and North African theater.

Jonathan M. Weiss received his doctoral degree from Yale University. He has taught at the University of Warwick in England and is at present Professor of French at Colby College, Maine, where he is also the Director of Overseas Studies Program. Professor Weiss has written numerous articles on *québécois* literature and is the author of the well-known volume, *French-Canadian Theater*, which appeared in the Twayne Series.

Works Cited

Ackroyd, Peter. *Dressing Up: Transvestism and Drag: The History of an Obsession*. London: Thames and Hudson, 1979.

Adorno, Theodor W., and Max Horkheimer. *La Dialectique de la Raison* [1947], traduit de l'allemand par Éliane Kaufholz. Paris: Gallimard, coll. "Tell," 1974.

Anthony, Geraldine., ed. *Stage Voices: Twelve Canadian Playwrights Talk about Their Lives and Work*. Toronto: Doubleday Canada, 1978.

Balibar, Renée. *L'Institution du français: Essai sur le colinguisme des Carolingiens à la République*. Paris: Presses Universitaires de France, 1985.

Barbaud, Philippe. *Le Choc des patois en Nouvelle-France: Un Essai sur la francisation du Canada*. Sillery: Presses de l'Université du Québec, 1984.

Barbeau, Jean. "A propos du *Théâtre de la Maintenance*." In *Le Théâtre de la maintenance*. Montréal: Leméac, 1979.

_____. *Joualez-moi d'amour*. Montréal: Leméac, 1972.

_____. *Ben-Ur*. Montréal: Leméac, 1971.

_____. *Goglu* [précédé de] *Le Chemin de Lacroix*. Montréal: Leméac, 1971.

_____. *Joualez-moi d'amour* [précédé de] *Manon Lastcall*. Montréal: Leméac, 1972.

Barthes, Roland. "Littérature et signification." In *Essais critiques*. Paris: Seuil, 1964.

Beauchamp, Hélène. *Le Théâtre pour enfants au Québec: 1950–1980.* Montréal: Hurtubise HMH, 1985.

Beauchamp, Hélène, and Jean-Marc Larrue. "Les Cycles Repère: Entrevue avec Jacques Lessard." *L'Annuaire théâtral* 8 (1990): 139.

Beaudet, Marie-Andrée. *Langue et littérature au Québec 1895–1914: L'Impact de la situation linguistique sur la formation du champ littéraire. Essai.* Montréal: L'Hexagone, 1991.

Beaulieu, Jocelyne. *J'ai beaucoup changé depuis. . . .* Montréal: Leméac, 1981.

Bédier, Joseph. *Le Roman de Tristan et Iseut.* Paris: L'Edition d'Art H. Piazza, 1946.

Bélair, Michel. *Le Nouveau Théâtre québécois.* Montréal: Leméac, 1973.

Bellefeuille, Pierre de, et al. *La Bataille du livre au Québec: Oui à la culture française non au colonialisme culturel.* Montréal: Leméac, 1972.

Benson, Eugene, and L.W. Conolly, eds. *The Oxford Companion to Canadian Theatre.* Toronto: Oxford University Press, 1989.

Blodgett, D. "How Do You Say Gabrielle Roy?" In *Translation in Canadian Literature.* Edited by Camille R. Labossière. Ottawa: University of Ottawa Press, 1983.

Bouchard, Michel Marc. *Les Feluettes.* Montréal: Leméac, 1988.

Boucher, Denise. *Les Fées ont soif: Théâtre.* Montréal: Éditions Intermède, 1978.

Bouet, Jeanne. "Le Dix Ans de Repère." *L'Annuaire théâtral* 8 (4th trimester 1990): 102.

Bourdieu, Pierre. *Ce que parler veut dire: L'Économie des échanges linguistiques.* Paris: Fayard, 1982.

_____. "Le Marché des biens symboliques." *L'Année sociologique,* 22 (1971): 49–126.

_____. *La Distinction, critique sociale du jugement.* Paris: Éditions de Minuit, 1979.

_____. Les Régales de l'art, Genèse et structure du champ littéraire. Paris: Seuil, coll. "Libre Examen," 1992.

_____. *Réponses avec Loïc J.D. Wacquant.* Paris: Seuil, coll. "Libre Examen," 1992.

Bourhis, Richard, ed. *Conflict and Language Planning in Quebec.* Avon, England: Multilingual Matters, 1984.

Bouthillier, Guy, and Jean Meynaud, eds. *Le Choc des langues au Québec, 1760–1970*. Montréal: Les Presses de l'Université du Québec, 1972.

Brisset, Annie. *Sociocritique de la traduction: Théâtre et altérité au Québec*. Montréal: Éditions Balzac-Le Préambule, coll. "L'Univers des discours," 1990.

_____. "Shakespeare, poète nationaliste québécois: la traduction per-locutoire." In A. Brisset, *Sociocritique de la traduction. Théâtre et altérité au Québec*. Montreal: Éditions Balzac-Le Préambule, coll. "L'Univers des discours," 1990.

Burgoyne, Lynda. "Carole Fréchette: Les Blues d'un chant intérieur." *Cahiers de Théâtre Jeu* 61 (1991): 22–26.

_____. "Critique théâtrale et pouvoir androcentrique: Réception cri-tique de *Leçons d'anatomie* et de *Joie*." *Cahiers de Théâtre Jeu* 65 (1992): 46–53.

Canac-Marquis, Normand. *Le Syndrome de Cézanne*. Montréal: Les Herbes Rouges, 1988.

Caron, Louis. *La Vie d'artiste, Le Cinquentenaire de l'Union des Artistes*. Montréal: Boréal, 1987.

Champagne, Dominic. *La Répétition*. Montréal: VLB Editeur, 1990.

Chaurette, Normand. *Provincetown Playhouse*. Montréal: Leméac, 1981.

Chekhov. *Les Trois S_urs*. Translated by Robert Lalonde. Montreal: École nationale de théâtre.

_____. *Oncle Vania*. Translated by Michel Tremblay with the cooper-ation of Kim Yaroshevskaya. Montreal: Leméac, 1983.

Chodorow, Nancy. *The Reproduction of Mothering: Psychoanalysis and the Sociology of Gender*. Berkeley: University of California Press, 1979.

Chodorow, Nancy, and Susan Contratto. "The Fantasy of the Perfect Mother." *Rethinking the Family: Some Feminist Questions*. Edited by Barrie Thorne and Marilyn Yalom. New York: Longman, 1982, 54–75.

Cloutier, Rachel, Rodrigue Gignac, and Marie Laberge. "Entrevue avec Michel Tremblay." *Nord* 1 (1971): 49–81.

Crémazie, Octave. "[Lettre à l'abbé Casgrain]," *Œuvres complètes*, volume II: *Prose* (1866). Edited by Odette Condemine. Ottawa: Presses de l'Université d'Ottawa, 1976.

Dagenais, Angèle. "La Ligue des droits de l'homme condamne toute censure artistique." *Le Devoir* (13 June 1978): 14.

Dalpé, Jean-Marc. *Le Chien*. Sudbury: Prise de Parole, 1987.

Dancy, Paula. "Tremblay at Tarragon 1972–1981: The Plays, the Productions and the Critics." Master's Thesis, University of Guelph, 1985.

Dassylva, Martial. "La Veuve, l'orpheline et le jardinier." *La Presse* (21 January 1981): A11.

David, Gilbert. "Un nouveau territoire théâtral, 1965–1980." In *Le Théâtre au Québec 1925–1980*. Edited by René Legris, et al. Montreal: VLB Editeur, 1988. 141–71.

Delcourt, Marie. *Hermaphrodite, mythes et rites de la bisexualité dans l'antiquité classique*. Paris: P.U.F., 1958.

Delisle, Jeanne-Mance. *Un reel ben beau, ben triste*. Montréal: Editions de la Pleine Lune, 1980.

Desbiens, Jean-Paul. *Les Insolences du frère Untel*. Montréal: Éditions de l'Homme, 1960.

Dictionnaire des Œuvres littéraires du Québec. 6 vols. Edited by Maurice Lemire. Montréal: Fides.

Donnelly, Pat. "Gélinas and Oligny: A Match Made in Theatrical Heaven." *The Gazette* (20 January 1987): D11.

_____. "*Les Belles-Sœurs* in Scottish? It Works: Tremblay Play Loses Nothing by Translation into Dialect." *The Montreal Gazette* (June 1990): B8.

Dube, Yves. "Théâtre: Figures actuelles." *Lettres québécoises* 58 (1990): 38–40.

Dubé, Marcel. *De l'autre côté du mur*. Montréal: Leméac, 1973.

_____. *Zone*. Montréal: Leméac, 1969.

Dubois, Jacques. *L'Institution de la littérature*. Bruxelles: Fernand Nathan-Éditions Labor, coll. "Dossiers Media," 1978.

Dubois, René-Daniel. *Being at Home with Claude*. Montréal: Leméac, 1986.

_____. *26 bis, Impasse du Colonel Foisy*. Montréal: Leméac, 1982.

Ducharme, André. "Le Théâtre qu'on joue." *Lettres québécoises* 54 (1989): 35–37.

Dussault, Louisette. *Moman*. Montréal: Boréal Express, 1981.

En Collaboration. *La Nef des sorcières: Théâtre*. Montréal: Quinze, 1976.

Even-Zohar, Itamar, ed. *Polysystemic Studies, Poetics Today* 11(1) (1990).

Fennario, David. *Balconville: A Play* (1979). Vancouver: Talonbooks, 1980.

Féral, Josette. *La Culture contre l'art.* Sillery, Québec: Presses de l'Université du Québec, 1990.

_____. "La théâtralité." *Poétique 75* (September 1988): 347–61.

Fichte, Johann-Gottlieb. *Addresses to the German Nation.* New York: Harper & Row, 1968.

Filewood, Alan. "Diversity in Deficits: Theatre in Canada 1986–1988." In *Canada on Stage.* Toronto: PACTS Communications Centre, 1991.

Firestone, Shulamith. *Dialectic of Sex: The Case for Feminist Revolution.* New York: Bantam Press, 1971.

Foucault, Michel. *Un Parcours philosophique: Au-delà de l'objectivité et de la subjectivité.* Paris: Gallimard, 1984.

Frangi, F. *Préface à la Duchesse de Langeais.* Paris: Livre de Poche classique, 1972.

Fréchette, Carole. "Questions et confidences." *Cahiers de Théâtre Jeu* 61 (1991): 27–28.

_____. *Baby Blues.* Montréal: Les Herbes Rouges, 1989.

Fréchette, Louis. *Félix Poutré: Drame historique en quatre actes.* Montréal: s.é., 1862.

Gagnon, Dominique, Louise Laprade, Nicole Lecavalier, and Pol Pelletier. *A Ma Mère, à ma mère, à ma mère, à ma voisine.* Montréal: Les Editions du remue-ménage, 1979.

Garber, Marjorie. *Vested Interests: Cross-Dressing and Cultural Anxiety.* New York: Routledge, 1992.

Garcia Méndez, Javier. *La Dimension hylique du roman.* Montréal: Le Préambule, 1990.

Garneau, Michel. *Les Guerriers: Théâtre.* Montréal: VLB, 1989.

_____, tr. *Macbeth.* Montreal: VLB Editeur, 1978.

Garner, Shirley Nelson, Claire Kahane, and Madelon Sprengnether. *The (M)Other Tongue: Essays in Feminist Psychoanalytic Interpretation.* Ithaca: Cornell University Press, 1985.

Gauthier, Gilles. *On n'est pas des enfants d'école.* Montréal: Québec/Amérique, 1984.

Gélinas, Gratien. *Les Fridolinades.* 4 vols. (1:1945-46; 2:1943-44; 3:1941-42; 4:1938-40). Montréal: Les Quinze, éditeur, 1980, 1981, 1981, 1988.

_____. *Tit-Coq*. Montréal: Editions de l'Homme, 1968.

Genette, Gérard. *Palimpseste*. Paris: Seuil, 1982.

Germain, Jean-Claude. "C'est pas Mozart, c'est le Shakespeare québécois qu'on assassine." *Cahiers de Théâtre Jeu*, no. 7. Montréal: Editions Quinze, 1978.

_____. "Du décor et des costumes" [preface]. In *Les Faux Brillants de Félix-Gabriel Marchand*. Montréal: VLB, 1977.

_____. *Les Hauts et les bas de la vie d'une diva, Sarah Ménard par eux-mêmes*. Montréal: VLB, 1976.

_____. *A Canadian play/Une plaie canadienne*. Montréal: VLB, 1979.

_____. *Si les Sansoucis s'en soucient, ces Sansoucis-ci s'en soucieront-ils? Bien parler, c'est se respecter!* [précédé de] *Diguidi, ha! ha! ha!* Montréal: Leméac, 1972.

_____. *Les tourtereaux*. Montréal: l'Aurore, 1974.

_____. *Le Buffet impromptu ou la nôsse chez les propriétaires de bungalow*. Adapted from Bertolt Brecht's *Die Kleinbürgerhochzeit*. Montreal: École nationale de théâtre manuscript, 1976.

_____. *Diguidi, diguidi, ha! ha! ha!* and *Si les Sansoucis s'en soucient, ces Sansoucis-ci s'en soucieront-ils? Bien parler, c'est se respecter!* Montreal: VLB, 1972.

_____. Preface. In *A Canadian Play/Une plaie canadienne*. Montreal: VLB, 1983.

Girard, Gilles. "Du théâtre de Robert Lepage: quelques points de repère." *Québec français* 89 (Spring 1993): 95–96.

_____. "Le Théâtre de Ronfard ou l'opération démythification." *Québec français* 69 (March 1988): 70–74.

Gobard, Henri. *L'Aliénation linguistique: Analyse tétraglossique*. Paris: Flammarion, 1976.

Gobin, Pierre. *Le Fou et ses doubles: Figures de la dramaturgie québécoise*. Montréal: Presses de l'Université de Montréal, 1978.

Godin, Jean-Cléo. "Héros ambigus, rois sans royaumes." In *Small Is Beautiful*, under the direction of Claude Schumacher and Derek Fogg. Glasgow University: Theatre Studies Publications, 1990.

Godin, Jean-Cléo, and Laurent Mailhot. *Théâtre québécois I*. Montréal: Edition Hurtubise HMB, 1988.

Gravel, Robert. *TRAC 3*. National Archives of Québec, Montréal.

Gurik, Robert. *Hamlet, prince du Québec*. Montréal: Leméac, 1977.

_____. *Hamlet, prince du Québec*. Montréal: Editions de l'homme, 1968.

_____. *Les Tas de siège*. Montréal: Leméac, 1971.

Habermas, Jürgen. *L'Espace public: Archéologie de la publicité comme dimension constitutive de la société bourgeoise* [*Strukturwandel der Öffentlichkeit: Untersuchungen zu einer Kategorie der bürgerlichen Gesellschaft* (1962)]. Translated into French by Marc B. de Launay. Paris: Payot, 1986.

Hébert, Chantal. *Le Burlesque au Québec: Un divertissement populaire*. Montréal: Hurtubise HMH, 1981.

_____. "Une mutation en cours." *Théâtre/Public* 117(May-June 1994): 64-73

Hébert, Chantal, and Perelli-Contos. *Les tendences actuelles de l'écriture scénique*. CRSH, 1992–95.

_____. *Le théâtre de recherche et la référence aux formes populaires du spectacle*. FCAR, 1990–93.

Hébert, Marie-Francine. *Cé tellement "cute" des enfants*. Montréal: Quinze, 1975.

Hébert, Pierre. "La Réception des romans de Roch Carrier au Québec et au Canada anglais ou le syndrome de Krieghoff." In *Le Roman Contemporaine au Québec (1960–1985)*. Montréal: Fides, 1992.

Hirsch, Marianne. *The Mother/Daughter Plot: Narrative, Psychoanalysis, Feminism*. Bloomington: Indiana University Press, 1989.

Homel, David. "Dans les deux sens (la traduction littéraire au Canada)." *Liberté* 205. 35(1) (1993): 132–39.

Homel, David, and Sherry Simon. *Mapping Literature*. Montreal: Véhicule Press, 1988.

Honzel, Jindrich. "La Mobilité du signe théâtral." *Travail théâtral* 4 (1971): 5–20.

_____. *Introduction à l'oeuvre sur le Kavi*. Translated by Pierre Caussat. Paris: Seuil, 1974.

Kaplan, Jon. "Warriors Misfires." *Now* (3–9 March 1994): 51.

Karch, Mariel. "Les Guerrriers de Michel Garneau." *Sameplaît*, Radio CJBC (26 February 1994).

Karch, Pierre. "Au Canadian Stage, *Les guerriers*: Le salut de l'armée par la pub." *L'Express* (1–7 March 1994): 7.

Koustas, J. "*Hosanna* in Toronto, 'Tour de force' or 'Détour de traduction?'" *Traduction, Terminologie, Rédaction* 2(2) (1989): 129–39.

Kristeva, Julia. "About Chinese Women" ["Des Chinoises"].
Translated by Sean Hand. In *The Kristeva Reader*. Edited by Toril
Moi. New York: Columbia University Press, 1986.

_____. "Stabat Mater" ["Hérétique de l'amour"]. Translated by Léon
S. Roudiez. In *The Kristeva Reader*. Edited by Toril Moi. New
York: Columbia University Press, 1986.

_____. "Women's Time" ["Le Temps des femmes"]. Translated by
Alice Jardine and Harry Blake.) In *The Kristeva Reader*. Edited by
Toril Moi. New York: Columbia University Press, 1986.

Laberge, Marie. *C'était avant la guerre à l'anse à Gilles*. Montréal:
VLB, 1981.

_____. *Deux Tangos pour toute une vie*. Montréal: VLB, 1985.

_____. *L'Homme gris* suivi de *Éva et Évelyne: Théâtre*. Montréal:
VLB, 1986.

Labsade, Françoise Tétu de. "Langue et politique." In *Un Pays, une
culture*. Montréal: Editions Boréal, 1990.

Lacroix, Jean-Guy. *La Condition d'artiste: une injustice*. Montréal:
VLB, 1990.

Ladmiral, Jean-René. *Minima Moralia, Reflexions sur la vie mutilée*.
Paris: Payot, 1991.

Laillou Savona, Jeannette. "Didascalies as Speech Act." Translated by
Fiona Strachan. *Modern Drama* 25(1) (March 1982): 25–35.

_____. "Narration et actes de parole dans le texte dramatique."
Études littéraires 13(3) (December 1980): 471–93.

Lalonde, Michèle. *Défense et illustration de la langue québécoise*.
Paris: Seghers-Laffont, 1979.

Lamontagne, Gilles. "Baby Blues navigue entre de beaux moments et
l'insignifiance." *La Presse* (23 March 1991).

Lane-Mercier, Gillian. "Pour Un Statut sémiotique du dialogue
romanesque." *Versus* 54 (September–December 1989): 3–20.

_____. "Pour Une Analyse du dialogue romanesque." *Poétique* 81
(February 1990): 43–62.

Languirand, Jacques. *Klondyke* (suivi d'une étude: "Le Québec et
l'Américanité"). Montréal: Cercle du Livre de France, 1971.

_____. *Les Grands Départs*. Montréal: Cercle du livre de France,
1958.

Larocque, Pierre A. "Projet pour un bouleversement des sens ou
visions exotiques de Maria Chaplin." *Le Baroque* 2 (April 1977):
3–4.

Larrue, Jean-Marc. "Le Théâtre expérimental et la fin de l'unique," *Cahiers de Théâtre Jeu* 52 (September 1989): 41.

Lavigne, Louis-Dominique. *Où est-ce qu'elle est ma gang?* Montréal: Québec/Amérique, 1984.

Lavoie, Pierre. "Il y a 20 ans, *Les Belles-Sœurs* par la porte d'en avant." *Cahiers de Théâtre Jeu* 47 (1988): 57–74.

_____. "L'Improvisation: l'art de l'instant." *Etudes littéraires* 18(3). Québec: Presses de l'Université Laval, 1985.

Le Blanc, Alonzo. "Ronfard: dérive organisée et conflit des cultures." *Etudes littéraires* 18(3) (Winter 1985): 134.

Lebeau, Suzanne. *Une lune entre deux maisons.* Montréal: Québec/Amérique, 1980.

_____. *La Marelle.* Montréal: Leméac, 1984.

Legris, Renée, André-G. Bourassa, Jean-Marc Larrue, and Gilbert David. *Le Théâtre au Québec 1825–1980.* Montréal: VLB Editeur SHTQ-BNQ, 1988.

Lemire, Maurice, ed. *La Vie littéraire au Québec 1763–1805.* Québec: Presses de l'Université Laval. 5 vols. 1991–. (1: 1991; 2: 1992; vols. 3, 4, and 5 forthcoming.)

Leonard, Paul. "Critical Questioning." *Canadian Theatre Review* 57 (Winter 1988): 4–10.

Lepage, Roland. *La Complainte des hivers rouges.* Montréal: Leméac, 1974.

Lépine, Stéphane. "Le Théâtre qu'on joue." *Lettres québécoises* 55 (Fall 1989): 38–40.

Levesque, Robert. "Les Grandes Langues des *Belles-Sœurs. Le Devoir* (29 September 1992): B3.

_____. "Michel Tremblay: 'Quand je mourrai, peut-être que la duchesse de Langeais sera un personnage complet." *Le Devoir* (15 September 1990): n.p.

_____. "Un blues timide," *La Presse* (30 March 1991).

Linton, Ralph. *The cultural Background of Personality.* New York-London: Appleton-Century, 1945.

Loranger, Françoise. *Médium Saignant.* Montréal: Leméac, 1970.

Lord, Barry. *The History of Painting in Canada.* Toronto: NC Press, 1974.

Lyotard, Jean-François. *Le Postmoderne expliqué aux enfants.* Paris: Galilée, 1987.

Maillet, Antonine. *Le Bourgeois gentleman.* Montréal: Leméac, 1987.

Maltais, Murray. "L'Éveil d'une femme et d'une Québécoise." *Le Droit* (30 December 1981): 24.

Marchand, Félix-Gabriel. "Fatenville: Pièce en un acte." *La Revue canadienne* (September 1869): 666-710.

Marsolais, Gilles. "Traduire et Monter *Mademoiselle Julie*." *Cahiers de la Nouvelle Compagnie Théâtrale* 11(2) (1977): 12.

Melançon, Joseph, Clément Moisan, and Max Roy, eds. *La Littérature au Cégep (1968–1978): Le Statut de la littérature dans l'enseignement collégial.* Québec: Nuit Blanche Éditeur, 1993.

Messier, Jean-Frédéric. *Le Dernier Délire permis.* Montréal: Les Herbes Rouges, 1990.

Micone, Marco. *Gens du silence.* Montréal: Québec/Amérique, 1982.

Miron, Gaston. *L'Homme rapaillé.* Montreal: Presses de l'Université de Montréal, 1970.

Moss, Jane. "`All in the Family': Quebec Family Drama in the 1980s." *Journal of Canadian Studies* 27(2) (1992): 97–106.

_____. "Filial (Im)pieties: Mothers and Daughters in Quebec Women's Theatre." *American Review of Canadian Studies* 19(2) (1989): 177–86.

_____. "Living with Liberation: Quebec Drama in the Feminist Age." *Atlantis* 14(1) (1988): 32–37.

_____. "Marie Laberge and Women's Theater in Quebec." *Writing Beyond the Hexagon: Women Writing in French.* Edited by Karen Gould, Mary Jean Green, Micheline Rice-Maximin, Keith Walker, and Jack Yeager. [Forthcoming.]

_____. "Sexual Games: Hypertheatricality and Homosexuality in Recent Quebec Plays." *The American Review of Canadian Studies* 17(3) (Autumn 1987): 287–96.

_____. "Living with Liberation: Quebec Drama in the Feminist Age."

_____. "`All in the Family': Quebec Family Dramas in the 1980s."

_____. "Filial (Im)pieties: Mothers and Daughters in Quebec Women's Theater." *American Review of Canadian Studies* 19(2) (1989): 177–86

_____. "Marie Laberge and Women's Theater in Quebec." In *Writing Beyond the Hexagon: Women Writing in French*, edited by Karen Gould, Mary Jean Green, Micheline Rice-Maximin, Keith Walker, and Jack Yeager. [Forthcoming.]

Nardocchio, Elaine F. "The Critic as Expert: Part II." In *Reader Response to Literature: The Empirical Dimension*. Edited by Elaine Nardocchio. Berlin: Mouton de Gruyter, 1992.

Noel, Danièle. *Les Questions de langue au Québec, 1759–1850: Étude revue pour le Conseil de la langue française*. Quebec: Éditeur Officiel, 1990.

Nunn, Robert. "Cognita: Has Quebec Discovered English Canadian Plays?" *Theatrum* (June/July/August 1991): 15–19.

O'Neil-Karch, Mariel, and Pierre Paul Karch. "Le Théâtre québécois à Toronto." In *Revue d'histoire littéraire du Québec, le théâtre*. Ottawa: Editions de l'Université d'Ottawa, 1984.

Ovid. *Metamorphoses*. Translated by Rolfe Humphries. Bloomington: Indiana University Press, 1955.

Paglia, Camille. *Sexual Personae: Art and Decadence from Nefertiti to Emily Dickinson*. New York: Vintage, 1991.

Paré, François. *Les Littératures de l'exiguïté*. Hearst: Les Editions de Nordic, 1992.

Pavolic, Diane, and Lorraine Carmelain. "Le Québec des années 1980: éclectisme et exotisme." In *Canada on Stage*. Toronto: PACTS Communications Centre, 1991.

Pednault, Hélène. *La Déposition: Théâtre*. Montréal: VLB, 1989.

Pelletier, Maryse. *La Rupture des eaux*. Montréal: VLB, 1989.

Pelletier, Pol. *La Lumière blanche*. Montréal: Les Herbes Rouges, 1989.

Petitclair, Pierre. "*La Donation*: Comédie en deux actes." *L'Artisan* (December 1842): 15–29.

Pierre, Gaston Saint. *The French Canadian Experience*. Toronto: Macmillan, 1979.

Pontaut, Alain. "Tremblay s'explique: *Hosanna*." *Le Jour* (24 May 1975): 11.

Quesnel, Joseph. "L'Anglomanie ou le Dîner à l'anglaise" (1803). *La Barre du Jour* (July–December 1965): 117–41.

Robert, Lucie. "Changing the Subject: A Reading of Contemporary Feminist Drama." In *Women on the Canadian Stage: The Legacy of Hrotsvit*. Edited by Rita Much. Winnipeg: Blizzard Publishing, 1992.

_____. "Le Statut littéraire de la dramaturgie." In *La Littérarité*. Edited by Louise Milot and Fernand Roy. Sainte-Foy: Presses de l'Université Laval, 1991.

_____. "Towards a History of Quebec Drama." *Poetics Today* 12(4) (Winter 1991): 747–67.

_____. "The New Québec Theatre." In *Canadian Canons: Essays in Literary Value*. Edited by Robert Lecker. Toronto: University of Toronto Press, 1991.

Ronfard, Jean-Pierre. *Vie et mort du Roi Boiteux*. 2 vols. Montréal: Leméac, 1981.

_____. *Le Titanic*. Montreal: Leméac, 1986.

Rossi, Vittorio. *Scarpone*. Montréal: Nu-Age Editions, 1990.

Rougemont, Denis de. *L'Amour et l'occident*. Paris: Plon, 1972.

Rousseau, Guildo. *L'Image des Etats-Unis dans la littérature québécoise (1775–1930)*. Sherbrooke: Editions Naaman, 1981.

Rouyer, Charles-Antoine. "Qu'est-ce que vous en pensez. . . ." *L'Express* (1–7 March 1994): 7.

Ruddick, Sara. "Maternal Thinking." In *Rethinking the Family: Some Feminist Questions*. New York: Longman, 1982.

St. Pierre, Paul. "Translation as a Discourse of History." *Traduction, Terminologie, Rédaction*. 4(1) (1993).

Saussure, Ferdinand de. *Cours de linguistique générale* (1916). Edited with an introduction by Tullio de Mauro. Paris: Payot, 1982.

Savona, Jeannette Laillou. "Didascalies as Speech Act." *Modern Drama* 25(1) (March 1982): 25–35.

_____. "Narration et actes de parole dans le texte dramatique." *Études littéraires* 13(3) (December 1980): 471–93.

Searle, John. *Speech Acts: An Essay in the Philosophy of Language*. Cambridge: Cambridge University Press, 1969.

Shaw, George Bernard. *Pygmalion* (1912). Translated into French by Éloi de Grandmont. Unpublished.

Sinclair Robinson, and Donald Smith. *Manuel pratique du français canadien*. Toronto: Macmillan, 1973.

Stanton, Domna C. "Difference on Trial: A Critique of the Maternal Metaphor in Cixous, Irigaray, and Kristeva." In *Poetics of Gender*. Edited by Nancy K. Miller. New York: Columbia University Press, 1986.

Suleiman, Susan Rubin. "Writing and Motherhood." In *The (M)Other Tongue*. Edited by Shirley Nelson Garner, Claire Kahane, and Madelon Sprengnether. Ithaca: Cornell University Press, 1985.

Taylor, Kate. "Les Guerriers' Staging Is at War with the Script." *The Globe and Mail* (28 February 1994): C3.

Tessier, Rudel. Afterword. In Gratien Gélinas, *Hier les enfants dansaient.* Montreal: Leméac, 1968.

Tétu de Labsade, Françoise. "Langue et politique." In *Un Pays, une culture.* Montréal, Editions Boréal, 1990.

Théâtre des cuisines. *As-tu vu? Les Maisons s'emportent!* Montréal: Les Editions du Remue-Ménage, 1980.

_____. *Môman travaille pas, a trop d'ouvrage!* Montréal: Les Editions du remue-menage, 1976.

Toronto: PACTS Communications Centre, 1991.

Tougas, Francine. *Histoires de fantômes, L'Age d'or, Grandir.* Montréal: Leméac, 1985.

Toury, Gideon. *In Search of a Theory of Translation.* Tel Aviv: The Porter Institute for Semiotic and Structural Studies, 1980.

Tremblay, Michel. "Anne." Unpublished short story. National Library of Canada, Fonds Michel Tremblay [14 ch. 8].

_____. *Damnée Manon, Sacrée Sandra.* Montréal: Leméac, 1977.

_____. *Des Nouvelles d'Edouard.* Montréal: Leméac, 1984.

_____. *Hosanna suivi de La Duchesse de Langeais.* Montréal: Leméac, 1973.

_____. Interview. *La Presse* (2 September 1989): 3.

_____. *L'Impromptu d'Outremont.* Montréal: Leméac, 1980.

_____. *La Grosse femme d'à côté est enceinte.* Montréal: Leméac, 1978.

_____. *Les Belles-Sœurs.* 2nd ed. Montréal: Leméac, 1971.

_____. *Les Belles-Sœurs.* Montréal: Leméac, 1972.

_____. *A toi pour toujours ta Marie-Lou.* Montréal: Leméac, 1971.

_____. *Le Vrai Monde?* Montréal: Leméac, 1987.

Usmiani, Renata. "Discovering the Nuance." *Canadian Theatre Review* 24 (Fall 1979): 38–41.

_____. "Where to Begin the Accusation." *Canadian Theatre Review* 24 (Fall 1979): 26–39.

_____. *Michel Tremblay.* Vancouver: Douglas & McIntyre, 1982.

_____. "Tremblay Opus: Unity in Diversity." *Canadian Theatre Review* 24 (Fall 1979): 12–25.

_____. *The Guid Sisters* [*Les Belles-S_urs*]. Translated by Martin Bowman and Bill Findlay. Toronto: Exile Editions, 1988.

Vanasse, Andre. "Michel Tremblay: 'Les Bibittes des autres.'" *Le Maclean* (September 1972): 20–39.

von Humboldt, Wilhelm. "Man's Intrinsic Humanity: His Language." In *Humanist Without Portfolio*. Translated by Marianne Cowan. Detroit: Wayne State University Press, 1963.

_____. *Werke*. Berlin: Walter de Gruyter, 1968.

Wallace, Robert. "Homo création: pour une poétique du théâtre gai." *Cahiers de Théâtre Jeu* 54 (1990): 24–42.

_____. *Producing Marginality: Theatre and Criticism in Canada*. Saskatoon: Fifth House Publishers, 1990.

_____. "Towards an Understanding of Theatrical Difference." *Canadian Theatre Review* 55 (Summer 1988): 5–14.

Weil, Kari. *Androgyny and the Denial of Difference*. Charlottesville: University Press of Virginia, 1992.

Weiss, Jonathan M. *French-Canadian Theater*. Boston: Twayne, 1986.

Index